SNAKE

Also by Berry Stainback

It's What You Learn After You Know It All That Counts (with Earl
    Weaver)
Joe, You Coulda Made Us Proud (with Joe Pepitone)
A Very Different Love Story

SNAKE

Ken Stabler
and
Berry Stainback

DOUBLEDAY & COMPANY, INC.
GARDEN CITY, NEW YORK
1986

For Rose Molly Burch Stabler and all the guys who
played the game with me

For Rita Hourigan Stainback, who's still playing the
game with me

Library of Congress Cataloging-in-Publication Data
Stabler, Ken.
    Snake.
    1. Stabler, Ken. 2. Football players—United States
—Biography. 3. Oakland Raiders (Football team)
I. Stainback, Berry. II. Title.
FV939.S68A37 1986 796.332′092′4 [B]   86-2115
ISBN 0-385-23450-3

Contents

Introduction

When I first started to scribble down notes for *Snake,* I wondered if I could possibly cover the whole story in one book. The memories seemed endless. Just the football highlights could go on and on. Taking over the Alabama team in 1966 and leading it to an 11–0 record, then beating Nebraska in the Sugar Bowl and being named MVP of the game, that was my first big thrill. Coach Bryant later called me "the best quarterback I ever had at Alabama," and John Madden would say the same thing about me when I played for the Oakland Raiders. Those were the renegade Raiders, the team everyone loved to hate, except those of us who loved to play for them. Three times my teammates in Oakland voted me MVP of the Raiders, and that meant more to me than anything.

I knew the 1976 season would have to be a full chapter, the year we finally won the Super Bowl. It was my best year. I was named the National Football League's Player of the Year by *The Sporting News* and won the Hickok Award as the Professional Athlete of the Year, after completing 66.7 percent of my passes that season. Only Sammy Baugh, who hit on 70.3 percent of his passes in 1945, did better.

But the inside stories of myself and my teammates, off the field as well as on, those were what would bring the book to life. I had a ton of them, some twenty years' worth of wild and woolly tales. But wanting even more details, I made some phone calls to guys who shared the experiences with me at Oakland when I was studying the game plan by the light of the jukebox and living life at 5,000 r.p.m.'s.

That was the only way I knew to do things until I met Rose Molly Burch in February 1984 and she turned my life around. When I married Molly that June, a friend who called to congratulate me was writer Jack Smith, who had covered the Raiders in my time and was now with the Seattle *Post-Intelligence*. "One of the guys here said it was nice that you finally married a former Miss Alabama," Jack said, chuckling. " 'For years,' he said, 'Snake dated Miss Alabamas as fast as they could turn them out.' "

So I phoned Jack for his recollections of the good times with Oakland, and he said, "The whole scene with that team was a social phenomenon that will never be seen again. You were the funniest of the bunch, but there was a full gang of great characters."

Then Jack got talking about the nights in training camp when he helped players sneak out after curfew to go drinking in Santa Rosa. I usually connected with a date, but Jack recalled a night when he drove around back of the motel where we stayed, car lights out, and picked up Gene Upshaw, Art Shell, and me. We went to The Hilltopper and sat out on the patio drinking. About 1 A.M. our waitress came out and said, "You know, there's a coach drinking inside."

Upshaw said to Jack, "You got us into this, now get us out of it."

Jack walked into the main bar just as the assistant coach went into the men's room. Jack followed him in and said, "Look, it's my fault three players are out there on the patio."

"Players!" the coach cried. "Holy shit, they can't see me here at this hour! Cover for me, Jack, and I'll slip out the front."

We laughed and ordered another round of drinks.

"Sometimes when we got back," Jack said, "Madden would call my room for the second shift and we'd go out. John would say, 'I can't wait for these guys to retire so I can drink with them.' "

Upshaw broke up when I called and reminded him of that night at The Hilltopper, and he talked about how we used to welcome the players who joined us from other teams. "They were always so happy to get with the Raiders," Gene said. "We'd take them out drinking and say, 'Welcome to the pros.' We had such a close-knit team, we all went out together, we drank together, and we all played ball together like an old-time football team—just line up and come right at you. But the best thing was, there was never any division whatsoever on that team. We were all Raiders."

"We couldn't do enough for each other," I said.

"Yeah, Snake," Gene said, "but you did have a tendency not to show up at functions, like certain banquets for teammates."

"I always meant to show up," I said. "It's just that I got waylaid en route sometimes."

"But when an offensive lineman asked you to attend an affair, you always showed up," Gene said.

Those Raider years were almost all great times, and I've put them all in here and more—the good, the bad, and the ugly.

I remember when Jack Smith, putting together a story on me, read me a quote from Jack London: "I would rather be a meteor, every atom of me in magnificent glow, than a sleepy and permanent planet. The proper function of man is to live, not to exist. I shall not waste my days in trying to prolong them. I shall use my time."

"What does that mean to you?" Jack Smith asked.

I thought for a long moment, and then I said, "Throw deep."

That's what I've tried to do throughout this book: Throw deep.

1

"The Santa Rosa Five" Go to Camp

Some of my most vivid memories are of training camps. Although many players have compared life in a National Football League training camp to being in a Turkish prison, I loved it.

The Oakland Raiders of my day trained in the long-sucking heat of Santa Rosa, California, where the sweat poured like rain for eight weeks. The workouts were scheduled for ninety minutes in the morning and ninety minutes in the afternoon. But I'd like to have an Al Davis pinkie ring for every workout that lasted over two hours. We got so much conditioning in during practice, we didn't have to do the extra running that other teams did. Which was fine—we weren't entering any marathons.

But we worked like hell in practice and tried to keep from snoring like hell in meetings: ninety minutes in the afternoon, ninety more in the evening. The meetings were so boring they made leaf-raking seem like an exciting occupation. I can understand why so many players hated training camp.

But, as I said, I loved camp. First, because with the Raiders we went in knowing we were going to win every year; and second, because we also knew we were going to have fun. In fact, we expended almost as much energy devising and executing good times as we did

getting ready for the season. But then the two disciplines went together like victory and celebration.

The monotony of camp was so oppressive that without the diversions of whiskey and women, those of us who were wired for activity
and no more than six hours' sleep a night might have gone berserk. I
was fortunate to have four let's-party-hearty roommates to pal with
most of my years in Oakland. The roomies were halfback Pete
Banaszak, wide receiver Freddy Biletnikoff, defensive end Tony
Cline, and middle linebacker Dan Conners. We lived for the weekly
football games and the football-player nights in between. I liked to
think of us as "The Santa Rosa Five."

We stayed at the El Rancho Motel in Santa Rosa, about sixty miles
north of Oakland, a one-story quadrangular building of some sixty
rooms. Most of them accommodated two players, but we shared one
of the five two-room suites. Tony, Freddy, and myself had the large
main room, with Pete and Dan in the adjoining one. We needed space
to socialize.

At a used-appliances store we bought three ancient refrigerators
for $10 apiece and installed them in the suite. Those machines
whined and groaned twenty-four hours a day, probably costing the
motel a fortune in electricity charges. We kept the fridges full of beer,
soft drinks, candy bars, and fruit. Mostly beer.

Pete had a girl one year who baked us a pie every week. The pies
were also stored in the fridge. The girl was strange. Given all the
female "players" who moved through our abode, it was inevitable
that the girl would be replaced by new talent, and she was. Yet she
kept bringing pies.

"Why don't you ease her out gently?" I asked Pete.

"I like pie," he said.

"She's a tad weird."

"Her pies ain't."

The final week of camp, on her last pie delivery, the girl heaved it
at Pete, who ducked. The gooey concoction hit me right in the chest
and dribbled down my shirt.

"You're right, Snake," Pete said. "She's weird."

After you've played a few years and have the offense down pat,
meetings are the most boring aspect of training camp. Freddy

Biletnikoff taught me how to deal with that. Freddy had already played eight years when I took over at quarterback and he had perfected a neat meeting trick.

We always sat together in the back of the room. One night I leaned over and whispered something to him and got no response. I nudged him with an elbow and whispered, "What the hell's wrong with you?" He had been staring straight ahead with the lifeless expression in his eyes that veterans get at meetings, but now he shook his head like a dog coming out of water and said, "I was asleep." "Goddamn," I said to myself, "he's been sleeping with his eyes open!" Well, it took some practice to get that one down, copping z's with your lids up and a semiattentive look on your face. I guess that's when I decided that a determined man can do about anything.

Most of the veterans brought playthings or projects to camp to help them break the boredom. In 1968, my first year in camp, defensive tackle Dan Birdwell brought a junk car to work on. It appeared to me to be well beyond repair. But a teammate explained, "Dan'll fix it or kill it with his bare hands."

I kept hearing stories about how tough Birdwell was, how he liked to not just beat opponents but punish them. "Dan's not happy when he comes off the field after a series," Dan Conners told me, "unless he's got blood and bits of flesh under his fingernails."

Birdwell soon showed me how tough he was. One day he was working on the exhaust manifold of his junker while it was hot. Someone told him he was going to get burned. "Fuck it," he said. "Gotta get this heap together."

The following morning he showed up at practice with great big blisters on his fingers. Guys saw them and told him to see the trainer, take a day off. "These don't bother me," Birdwell said. Then he started popping the blisters and squirting the juice at people.

After working on the car's brakes, Birdwell decided to try them out in the driveway that circled the motel. There was a wooden fence on the side where the dressing room and two playing fields were situated. Birdwell drove around the driveway until he built up speed. As he approached the turn by the fence, he slammed on the brakes. They apparently needed a bit more adjusting. The car hopped off the driveway and crashed right through the fence.

Center Dave Dalby brought the first money-making toys to camp.

He hauled in two coin-operated pinball machines and set them up in his room. It cost 25¢ per game, and there was usually a line waiting to play that stretched out of Dave's room and all the way down the hall. You don't know the meaning of the word "tilt" until you've seen a defensive lineman get mad at a pinball machine. But those two machines paid for all of Dalby's preseason bar bills, which about equaled the national debt of Chad.

One rookie came into one camp with a huge jigsaw puzzle. That guy might as well have posted a sign that read: I AM NOT RAIDER MATERIAL. He began assembling the puzzle on two card tables he'd pushed together in his room. As we passed his open door going to and from practice every day, we would check his steady progress. On Friday of the third week, the rookie had about 75 percent of the puzzle together and he said, "By Monday I'll be finished."

"No way," Tony Cline said as we walked on.

"He's pretty fast with that thing," I said.

"Not fast enough," Tony said.

On Monday the kid was cut and the puzzle was still there, incomplete. Of course, he couldn't have finished it anyway. Tony explained, "I stole three pieces."

Another young player who didn't make it with us that season may have sealed his fate with one pass. Don Milan was a quarterback from Cal Poly–San Luis Obispo with a real strong arm. Al Davis, the managing general partner and self-proclaimed genius of the Raiders, liked to stand in the end zone behind the secondary at practice and watch the pass routes and coverage when the ball was delivered. Al seldom misses anything, but even geniuses get distracted on occasion. Somehow Al looked away as Milan released a pass. It went high and sailed over everyone except Al. The ball peeled his head like an onion.

After practice I hurried to Milan's locker and collected the pair of football shoes I'd lent him. Freddy was right behind me asking for repayment of a $5 loan and someone else asked that Don return the jacket he had borrowed. We all knew that the odds on Milan's being in camp very long were not good. He became a backup in Green Bay that season.

George Buehler, a six-four, 285-pound guard, inevitably brought the most interesting toys to camp, intricate models that he would assemble. Once he brought a remote-controlled model airplane that cost about $700. He spent every free moment in camp working on that plane. We'd watch him in his room, his thick, gnarled lineman's fingers fastening tiny parts. Finally, after weeks of labor, he took his plane out for its maiden flight.

Naturally, we all went out on the field to see if his slick-looking craft would actually fly and if George could control it. The plane was terrific and so was George. He had it doing loops, diving, climbing, banking, all kinds of maneuvers. A group of us stood there watching with admiration as George put his plane through its paces like a prized hunting dog. We let out cheers and he was rightly proud.

Then, as he brought the plane down low for some lazy circles and figure eights, Dave Casper came walking by. Casper didn't know what was going on, which in itself was not that unusual; I never knew what was going on with Dave Casper either. He was a very intelligent individual, able to hold two or three conversations at the same time. One-on-one, though, he was sometimes a tad hazy.

The plane dived once right over Casper, a six-four, 245-pound tight end, and he sort of waved it away, like King Kong swatting at the bothersome planes that dove at him in the movie. When Buehler's plane made a second pass, Casper was ready. He grabbed a handful of lava rocks from the path and threw them at the plane—hitting the engine. The plane pitched straight down and crashed, pieces flying in every direction.

Casper just kept walking, without a word to anyone.

I went to George, who stood there dumbfounded. "Maybe you're just too big to play with model airplanes," I said.

I'd usually bring firecrackers to camp. Hundreds of firecrackers. My roommates and I would periodically toss them behind unsuspecting victims, scaring the shit out of guys. We got Casper so many times one week that whenever he saw us coming he'd change directions and give us the finger.

The year after his plane crashed, Buehler constructed a high-dollar remote-controlled tank. This machine was virtually indestructible. Just to make sure it stayed that way, though, George told Casper that if he so much as looked at the tank he was going to bite Dave's face off.

Inside the quadrangle of rooms at the motel was a sidewalk that

skirted a courtyard of flowers, bushes, grass, and rocks. The courtyard was about fifty feet by fifty feet, and George ran his tank all over
it, over rocks, around flowers, through bushes. I saw that, remembered my firecrackers, and decided they would make a great combination. Especially when Coach John Madden was in his office.

One afternoon between practice and dinner Pete Banaszak and I
requisitioned Buehler's tank. I left a note in his box: DON'T WORRY.
THE SNAKE WILL RETURN. We went to our rooms, which were di-
rectly across from the coaches' offices, and timed running the tank
over to them. We taped a handful of firecrackers to the tank and
attached a long fuse that we calculated would be just the right length
to set off the fireworks as the tank rolled into the coaches' offices. Our
calculations proved to be accurate.

Seconds after the bombs burst, a frantic Coach Madden came running out of the office, jabbing index fingers into his ears and screaming, "Who the hell did that? Where'd you go?" Meanwhile we turned
the tank around. And while John stood there hollering and turning
pink and pulling at his hair as he tended to do whenever he got
excited, we ran that little tank between his spread legs and brought it
on home.

After that we blew up the coaches' room maybe once a week. Good
old John never got after us. At first I thought he just got used to the
explosions. Then I noticed that whenever he entered his office he
stuffed wads of cotton in his ears.

You never knew what oddity a placekicker might bring to camp.
Placekickers are a breed apart, and I don't mean George Blanda, a
placekicker who was also a football player. I mean the guys who
make a living using no other part of their bodies but their feet, like
grape stompers. I have never known a placekicker who wasn't more
than a little strange, if not a full-time Twilight Zoner.

Errol Mann, the veteran placekicker from the Lions, signed on
with us for the last years of his career. Mann had only two interests:
horses and airplanes. So one year he came to camp with a six-foot-
high stack of horse magazines and airplane magazines. The next year
he brought a horse to camp. The following year he brought an airplane to camp.

"How'd you get the plane here?" I asked him.

"I flew it," he said. "Just got my license this spring. I'll take you up for a spin this afternoon after practice."

"No you won't," I said.

"Why not?"

"I have one rule in life I will not break," I said. "I will not get into an airplane with a placekicker in the pilot's seat."

"That's ridiculous."

"Errol, no offense," I said. "But all of your skills lie in your feet. You really shoulda took up tap-dancing."

None of the players would fly with Mann. In fact, Errol Mann just may be the only pilot ever to have to fly solo for his entire life.

John Madden knew he was coaching a gang of distinctive individuals. Characters, some called us. Others called us ruffians, mavericks, renegades, oddballs, intimidators . . . and there's no point in mentioning the curse words. But all the labels were fair enough. And I think John decided with the type of people we had that it was necessary to give us a certain amount of room to roam. We had more characters than any other team and John realized that we didn't care for a lot of restrictions, were happier without them, and as a result played better. John handled individuals very well, and I feel that was a prime reason why the Raiders had the best won-lost record in pro football while he was coaching the team.

Al Davis liked to pick up so-called misfits from other teams. He obviously figured that, while they may not have fit in elsewhere, they sure as hell could fit in with us. And those of us who were already Raiders welcomed anyone who could help the ball club, and maybe even add another dimension to our festive occasions.

In August 1975 Al grabbed veteran linebacker Ted Hendricks from Green Bay, where he had not meshed in the Packers' defensive system. His nickname was "Kick 'em in the Head Ted" because he had no qualms about applying his feet to opponents when the urge seized him. Hendricks had no qualms about anything.

The day he reported at Santa Rosa he didn't turn out with the rest of us for practice, and we wondered where he was. Then we saw him coming over the hill that rose just beyond the field. He was riding a horse, in uniform. Except on his head was a spike-topped World War I German helmet that he'd painted silver and black, and on the sides were Raider-symbol patch-eyed pirate decals. Everyone cheered.

Hendricks rode right up to John Madden and said, "Okay, Coach, I'm ready to play some football."

Early in the next season, when the Washington Redskins released John Matuszak, it didn't bother Al Davis that this was the third team to dump "The Tooz." Al snapped him right up. George Allen was the Redskins' coach at the time and writers could not understand why a man who loved veterans the way Allen did would cut one who was six-eight, 280 pounds, and under thirty years of age. "Vodka and Valium," was George's explanation. "The breakfast of champions."

I didn't believe that for a minute. Anytime I celebrated with The Tooz, all he ever drank was Crown Royal and the only pills he popped were occasional Quaaludes. "Crown and ludes, the late supper of champions," The Tooz might say.

The day Matuszak arrived at practice he suited up with us, but also delayed joining us on the field. Then he came running at full speed and let out a god-awful scream that made spectators cringe and the rest of us laugh like hell. Al Davis was not amused. He was standing next to Hendricks and Al, kind of thinking out loud, said, "I wonder if John's worth the gamble?"

Hendricks gave him a you've-got-to-be-kidding look and said, "Al, what difference will one more make?"

What was most interesting was how many of the outcasts we acquired played better football for us than they ever had with other clubs. Even Hendricks, who'd had excellent years with the Baltimore Colts before his brief decline in Green Bay, had his finest years with the Raiders. Matuszak was much more effective than he had been at Houston or Kansas City. Errol Mann led the AFC in field goals and scoring in 1977. Willie Hall, Warren Bankston, Dave Rowe, Mike McCoy, Pat Toomay . . . the list goes on and on of players whose performance improved in the Raider environment. They became fond of our life-style and our game-style. Al Davis's "Pride and Poise" theme for the Raiders was dead right. For all the fun, Raiders got serious on Sunday. Real serious.

When Toomay joined us he was ecstatic, after playing with the Dallas Cowboys, the Buffalo Bills, and the Tampa Bay Bucs. "All my life," he said, "I knew that somewhere in the league there must be a club like this."

Most of the Raider players who were not married drank hard and chased women harder. It relieved the monotony of training camp and the pressure of games. And, goddamn, it was fun.

I was married twice while a Raider, but I never felt like a husband. Perhaps because both of the women I married were more like sparring partners than wives. Obviously, the fault was not all theirs. But I was never deterred from the endless game of prowl-and-party.

My roommates and I had a pact. We all took seats by the door at the 8:00 P.M. meeting and the moment it broke up—around 9:30—we sprinted to our rooms. We'd comb our hair, slap on face juice, and dash to the biggest car we had, usually a Banaszak Buick. We only had ninety minutes to complete what we called "The Circuit." That consisted of hitting at least five bars before we had to be back for the 11:00 P.M. curfew.

The Circuit started each night at Melendy's, the nearest bar, and we never missed stopping at The Music Box. It had a large dance floor, the best live music in Santa Rosa, and The Box was also where the best-looking women usually hung out. No minor consideration.

Every year during training camp the women of Santa Rosa turned out in droves to greet the Raiders, many bearing dance cards that just had to be filled in. Some of the women were beautiful, a great many were attractive, and the balance ranged from plain to ugly as a mud fence. We tried to be selective.

We usually played Boss dice on The Circuit to see who would pay for the drinks. All the while, at each stop, we'd check out the women who appeared to be what we called "players." As we had to be in by curfew, all cars parked, dates would be set for eleven-thirty. The experienced female players knew the routine; others were quick learners. They would drive to the El Rancho, pick you up, and haul you to their place or to another motel. Those players not familiar with the word "shy" would join you in your room, uninhibited by the witnesses to the performance. There were a few tireless spirits who would attend to all five of us. They were known as "60-Minute Players," or "The OT Girls."

When one of the roomies came in real late with a girl, those of us who appeared to be (but were not quite) asleep would peek at the action. Freddy liked to crawl on the floor and get right up close. I bought a kid's plastic periscope to peek around the door frame into the inner room. But the damn thing didn't work unless all the lights in there were on.

One night, when Freddy was between marriages, he was going at it with a girl in his bed for about forty minutes. Pete was under the covers in the next bed, seemingly asleep. When Freddy finished, he whispered to the girl, "You know, Pete Banaszak over there has one of the biggest dongs in camp."

"No kidding!" the girl said, sitting up and eyeing Pete in the semi-darkness. He was lying on his back, his closed eyes facing her, his chest rhythmically rising and falling.

"I'm serious. Pete's hung. Go on over there and pull back the covers. You can see he's out cold."

Pete, of course, had been watching the show slit-eyed. The girl bent down for a good look and when she flipped back the covers, a blue-diamond boner popped up and quivered in her face. The girl let out a muffled cry and hopped back to Freddy. Seeing that Pete's eyes were still shut, Freddy said, "You should see that thing when he's *awake!*"

"Maybe I'll have to come back," the girl whispered, giggling.

Pete's eyes opened and he smiled.

Many nights we'd go right back out after curfew, and many times I didn't return until just before breakfast. We left and returned the same way—through a back door and a hedgerow of bushes rimming the driveway. If I had a midnight date, she would pull in, turn off the headlights, then slowly circle the driveway. Meanwhile I'd creep through the bushes in a crouch and look up the driveway for her— and usually see about fifteen other veterans hunched down waiting for pickups.

We had a teammate who kept professing how religious he was. He enjoyed chiding some of us for our womanizing. Then one night I went through the hedgerow and who was right beside me but that God-spouting hypocrite. A woman stopped her car and he made for it as if she had the keys to the pearly gates. "Caught, caught!" I half hollered. The next day he denied that it was him I'd seen. For the next week, though, whenever I saw him I'd yell, "Caught, caught!" and watch him turn red.

Then there was the night a car pulled up by me and I slipped in and kept my head down on the seat as usual. The young woman pulled up to the exit under the lighted EL RANCHO MOTEL sign and I looked up. I couldn't believe it. The driver was gorgeous, a girl I'd never seen before—not my date.

She glanced at me as she pulled away and I sat up. "Oh, I thought you were Tony!" she said.

"Well, I thought you were Sue," I said. "But the coaches are on patrol," I lied. "We can't turn back."

"Tony will be upset."

It had to be Tony Cline, who was getting all spiffed up when I hurried out. "He'll be fine," I said. "He's used to disappointment."

"What about you?"

"I've always relied on the kindness of strangers," I said, and she laughed.

All of the surprises during our night forays were not so pleasant. One precurfew evening all of The Santa Rosa Five made connections at The Music Box and later went back there to party with our dates. We were dancing and drinking and having a great time. My girl was a sexy little blonde who danced real close, applying more pelvic action than Tina Turner. I began to get anxious to press on her in private. So I invited her to step out of the smoke-filled bar for a few minutes of fresh air. Then I started trying to sell her on going to her place or a motel.

She was leaning back against the door of a car and I was standing in front of her, a hand on either side of her on the car, just sweet-talking away. All of a sudden, I felt someone else's hand on my shoulder from behind. I turned my head and saw that the person attached to that hand was my second wife.

"I hope she's worth it!" my wife said and stormed away.

She was. I had already been busted for a crime, so I figured I might as well go ahead and do the crime.

Of course, I had to tell the girl that my wife and I were separated (which was true, as long as I was in camp and she stayed home) and going to get a divorce (in a year or so, but why be picky?). I had heard about a couple of other Raider wives who had driven the sixty miles from Oakland to search the bars of Santa Rosa for their husbands, but this was the first trip for my wife. I felt kind of bad that the very first time she had driven up she'd caught me. But then I said to myself, "Almost any night she came she would have caught me." I felt better.

I never got caught with a woman in the El Rancho, though roughly half of our partying occurred right there. But every year in camp a few guys would get nabbed by coaches. They knew the program. The coaches had been around longer than us and periodically they would run a spot check after curfew, around 1 A.M. Invariably, it was a veteran who was found with a girl in his sack.

John Madden did this just to maintain some kind of control. He was not a guy to lay down rules and try to stop the fun completely, as most coaches did, because he knew that football players needed some relaxation. He drew a line, and it was a long one, beyond which you were not to tread. We just rubberized that line and stretched the hell out of it.

Of course, none of the carousing would have been allowed if we weren't winners. When we won the Super Bowl in January 1977, we were coming off our eighth appearance in the AFC Championship Game in the last ten years. And our training camp suite was plumb full of winning football players.

Freddy Biletnikoff was an all-time great possession receiver. Halfback Pete Banaszak had a knack that few could match for putting the ball into the end zone. Dan Conners was the best middle linebacker the Raiders ever had until Matt Millen arrived in the eighties. Tony Cline was a superquick pass-rushing defensive end, an undersized overachiever whose knees couldn't take the punishment from down blocks or he would have played much longer than six years with us. But who would mess with the minds of performers like those guys? Not John Madden. He wanted players, and whether they drank milkshakes or double Mai Tais was all the same to him.

Still, there had to be some policing, and at each camp six or eight players would be fined $200 for missing curfew and four or five spotcheck felons would have to cough up $500. The fine dollars went into a fund for the year-end team party.

John Madden enjoyed standing up in the dining room and announcing the fines at breakfast, particularly when a player got busted with a woman in his room. "I'd like to thank John Matuszak [or whoever]," John would say, "for his contribution to the party fund. He was found to have given some poor, homeless young woman shelter last night. She had to be homeless to stay with him. And while we admire his big heart, we appreciate more his $500 party donation."

Then everyone would laugh and raise hell razzing the guy who had gotten caught.

"Look forward to the drinks on you, Tooz!"

"For $500—she better been good!"

"You coulda got five high-class hookers, sucker!"

"He can't handle high-class!"

At practice the coaches gave the fined player a hard time. They'd look down their noses at you and alternate giving you the cold shoulder and verbal abuse.

"You look like you're running in sand. Your legs dead?"

"Get off on the snap, Party Marty—not two counts late!"

"You'll be sucking air Sunday if you don't shape up."

Teammates gave you no sympathy either: Better you than them. They'd laugh and rub one index finger on top of the other at you, like school kids shaming someone who's been naughty.

I did get tapped for not making curfew once. Our standard procedure was to drink in the last bar on The Circuit until 10:50. Then we'd jump in the car and race back to camp looking like members of Joey Chittwood's Thrill Show. Joey's thrill was wrecking cars, which is what we almost did a number of times trying to reach our rooms before 11:00. We'd come screeching into the El Rancho parking lot and hook-slide the car into a spot by our room, fly through the back door, and dive into the suite at approximately 10:59.9.

But one night we blew a rear tire a couple of miles from the motel. "Leave the car until tomorrow," Freddy said. "We can run for it."

Given my bad knees and all that booze in me, I wasn't about to run two miles. "To hell with that," I said. "We'll speed-change the tire. Pete, you set the jack. Dan, you pop the hubcap. Tony, you get the spare. Freddy, you grab the lug wrench."

"What're you gonna do, Snake?" Freddy asked.

"My duty. Go down with the ship if necessary."

Pete was so drunk he couldn't set the jack properly. I jumped into the breach and it took me over ten minutes to get the flat off the blacktop. It's not real easy changing a tire in the dark drunk. We didn't stomp into our rooms until 11:35. There was a note on the floor: THAT'S $200 × 5.

Pete Banaszak liked to tell a story about his rookie camp when he roomed with Ken Herock, the veteran tight end. Herock decided to skip curfew one night and said he'd thought of a plan to beat getting caught. He plumped up two pillows and placed them in his bed the long way, then took the lamp off his night table and put it with the shade where his head would be in bed. He pulled the covers up over his dummy, and Pete said, "Looks pretty good."

"Cover for me," Herock said and took off.

A few minutes after eleven, a coach knocked on the door, opened it, and poked his head in. He nodded at the other bed and asked Pete, "That Herock?"

"Think he's asleep," Pete replied.

The coach turned on the wall switch—and the lamp in the bed lit up.

When Herock returned some hours later, Pete said, "You should've unplugged your head."

We partied so much in our rooms, they became very popular with various female players. At times we had to take reservations. We also began finding, the morning after, various bras and panties that women had left behind. That gave us the idea to start a collection of women's undergarments. Kind of our trophies. We tacked the garments up on the walls and watched the items multiply. Women readily contributed, with monogrammed panties being the choice donation of the elite. Those who wore bras also left them, though poor Big C apparently couldn't be without hers for too long without risking a backache.

Undergarment collecting became an annual rite of training camp. Someone called us the "Fredericks of Santa Rosa." In subsequent years, we tended to judge our preseason success not by how many passes were completed or receptions caught, not by how many tackles were made or how much yardage was gained. The bottom line was: How much lingerie did we collect?

There were some nights when we were all tired or maybe needed a night off the sauce and we'd decide not to go out on The Circuit. We'd all just sit around the rooms, read, talk, have a couple of beers. It felt damn good—for about an hour.

Then one of us would feel the need to get some entertainment going. A ball boy would walk past our open door and we'd tell him to go find the two rookies we named and send them to us.

"Tell them it's their ass and yours if they don't get here pronto," we'd add because some wise rookies would try to get the ball boys to say they couldn't be found.

Usually we'd just send the rookies out for pizza or hamburgers. But the really fun times were when their assigned mission, a bit more difficult but one of the most important in their young lives, was to bring us back women.

"This is a major test of your abilities," I'd tell them. "Raiders have to be resourceful, determined, and quick-witted at all times. This is one of them times. Raiders are also expected to know how to sweet-talk women. So regard this as just part of your training. Failure won't be looked on kindly."

"I'm sure," Pete would say, "you don't want to be standing on your chair at every meal singing your rotten school songs."

"Go get 'em," Tony would say.

"And remember," Freddy would always add, "no coyotes."

We never expected much from the rookies. After all, they didn't have the experience of us crafty old veterans. But the Raiders always seemed to have rookies who were outstanding performers in the women field. They never failed to fetch us at least one woman, usually a pair, some of them surprisingly attractive party people who would leap right into the festivities. Others who showed up simply were not players, saying they had just come by for a laugh, and we'd suffer our disappointment graciously. We'd offer them a beer, give them a laugh, and send them on their way.

One night, though, we suffered a terrible disappointment. The two girls were so cute I about felt my eyeballs sweat. Both girls were wearing white short-shorts that did little to disguise their real selves. They were also unencumbered by bras and walked into our doorway like players of the first rank. But when the redhead opened her mouth, it was like we were two TDs down to the Steelers with thirty seconds left to play.

"Are you guys *serious?*" she said with sarcasm you could chew on. "We just wanted to check out you jerks who had the balls to send kids to score dates for you." Her eyes scanned the room. "Did you really think we'd be a couple more of your playthings?" If looks could melt, all of the gadgets and lingerie would have gone up in smoke. "Well, you're not hanging these up there," Red said. She hooked a finger under the lower edge of her panties, tugged it down on the side of her thigh, and let it snap back.

Her girlfriend turned, bent, and mooned us through her shorts, saying, "Enjoy yourselves." Then they were gone.

"Win some, lose some," I thought. But within ten minutes we were out on the prowl again. No way we could stay in after that simmering short-short show.

Married veterans sometimes had to be even more resourceful than the rookies who fetched for us. For example, what do you do when you are about to go home to your wife from camp bearing crabs? This story concerns a former teammate who is still married to that wife, so he will remain anonymous.

Crabs are treated with an ointment called Pyrinate A-200. It was so popular with The Santa Rosa Five that we pasted a Pyrinate label on our bathroom mirror over a sign that read: COMBAT YOUR ENEMY. But it takes a week to kill off crabs, and my teammate would have to join his wife in two days, after the final preseason game. He would be expected to take care of his homework, and what could he do?

What he did was get lucky. In the game against the Rams, with his wife looking on from the stands, he was kicked in the nuts on a kickoff. It was the only time in his life he was thankful for a kick in the nuts, but he saw that as a solution to his problem.

After the injury he was carried off the field into the locker room. At game's end he had very swollen testicles, and to emphasize this he stuck two athletic socks into his Jockey shorts. Then he pulled on slacks and a sport coat and gingerly walked out to meet his wife.

"Sorry I can't go home with you, babe," he said, pointing at his bulging crotch. "I'm hurting and everyone who got hurt today has to go back to camp for treatment."

Every year, midway through training camp, guys would start coming up to me and saying, "Time for a party, Snake. See what you can get outta John." I had a good relationship with John, so I was always chosen to find out when he felt we could afford to lighten up in practice. The idea was to find a day when we weren't going to do any serious work at the morning workout. When I got the day, I'd say,

"The guys need a blowout, John. If we can move the morning workout back to eleven o'clock and curfew the night before back to, say, two in the morning, we can have our annual air hockey tournament. Everyone'll unwind and we'll get on with serious work in the afternoon."

"All right, Kenny," John said one year. "I'll set curfew at one, then people may be back by two. But I have one condition."

"What's that?"

"No more firecrackers."

"Deal," I said, laughing.

Dave Dalby, our unofficial social director, organized the annual air hockey tournament at Melendy's, which had one of those large Coleco tables. The day's celebration started with a parade through Santa Rosa, headed by the Raiders Queen. Dalby and Ted Hendricks would find the ugliest girl in town with a good figure and big tits and dub her our queen. A little crown would be set on her head and a sash descending across her breast would proclaim her RAIDERS QUEEN. Her throne was a wooden lawn chair that would be placed in the back of Hendricks's pickup truck. The beribboned truck would lead about twenty cars all through town, with the queen waving to the folks lining the route to Melendy's.

The only rule in the tournament was that sober contestants would be disqualified, though I never saw one of those. So what we ended up with was a bar full of large drunks smashing air hockey pucks at one another, throwing beer and maybe an odd chair or two, everyone having fun.

The Raider training camps were one of a kind. The players partied hard and played hard, and that combination may have been no small factor in why we won.

When I was traded to the Houston Oilers in 1980, I looked forward to training camp, too, because I knew Coach Bum Phillips didn't believe in a lot of rules or even stringent bed checks. He ran much easier practices and regularly gave players half days off.

But Bum was ready for me. He roomed me with center Carl Mauck, a six-five, 280-pound, totally dedicated football player and full-time drill instructor. He became "The Snake Keeper," determined to keep me from straying far or staying out late. I couldn't really argue with this truck-sized individual, a nice guy at heart but one from an entirely different school than I had attended for almost a decade. We did, however, discuss the situation.

"Carl, this is the goddamn *pre*season!" I said.

"We all want you ready for the season, Snake."

"I've always been ready for the fucking season," I said. "Unless I was physically injured. With your help, I may go into this season *mentally* injured. Carl, you can't let this game dominate your entire existence—it'll eat you alive."

"You got to learn a whole new system here, Snake," he said.

"Yeah, it's real complex," I said. "Turn and hand the ball to Earl Campbell."

That was just about all I'd done the first few days of workouts and it was getting me down, so I had to get out. Fortunately, Mauck was usually asleep by eleven, his snores rattling the windows and blowing all of the one-pound-and-under items off his night table, and I got out for a little partying. I discovered on returning that Mauck never knew I was gone. I could tell he hadn't even turned over because the ashtray was still on my night table.

In the bars of San Angelo, Texas, where the Oilers trained, I'd see Mauck early in the evenings after dinner. I'd usually be chatting it up with a woman when he'd come over and say, "How's it goin', Snake?"

"All right, Carl," I'd reply. "But just remember, I expect you back in the room before curfew."

He'd laugh and buy us a round.

During the third week, Bum Phillips announced we'd have Saturday afternoon off. That meant everyone would vanish and I'd have the room at Angelo State alone until Mauck came back at eleven. I'd met a beautiful girl, a Texan, just before leaving the Coast and I phoned her.

"Would you like to come down to training camp?" I asked. "Not to participate, just visit."

She flew in three days later and everything about her was just dynamite: big blue eyes, big tanned breasts, an itty-bitty waist. The only problem was, she brought her goddamn dog with her. It was one of those white, fluffy little shit-eating dogs, half midget poodle and half dust mop. So I had to get a bowl for the dog's food and a bowl for its water. It was happy. The girl and I started drinking and partying and I was soon so happy that I forgot the time. When I finally noticed the clock, it was ten-forty. That goddamn Snake Keeper Mauck would be back any minute!

We threw on our clothes, threw the booze and the girl's things into her bag, and hustled out of there. I drove her to a motel and we started playing again.

It was after twelve when I headed back to camp. "Mauck's already caught me," I thought, "so fuck it." I was humming, a warm glow still with me when I walked into our room. I stopped humming when I saw that big sonuvabitch leaning up against the wall, his railroad-tie arms folded across his chest and grim displeasure creasing his face. Even his hair, which resembled a Brillo pad, appeared to be clenched extra tight.

"Look at this place—you fucker!" he said.

We had forgotten the goddamn dog! And that dear little pile of white fluff had turned over its food, turned over its water, and also shit and pissed all over the room. I couldn't believe that an animal that size could hold all that crap. As I cleaned up, the dog went, "Yap, yap. Yap, yap." Over and over again.

Mauck finally smiled. "You know, Snake, I've seen you with a couple of dogs in town," he said, "but I've never seen you with one that barked before."

It all worked out fine. I had to take the dog back to the girl. I stayed with her till 7 A.M. and returned to camp for breakfast feeling right refreshed. Ready to go out and hand the ball to Earl.

There was some fun at the Oiler camp. But it wasn't anything like Santa Rosa. Nothing was the same after Oakland. With the Raiders we went to camp every year expecting to win, certain we would win —because we always won. With the Oilers and Saints, my last NFL stop, there was a palpable tension that permeated the camps. With those ball clubs it was: We've got to play extra hard this year not to lose.

They should have learned to relax some, starting in training camp. It should be fun.

2

〰〰〰〰〰〰〰〰〰

"Damn, That Boy Runs Like a Snake!"

My father, Leroy Stabler, was called "Slim" by everyone who knew him. But the nickname came from his slimmer youth. He was a big, strapping man, six-five, 215 pounds, with forearms and hands the size of a blacksmith's. And from as far back as I can remember he was a larger-than-life figure to me. He was the major influence in my life, even after that day his heart literally exploded and he died at age forty-seven. This was at a point, following years of bitter frustration, when Slim was finally happy, when he'd finally been able to buy his own house and the land it stood on, when at last my mother Sally could stop working. His dreams had come true, and then he was gone.

But he had given me all he could and then some. He gave me a love of sports, a love of fast cars, and a love of music. He also gave me a relentless desire to have fun, to live every day at 5,000 r.p.m.'s. Slim always tried to have fun, at work or play, and he usually succeeded when he didn't slip too deeply into the whiskey—because then he was no fun for anybody. But the sudden death of this man who appeared to be the picture of health told me that you cannot predict your final day, so go hard for the good times while you can.

Slim Stabler did not have an easy life. He had been an outstanding athlete at Blackshire High School in Uriah, Alabama, in the late thirties, a star baseball and basketball player. His contemporaries say he was a fierce rebounder and scorer around the basket and that he could have earned an athletic scholarship to college. But his father died and Slim had to quit school in the eleventh grade and find work to help his family.

Then came World War II, and he went off to fight in Europe. A machine gunner, he apparently went through some heavy combat. He was in the Anzio invasion, where he was wounded in the leg and hospitalized for three months. But he didn't talk about the war. Even when friends who also had been in combat asked him about his experiences, Slim would just grunt and say, "It was rough." I suspect it was too rough for him to speak of.

The only time he mentioned the war to me was one night when we were watching television. "Gunsmoke," his favorite program, was on and he said that James Arness had been on Anzio Beach too. Then he said, "You know, Bud," which was what he called me, "every fifth round in a machine gun belt was a tracer. There were times we fought right through the night. So I took out all of the tracers and replaced them with regular bullets. Tracers help you spot your target. But if you can see where they're going, I figured the enemy could damn well see where they were coming from."

The message was: You don't have to stick by the rules as long as you get the job done right.

Slim was discharged in 1944, went to work as a mechanic for a Foley, Alabama, car dealer, and married my mother, who worked in the office of Dr. John Foster. I was born on Christmas Day in 1945 and my sister Carolyn came along in 1950. Six weeks after each birth, my mother had to return to work, and all-day baby-sitters provided for us, because her income was needed.

"It hurt me that I couldn't ever be a mother to you kids," Sally told me many years later, "that I was only around you at night, Saturday afternoons, and Sundays. It hurt me that I couldn't be a housewife and mother, but I could handle it. I just think it hurt your father worse."

Slim had his escapes, and sports was one of them. For years he played basketball for the American Legion Post team and for the church team, and he became a solid supporter of all the athletic programs in Foley. He took my mother and me, and later Carolyn, to all the high school games: baseball, basketball, and football. He also took a bottle of booze, usually bourbon, or rather my mother carried it for him in her purse.

"I could never take a little bag to a game," she says, laughing. "All of his friends had their wives do the same thing. Nobody wanted to be seen walking in with a bottle, but they wanted it once they sat down."

A number of the Foley High players came to love Slim. One of them was Billy Walker, who is seven years older than me and is still a good friend of mine. To this day, Billy has Slim's Legion Post basketball shirt that my father gave him when he retired. But what Billy appreciated most about my father was that he would buy him and his underage pals beer after games.

"Other men would only buy you a beer if you won," Billy says. "Slim would buy us beer anyway. When we lost, he'd say, 'Hell, don't worry about it. You'll kick their ass next time.' "

My father didn't drink much in the early years when he had to work the next day, but on Friday and Saturday nights he always cut her loose. George Wenzel, a hunting buddy, owned George's Social Club where Slim hung out. He and my mom and I would pile in the truck, Slim would put his guitar in back, and we'd go to George's, a little cinder-block honky-tonk. He wouldn't take the guitar in. He'd just have a few beers, tell a few jokes, and listen to the jukebox.

Then someone would say, "Slim, got your guitar with you?"

"Nah," he'd say.

A few minutes later someone else would say, "You know you got your guitar, Slim."

"Not with me," he'd say.

It was a routine. My father was a ham who loved to entertain, but he wanted to be asked to perform. And after a few more requests, when he was properly primed, he'd nudge me and say, "Bud, go get the guitar out of the truck."

"All right!" people would say. "Slim's gonna sing us some Hank!"

I'd fetch his box, then my father would sing and play for hours, running through all of Hank Williams's songs—usually starting with "Your Cheatin' Heart." Everybody would cheer, and every time his glass was empty someone would set a fresh drink down in front of him.

My mother just sat there sipping one or two drinks all night. "Sometimes I had to leave him," she says, "because I had to work Saturday mornings. And sometimes the daylight brung us home."

Slim had two guitars, and one he restrung left-handed for me. He taught me a couple of chords, but then I got so involved in playing sports that I didn't learn to play the guitar until I was in training camp with the Raiders. Marv Hubbard taught me a lot. I even learned to play right-handed. But it was my father who made me love music. I've always had a top-quality music system wherever I've lived and in all the cars I've owned.

There were evenings in later years when I'd come in the house and find Slim sitting on his bed all alone, just strumming and singing. My father was always subject to falling into down moods, and I felt the music helped bring him out of them.

Another of his favorite relaxations was hunting and fishing, and he taught me how to do both before I was ten. He liked to go freshwater fishing and usually he'd take me up on the Magnolia River. We'd bring home a mess of catfish, and that sweet white meat was delicious. Occasionally he'd hook up with a friend who had a boat and we'd fish on the Intracoastal Waterway. And there were times when he would set out with a buddy and get diverted by whiskey, and then he had to stop at the fish store on the way home. But he always came in with fish—caught or bought—and he always said the same thing: "Sally, get the grease hot."

In the fall and winter we hunted rabbits and all kinds of good-eating birds. There was an endless abundance of quail, doves, woodcock, and snipe in the fields and woodlands around Foley, as well as ducks by the flock on the inland waters.

Slim always kept hunting dogs, first a pair of black Labradors and then a pack of four beagles that he field-trained. Rabbit hunting was kind of like shooting fish in a barrel. We'd stand in one spot and just let the beagles go. And the dogs would drive the rabbits right back into our shotgun sights.

Two of my father's friends—George Wenzel and Rex Lee—also

had beagles. They would all load their dogs into the back of Slim's truck at night, get themselves a couple bottles of bourbon, and drive to the woods. After turning the dogs loose, they'd sit in the truck drinking whiskey and listening to their dogs running down rabbits. Each dog had its own distinctive sound. When the dogs sniffed onto the trail of a rabbit, the yups and whoops became more and more pronounced as they closed on their prey. The men, between pulls on the bottles, would identify their dogs.

"That's old Red."

"Hey, listen at Zeke, he's closin' in."

"Big Foot's got one!"

Around midnight, feeling fine behind the bourbon, they would call in the dogs and come on home. The simple good times in Foley—I learned to love them as a kid.

My father would take anyone hunting. He even took our preacher, but he always took the whiskey, too.

He wasn't a real religious man, yet Slim took us all to church every Sunday. We went to prayer meetings, revival meetings, church picnics. Then, when I was in high school, we suddenly stopped going to church. One Sunday morning my father simply said, "I'm going down to the Legion Post," which was the only place you could get a drink on Sunday in Foley. He never said another word about church, and the family never went again. I don't know why, but there were a lot of things he wouldn't talk about.

He was a public man but a private person. He had scores of friends, yet he had no real close friend. He enjoyed being with people, but just beneath the enjoyment there often seemed to be something troubling my father, some unspoken dissatisfaction. It created a tension in the man that allowed his friends to get only so close and no closer. He could never reveal himself to anyone, to confide what was going on inside him.

"I'd ask him and he just wouldn't say—ever," my mother says sadly. "He'd get in one of his moods and I couldn't get a word out of him."

Looking back, it's a shame that my father couldn't get things out, couldn't release his tension. That's just how he was, and I know how it is. I came to be pretty much the same way.

But everyone liked Slim, respected him. He was the best mechanic in Foley, a guy who could repair any vehicle. He soon rose to the position of service manager, and he became tops at that job too. His only problem was a bad temper that often flared at his employers. He felt they never paid him what he was worth. As a result, Slim changed jobs every two or three years.

He was service manager for the Chevrolet dealer, got mad and quit. He went right over to the Ford dealer as service manager and got a few more dollars in his pay envelope. When he flew off the handle with his boss at Ford, he became service manager for the Heavy Equipment Company, which was in a town fifty miles away. He was soon back at the Chevy dealer, who welcomed him with a little more money. For a couple of years my father even tried running his own gas station, but that was no big income producer either. I'm sure he was also mad at the boss there—himself—when he quit.

Wherever Slim went, though, folks would follow him with their cars. Or they'd buy cars from the dealer where he worked because they knew he would keep their machines in first-class shape.

Another reason why my father was so popular was that he was a funny guy most of the time. He was a joke teller and practical joker who kept his friends and fellow workers loose and laughing. As I got older, from about twelve on, I periodically worked with him, cleaning up his shop, washing and waxing cars, and keeping tools in their cabinets.

Other mechanics were always borrowing parts my father had out on his workbench. He got tired of people taking his condensers whenever he was working on a distributor. So one day he put a charge in several condensers and left them out. If you picked one up and touched the two metal ends, it would shock the hell out of you. Sure enough, another mechanic came over and grabbed a charged condenser—and jumped as if he'd been snakebit.

"Goddamn, Slim!" he yelled, dancing around shaking his hand.

"What's the problem?" Slim asked innocently as the whole shop broke up. "Take something that wasn't yours?"

My father's most electrifying trick was wiring his pickup truck to shock people. He took a coil from a Model T Ford and hooked it up to the truck battery. Then he grounded it to the block and installed a button under the dash. When he pushed the button, the whole truck was hot. The shock wouldn't hurt, but it stung right smartly.

He introduced the trick at one of my baseball games. As I was growing up, I became a real good basketball and baseball player, and my father never missed any of my games. He'd drive his truck to my baseball games and usually park on the first-base side of the field, as I either pitched or played first. He always had a cooler of beer in the bed of the truck for his friends, and a bottle of bourbon in the glove box for himself and whoever else wanted a hit. He'd watch my games sitting in the cab of the truck or up on the hood.

One day he stayed in the cab. As usual, a couple of his friends were sitting on the hood and others were leaning on the truck. They were all talking, laughing, drinking, and cheering for me. Then Slim pushed the button and knocked everyone off the truck, their beer cans flying.

"Hot damn, Slim, what the hell'd you do!" they hollered, hopping away and rubbing at the stings.

I heard the hollering and looked over from the field. My dad was laughing so hard he had to get out of the driver's seat to double over.

He told them he suspected he had a short in the electrical system that he'd see to, then he tinkered under the hood a minute. "That'll do her," he said, just so he could later give the men another shock.

No one seemed to hold the gags against Slim, or at least they didn't say anything. I'm sure nobody wanted to offend him. My father was also among the toughest men in Foley.

I remember the night he took my mom and me to a Foley basketball game in nearby Robertsdale. Billy Walker was on the Foley team then and he got some big rebounds near the end of the game as we won by two points.

Slim was real happy on the drive home and he said to my mother, "Let's stop for a sandwich and a beer, Sally. You get a Coke, Bud," he said to me. I was only eight years old.

We pulled into the Summerdale Social Club, which was about halfway between Robertsdale and Foley. Four men from Robertsdale were already in there putting down beers and complaining about the game's outcome. "I'll tell you one thing. At the next game I'm gonna be sitting right by the court," said one man, "and I'm gonna trip up that roughneck Walker kid."

My dad stood up and said, "You just step outside and we'll see what we can do about that little plan right now."

He walked out the door and my mom and I went to the window. All four Robertsdale men followed him out and started beating on him. I was scared, seeing him surrounded, men hitting my dad from all sides. He knocked down one of the men, but then another caught him with a shot from the side. Slim went down, but he landed next to an asphalt shingle left on the ground by workmen who were re-siding the building. Slim came up swinging that shingle like a machete. He sent all four men to the hospital.

During the next Foley–Robertsdale game, Billy Walker played his usual elbows-scything, bang-the-boards game. No one from the Robertsdale crowd bothered him.

Some years later Billy told me about the fight my dad had had with his brother Harold. My uncle Harold owned the Foley Pool Room, which was within walking distance of the high school. Most of the kids and a lot of older men who liked to shoot pool for money hung out there. When I was older and working with my dad, we'd go there at lunchtime for pickled eggs. Harold was a few inches shorter than my dad, but real thick through the upper body, a powerful man, about twenty pounds heavier than Slim.

"Your daddy and uncle Harold love each other," Billy told me, "but they just don't get along. The other day they got into an argument at the pool room and Harold said, 'I'm just gonna have to whip your ass, Slim.' So they went out to the city dump to have it out.

"Now, your uncle's a rough, tough sonuvabitch and he's whipped a lotta ass in this town. Everyone was saying that was what he was gonna do to Slim, particularly the older men. I'll be goddamned if I believed that. 'Harold's strong, but he's in trouble,' I said."

Word of the fight spread quickly. It would be at the city dump so the police could not interfere, kind of like in the 1890s when other bare-knuckle fighters went out on barges to brawl.

"This was definitely a main event," Billy said. "The kids piled into four cars and the adults piled into six or eight more. It was like a caravan to the dump. Everyone formed a wide circle around Slim and Harold, but it didn't hold. Slim tore into Harold and knocked him all around the place, didn't give him a chance to come back. In five minutes it was over."

As a little kid, the first thing I noticed about my father was how strong he was. His arms bulged from all those years of busting frozen nuts on vehicles. Many times I saw him put a pull handle on threaded steel that no one else could budge, and he'd torque the metal free with the power in those arms.

His hands were the size of a baseball glove, with long, thick fingers. There was always grease under his nails, and skinned marks on his scarred hands. I knew that big workhorse could just snuff me out like a flea, and I was afraid of him.

He was so moody. He'd be fine 90 percent of the time, then he'd plunge into a foul mood. He was as easy to read as seeing black clouds in the sky and knowing it was going to rain. When he got in one of those moods, I learned to stay real quiet around him or get out of his sight.

He only spanked my sister and me when we were young kids, thank God, but he taught us he demanded instant obedience. The threat of physical punishment was always there, like a birthmark. When he was drinking, it would be even more frightening.

My father's drinking increased steadily as I grew older, probably in direct proportion to the frustration he felt as a provider. We all knew he thought he should be doing more for his family, that my mother should not have to work. Few of their friends' wives worked. That wasn't a married woman's place, in his view. He wanted to own his own house, as his friends did. Instead he had to rent a small house. He wanted to buy air conditioners for the bedrooms. Instead he told us we didn't need them. He wanted a quality music system. He wanted a little boat. We had plenty of food and decent clothes, but there was never enough money for those extras. And he carried that fact around like a stone in his shoe, a stone that with the passing years kept growing.

I couldn't understand my father's frustration then. My mother, sister, and I weren't upset by our circumstances. Others had far less than we had. My father loved cars and he traded for a new car every two years. He drove an old pickup, but kept it in good shape. I knew he wanted to get a real hot car someday and turn it into a racer. Just with his own knowledge and skills with machinery to create a dragster that would win on the tracks in the area.

But in my youth he didn't feel fulfilled, and he turned more and more to booze. He kept a bottle of Ezra Brooks or Early Times bourbon in the glove box of his truck. "C'mon, Bud, let's go riding," he'd tell me. We'd climb in the truck and off we'd go, just ambling about. He'd take out his bottle and turn it up to his lips and literally put bubbles in it, just like you see in movies. Except in movies the bubbles are in tea, not in 86.6 proof whiskey. Then my father would lower the bottle to his lap and let out a breath that was more like a sour sigh. But he kept after the bottle, smoking his Lucky Strikes steadily between hits, until he had lowered its level to where he felt satisfied.

I know my father loved his family and we all loved him. In fact, I idolized him. But when he got to drinking hard, the idol tarnished. He tended to get mean.

Then he'd make some cutting remark about something I'd done, petty little things that I can't even remember. He'd holler, rap me on the shoulder, push me around. Drinking, he was like a different person, as if the bourbon touched some inner demon he was harboring and brought it to the surface. I hated to see him at my baseball games when he was sitting in that truck drinking hard.

At thirteen I was pitching and playing first in the Pony League. I was already almost six feet tall and real skinny at 125 pounds. But on the mound I could just blow the ball past batters, and being left-handed I also had a good curveball. And I could hit, so I played first between starts. The manager, Raymond Christianson, made it clear that I was the star of the team. But I wasn't perfect.

My father wanted me to be because he thought I could go on and get a lot out of my athletic ability in the future. And knowing I wouldn't have to quit school and give up athletics to take a job as he'd had to, at times my father had too much desire for me to be perfect in sports. When I messed up a play, he could be nasty.

Playing first base one day, I made an error in the ninth inning that cost us the game. Well, I felt bad enough as I trudged off the field. My father capped his bottle, tossed it in the truck, and angrily walked toward me.

"Damn it, Bud, you play this game, you gotta concentrate!" he shouted. "You know you got to get down on the ball! Now, go on over and apologize to your teammates for losing the game."

He pushed me hard and I stumbled backward, looking at him in disbelief, hurt. Tears filled my eyes.

"Go on!" he said and stepped toward me as if to shove me again.

I turned and trotted over to the guys, eyes lowered, rubbing the back of my hands at the tears running down my cheeks.

"I'm sorry," I blurted. "Sorry I lost the game for us."

I was so embarrassed, I'll never forget that scene. I could see my teammates felt bad for me, and that made it worse. And Coach Christianson, who I was close to because he'd given me a lot of attention and encouragement, I think he was hurt about as much as I was.

"It's all right, Kenny," he said. "Everyone makes errors, even Mickey Mantle."

"Not Slim Stabler," I thought as I jogged to the truck, choking to hold back the tears, refusing to let him see me cry any more.

He didn't say a word to me for the next three days, and I didn't speak to him. I guess my father knew he had done the wrong thing, a hateful thing, but he couldn't bring himself to say that to me.

That was the way my father reacted any time the whiskey launched his demons at me or my sister or my mother. With silence. It must have been painful for him, but it could not have hurt him as much as the agony that was gnawing at his insides.

Yet my father cheered and supported my athletic abilities far more than he abused them. No son had a father who was a bigger fan. Whenever I needed some new athletic equipment, he'd go right out and buy it. And I kept improving in baseball and basketball.

My performance out of uniform wasn't always as impressive. About this time I discovered beer. On Friday and Saturday nights I'd slip out with some friends in junior high school and share a six-pack. One guy had a car, and the night before I was to play in a junior high basketball tournament we took a joyride to Pensacola, Florida. By the time we got there we were out of beer and out of money. So we turned down a dark street and two of the guys got out with screwdrivers and began popping hubcaps off parked cars. The plan was to sell the hubcaps and buy more beer. Real smart.

In two minutes the police caught us. They didn't arrest us because we were so young. But they reported us to the Foley police, who in turn notified our parents and the principal of our school. He suspended us from school for three days. I was the only basketball player in the group. While the other guys regarded the three days off from school as a vacation, I was heartbroken. I'd have to miss the tournament. I also had to go home and face my father. I was afraid he might kill me.

He handled the situation very well. "You can have a good athletic career ahead of you," he said, "maybe even get yourself to college playing ball. But you get a reputation as a thief, you won't get no chance. You've seen good athletes in high school not get scholarships because they couldn't stay out of trouble. Colleges don't take trouble-makers. Now, you keep that in mind."

"Yes, sir," I said.

My father always wanted me to play football, but I wanted to concentrate on baseball and basketball and Slim didn't push me. He kidded me.

"Maybe it's just as well you don't play football," he said. "You're so thin I believe you could drink a strawberry soda and look just like a thermometer."

I wasn't interested in getting beaten up in a sport I hadn't played since I was on a Tiny-mites team at the age of eight.

My father nudged me about football again in the eighth grade, but gently. "Baseball and basketball, Dad, those are my games," I said.

He nodded and turned to my mother. "Sally, we're gonna have to put some meat on Bud's bones. He's so thin he can stand sideways with his tongue out and look just like a zipper."

Just before I started the ninth grade, my father took me to an exhibition game in Mobile between the Houston Oilers and the New York Titans. It was 1960, first year of the American Football League. Afterward I went down on the field and got George Blanda's auto-graph. Eleven years later I would be holding the football for his placekicks with the Raiders. But I wasn't interested in playing foot-ball at the age of fourteen.

Entering my first year of high school, the tenth grade, I had grown to six-one. But at 140 pounds I was whippet-thin, and I still had no intention of playing football. Until I came home one evening and saw a black '54 Ford sitting in the yard and my father tinkering with it.

"Whose is that?" I asked him.

"It's yours if you play football, Bud."

Now, to get a car—my own car—I would have tried to play ice hockey in the Gulf of Mexico.

"I'm gonna be a real good football player, Dad," I said.

The car needed a little work. Of course, my father took care of that in three days, me handing him tools and waxing the Ford twice while he got her tuned up. Goddamn, was I thrilled when I drove off!

I went right to the pool room to show everyone my car. Billy Walker was coming out as I pulled in. Billy said, "Slim told me he was gonna have to do one of two things to get you to play football—either whip your ass or buy you a car. I'm glad to see you driving and not hobbling." He laughed.

I wasn't real fast, but I was quick, and I made the junior varsity team as a defensive back and kick returner. In running back one punt about sixty yards for a touchdown, I zigzagged across the field four times, probably covering two hundred yards. Coach Denzil Hollis watched on the sideline and said, "Damn, that boy runs like a snake!" From then on, my nickname was "Snake." I loved it.

We had a truly amazing high school team for a town of four thousand. In my three varsity years we compiled a 29–1 record against schools with student bodies two and three times the size of Foley High's. My graduating class numbered forty-seven. It was a case of a lot of outstanding athletes coming together in the same place at the same time. My senior year, nine of the eleven starters on offense received college football scholarships.

My first year on the team, as a sophomore, the offense averaged forty-three points a game. The defense gave up exactly six points—thanks to me. Playing defensive back, I got beat for the TD pass.

In addition to starting at defensive back and returning kicks, I was also vying for the backup quarterback job with Jimmy Paul, another good runner (we threw only ten passes a game). Whoever established himself as the number two quarterback this season would be number one next year.

Coach Ivan Jones sent in the second team toward the end of a game that we were winning big. I was at quarterback and Jimmy Paul was playing halfback. We drove down to the goal line. The coach called for an option play, where I was to fake to the halfback going left and keep the ball going right. But I thought a dive play to the left would score. Instead of faking left, I decided to hand off to Jimmy Paul.

But I screwed up. Instead of turning left to hand off, I turned to the right and we didn't score.

Coach Jones was furious. He suspected, because I was fighting for the quarterback job with Jimmy Paul, that I had purposely blown the handoff to him. Coach asked Jimmy if he thought I'd done it purposely, and Jimmy said yes.

At practice the next day Coach Jones called the whole team together and asked me what had happened on that play. "I just turned the wrong way, Coach," I said. "It was just a mental mistake on my part."

He didn't believe me, and he proceeded to chew me out in front of the team. I became so choked with anger that I couldn't say anything. But I swore to myself that I was going to be the starting quarterback the following season and prove to Coach Jones that he had been wrong about me.

I managed to do just that. Coach Jones came to me and admitted his mistake, apologizing for it, and that made us much closer. To this day I have tremendous respect for Ivan Jones (who's now principal of Foley High), even though he did have to paddle my ass one day that junior year.

I was doing everything right on the field, running and passing and leading the team to victory after victory, and I guess I got a little full of myself. Probably our toughest opponent was Escambia High School of Pensacola. My Ford had recently died from a case of terminal transmission, and just before the big game my dad said to me, "Bud, you beat Escambia, I'm gonna buy us a new car. We got the one I want right on the floor—a 1963 Impala SuperSport, 327 engine, four-speed, black with a red interior."

We won by ten points.

The new Chevy was real quick, and I often got it on Saturday nights. I'd race it all over the back roads. Girls loved that Super-Sport, and I loved them back.

A few days after the Escambia win, I took a girlfriend off for a little romancing before practice. One thing led to another and I ended up skipping practice. I hoped Coach Jones would be understanding, seeing as we were playing so well.

The next day I showed up and tried some lame excuse. Coach Jones took me into his office and closed the door. I thought he'd chew on me pretty good. "Bend over and grab your ankles, Snake," he said. I looked up between my legs and saw him standing behind me with a paddle that looked like a cricket bat. He whacked me in the ass once, twice—and I started to reach up to rub the sting. "Grab your ankles!" he said, and whacked me again. "Next time," Coach Jones said, "you get ten."

After the incident my father had an oblique way of telling me not to get carried away with myself. "Bud," he said, "you know I've been in a buncha fights. I can't tell you how many guys have said about me: 'I'm gonna kick that big fucker's ass.' Well, I can tell you it takes a big man to kick my ass, but it don't take him long."

The message was: No matter how good you are, there's always someone better. There's always a better quarterback. I didn't skip practice any more.

But that spring I did get in trouble with the police again. I ran around with a senior named Otis Reed, one of the best all-around athletes I've ever played with anywhere. We combined to score eighty-four points in one basketball game, and both of us averaged close to thirty points a game for the season.

Otis's family was poor and I used to pick him up for school in my car, and later in the Chevy on weekends. We became good buddies. Otis was tough and kind of wild, and the police were always hassling him. We drove down to the beach at Gulf Shores, Alabama, one Sunday and got real deep into the beer. When we got back to Foley that night, we saw a police cruiser parked at the pool room. Being young and drunk and stupid, I said, "Let's get back at them for fucking with you."

I parked, we got out, took a running start, and jumped up on the hood of the police car. I kicked out the blue roof light and Otis kicked in the windshield, then we took off. Not a soul was in sight.

In class the next morning, I was summoned to the principal's office. Otis was already sitting in his outer office and I dropped down in the chair next to him. As the secretary knocked on the principal's door, Otis whispered, "We didn't do it."

"Sure," I whispered.

The police chief was in with the principal and he asked if we knew anything about the damages done to a police car last night. When we said we didn't, Chief Cobb nodded his head real slow. "I want you boys to come on down to the station house with me," he said.

When we got there, he sat us down and had us take off our shoes. I handed him my penny loafers and Otis also turned over the only pair of nonathletic shoes he owned. Chief Cobb carried them outside to the damaged car parked by the window. He placed my shoes in the footprints on the left side of the hood, and Otis's shoes in the prints on the right side.

"I guess it's time to 'fess up, Otis," I said. "He's got us."

Chief Cobb put us on probation, but said we'd have to pay the damages. "That's gonna come to a right good sum. About $400 apiece, I'd guess. I bet your fathers are gonna be real pleased with you."

I was sure my dad wouldn't be able to control himself this time. He was struggling to keep up the payments on my dead $500 Ford, plus the big note on the Impala. But what he did was probably worse than a beating. He made me feel guilty. After all he'd done for me, I had thanked him by adding to his financial burdens.

"Bud, I'm working just as hard as I can to take care of this family, and you know it," he said. "I'm trying to pay off those cars, and now I have to pay for your foolishness, too. I sure ain't got any $400 laying around. I can't hardly believe you did such a dumb thing as bust up a police car. Damn, you disappoint me."

That summer I was able to pay him back. Southeast Conference colleges had begun recruiting me my junior year, and an Alabama alumnus got me a job with a local lumber company. I drove a forklift truck in the yard and also made deliveries to construction sites. It put some cash in my pocket.

The recruiting intensified my senior year as we again went undefeated and won the Gulf Shores football championship. I was named to the All-State, All-Southern, and to two All-American teams. I was also named MVP in the annual postseason all-star game played by the top seniors in the state.

Auburn and Alabama alumni had each taken me to see their teams play, trying to convince me that their program would be best for me. The Auburn offense was closer to the style I was used to playing, with the quarterback running more than passing, and I was leaning toward that school. But Auburn wasn't winning and Alabama always won. Alabama also had Paul W. Bryant Hall, probably the finest athletic dorm in the land.

But the greatest thing Alabama had to offer was Paul W. Bryant himself, the legendary "Bear." With his big body and that face that looked like it should be carved in Mount Rushmore, Coach Bryant was the most imposing figure I had ever seen, next to my father. The amazing thing was how closely my father resembled Coach Bryant, who could have been his older brother. In fact, Slim wore the same style clothes that Coach Bryant favored—houndstooth hat, blue blazer, and gray slacks.

My sister Carolyn likes to tell about the time she and Slim were in the stands early for one of my Alabama games. "A woman came over and insisted that Daddy was Coach Bryant. 'No, ma'am, I'm not,' he said. She kept insisting that he give her an autograph. Daddy had already had a few drinks, of course, and he said, 'I'm not any damn relation to the man!' I told the woman that Kenny Stabler was his son, but she wouldn't believe that. 'I know you're Bear Bryant,' she said. Finally Daddy said to her, 'Wouldn't you think if I was Coach Bryant that I'd be with my team before a game and not up here in the goddamn stands?' He turned away from her and took a long drink from his bottle."

When Coach Bryant came down to Foley and had dinner with my family, he just filled our little dining room. He didn't make any sales pitches. He just talked about hunting and fishing in that deep, gravelly voice that all but hypnotized you.

I decided right then that if I was going to bust my ass playing college football, I was going to do it for the man they called "Bear." He knew how to win, and I was used to winning. "Snake is going from Slim to Bear," I thought, which had a nice ring to it.

I also had an opportunity to sign a professional baseball contract about this time. The Yankees drafted me and offered a $20,000 bonus for my signature on a contract. In truth, I was a better thrower of baseballs than a thrower of footballs in 1964. Foley didn't have a top baseball team, but I won nine games and had 125 strikeouts that spring. Don Sutton pitched for Tate High School in Pensacola, and every time we hooked up there would be about eight scouts in the stands. I won the only game that Sutton lost in high school, 1–0. I struck out 16 and Sutton had 14 that day. He was a better pitcher because he knew how to set up batters, change speeds, move the ball around. As it turned out, he knew how to win three hundred games in the major leagues.

From as far back as I can remember, the only thing I wanted to do with my life was to become a professional athlete. Somehow I just knew that eventually I was going to make a living playing ball. And I chose football over baseball simply because I felt I'd make more money in the long run pitching pigskin instead of horsehide.

Once I signed a letter of intent to Alabama, a celebration was called for. A bunch of us who were going to college on scholarships got together with some girls and a couple of cases of beer. We kept buying beer until our money ran out. Then, once again drunk and dopey, I did something stupid, along with the other guys. We drove up behind a grocery to steal several cases of empty Coke bottles stacked there. We planned to redeem them elsewhere and use the money to buy more beer. As usual, we got busted.

I also accumulated a number of speeding tickets in late spring, and word of my misdemeanors reached the Alabama coaches immediately. The university alumni network was incredibly efficient.

The day after I graduated, assistant coach Jimmy Sharpe showed up at the house and said the athletic department had found me a good job at the university for the summer. "Pay's not bad," he said. "And all you'll do is ride a machine that cuts grass. You get free room and board."

"Yes, sir," I said, "sounds good."

Actually, it sounded to me like one shit deal, the coaches taking me up on campus just so they could keep an eye on me because I'd had a little trouble. Most guys—at least the ones I knew—had trouble in high school.

So I went up to Tuscaloosa thinking the summer would be hell. I had $5 in my jeans. In my bag I had underwear, socks, another pair of jeans, a bunch of T-shirts and button-down shirts, my Foley High letter jacket, and a pair of sneakers. I was wearing my penny loafers. I wasn't going to make any points on wardrobe, and I couldn't get around much without a car.

But it turned out the coaches didn't bird-dog me at all. The job gave me spending money, and I made friends with some guys who also liked to play basketball, throw around a football, drink beer, and get close to girls. Girls were everywhere: blondes, brunettes, redheads. I had never seen so many great-looking women in one place.

The University of Alabama. It was definitely my kind of place.

3

"Stabler, You're Luckier Than a Shithouse Rat!"

In August 1964 all the football players came back to the university. One day before football practice started, I was shooting baskets in the gym with an assistant coach when Joe Namath walked in with another assistant. I liked Joe right away. He was the starting quarterback, a senior, but he was real friendly.

"You wanna play a little two-on-two, Ken?"

"Sure thing," I said.

I was thrilled. I was also a bit quicker than Joe because he had a bad knee, but he could play basketball. We went hard for almost forty minutes. And Joe and I ended up banging each other around pretty good. Just out of common courtesy.

Freshmen, who roomed on the dorm's top floor, didn't have much contact with upperclassmen. I was a little apprehensive and kind of low-keyed the whole year. I did quarterback the freshman team, though, and learned Coach Bryant's system, which was simple. We ran a rollout offense from the I formation, and we basically ran off-tackle to both sides. I rolled out, then pitched the ball out or back to a runner, or I carried it myself. When the defense brought the backs up to stop the run, we'd play-fake off tackle and throw to the wide receivers. Once the defensive backs fell off to try and stop the receivers, we'd run some more.

All plays to the right started with "Gee," those to the left started with "Haw." If you're driving a mule and want it to go right, you call out "Gee," to the left you call out "Haw." Apparently Coach Bryant had done some mule driving when he was growing up in Arkansas.

Alabama quarterbacks called their own plays, and the list of plays was worn in a plastic band on your wrist in case you needed to refer to it. I doubt that anyone ever had to, the list was so short. I remember in running option plays that defenders kept grabbing at my wristband when they tackled, why I don't know. Getting the list wouldn't tell them when we were going to call the plays, and everyone knew our plays anyway.

Our freshman season consisted of four games, which we split. I played fairly well, but I attempted to do too much by myself. We had a play called "55 Keep." It started like a rollout pass but was a keeper. Every time we got in a jam on third down, needing five yards or less for a first down, I called "55 Keep."

Coach Bryant called me over on the practice field and said, "Stabler, you can't do it all yourself. Every third-and-short you're calling the same play with you carrying. Defenses aren't blind, you know."

In the fall of 1965 I was given the jersey number 12, the same number Pat Trammell and Namath had worn. That suggested the coaches had high hopes for me. But not that season. Steve Sloan, a senior, led us to a 9–1–1 record, followed by a 39–28 victory over Nebraska in the Orange Bowl, and we won the national championship.

I backed up Sloan and improved my execution. Mainly, I ran out the clock, throwing maybe a dozen passes all season. I had a great opportunity in the Tennessee game. I was sent in late in the last quarter with the score tied 7–7. We drove about fifty yards, mostly carrying the ball myself, to about the Tennessee ten-yard line. Then I was thrown for a loss. The clock was running out and I wanted to stop it. I can't remember whether I checked the down on the down-and-distance marker on the sideline or on the scoreboard, but one of them said it was third down. I purposely threw a pass out of bounds to stop the clock. It was fourth down.

When I reached the sideline, Coach Bryant walked up to me and said, "Stabler, have you lost your fucking mind?"

He was furious. I had helped give Tennessee, not a strong team at the time, a major moral victory. I followed Coach Bryant to the visitors' dressing room at Neyland Stadium. The door was locked and our equipment manager had not arrived yet. Coach Bryant was not going to wait for the key.

He brought his right arm back and hit that door with a forearm smash that knocked it, literally, right off its hinges. We all walked in and when everyone was present, Coach Bryant said, "I want all the assistant coaches and nonplayers out of here. Right now."

Then he went over and tugged that splintered door closed and turned to us. No one made a sound. Coach Bryant cleared his throat and said, "I want to apologize for me and my staff for not preparing you people well enough to win the game today. It was us, not you, who lost that game. I'm sorry."

No wonder we all loved that man.

I had a lot of fun at Alabama. My roommate was Dennis Homan, and we always seemed to be in trouble with the dorm manager, Gary White, who lived with his wife in an apartment on the ground floor of the three-story building. Gary talked real slow and sounded like the cartoon character Deputy Dawg, so that's what we called him behind his back. He prided himself on keeping us in line.

You had to be in your room by eleven, lights out and no talking at eleven-thirty. "Deputy Dawg" would slip down the corridor and listen by your door to see if you were talking after lights-out. "Cut the shit, get to sleep," he'd call out.

"I wish someone would take the Dawg for a walk," I'd whisper to Dennis, who would laugh and bring another yell from Gary.

We had to be at study hall every weeknight until nine o'clock. Then Dennis and I would race to The Tide, the bar near campus where most of the athletes and a lot of fraternity guys used to hang out. Dennis had a black '65 Chevy Impala, and it allowed us to stay out till the last minute before curfew. At 11 P.M. Deputy Dawg was always waiting at the top of the first staircase or by the entrance to the dorm. There was no way to get past him if you were late.

One night Dennis and I got a pretty fair beer buzz on at The Tide and then needed something to eat. So we stopped at McDonald's, each bought a hamburger, and got back to the dorm at 10:55. We were jacking around as we ran into the dorm. Dennis, who'd finished his burger, snatched mine out of my hand and took off up the stairs. At the top of the stairs, I grabbed a fire extinguisher off the wall as I chased him. Dennis turned the corner and I turned, too, opening up the fire extinguisher full-blast. It fired a stream of water as big as your finger about twenty-five feet.

Dennis had run right past Deputy Dawg, who came toward me in the line of fire. The stream knocked him sideways. Dennis stood there laughing like hell.

"Stabler, meet me at the practice field at five-thirty tomorrow morning," Dawg said.

The next morning I had to run eight laps around the track—two miles—and do about twenty minutes' worth of grass drills. At Dawg's call, I'd dive to the grass, roll, get up, and dive again. He got me so many times for jacking around in the dorm, for not wearing slippers on the corridor carpeting, and for being late for curfew, it was ridiculous. Deputy Dawg was tough. I spent more time running in the early morning during my four years at Alabama than I did in my entire fifteen-year pro career.

But my room was always neat. Like me, Dennis believed in keeping all his gear in place and our room spotless. When Deputy Dawg ran a contest to see who had the neatest room in the dorm, Dennis and I each won a plaque that I still have. Capricorns are fanatical about neatness.

Money was a problem for me in school. The problem was, I never had much. The $15-a-month laundry allowance was usually spent before it arrived, and I'd have to do my own wash or ask a kind girl to help me out. Players were given books by the school, but as a phys ed major my classes were so easy that I sold most of my texts.

I also kited checks, not to beat anyone out of money but just in the interest of my survival. I'd cash a $10 check at the drugstore, say, then cash a $20 check at another store, and use half of the money to pay off the drugstore. Then I'd cash a $40 check someplace else and pay off the $20 debt. Eventually I'd come up with the money to catch the last one.

Usually I won the money playing shuffleboard at The Tide. There were two shuffleboards in the bar and everybody played them. Dennis and I almost never lost a game. Generally we just played for beer, which was why Dennis and I came in glowing many nights. But a couple of times a week we'd get in shuffleboard games with guys from the fraternities and play for $5 or $10 per game. I walked into The Tide one night with 50¢ and walked out of there with $50.

The guys in the frats wanted to beat us bad, which was why they became regular contributors to the Stabler fund. I enjoyed their company, as well as the parties they threw at the fraternity houses. Football players had open invitations to those affairs.

The only fraternity I wanted to be in was the A Club and, having earned my letter as a sophomore, I was inducted into the club at season's end. The initiation rite lasted a whole week, and about twenty-five of us from all sports went through it together. A few initiation highlights:

One night we were relieved of everything we had in our pockets, paired up, blindfolded, and driven into some woods about fifty miles from Tuscaloosa. Dennis and I were left there, in the pitch dark, not knowing where we were, and told we had to be back at the dorm by 7 A.M. I still don't know how we finally found our way to a road, but we did. Hitching four or five rides, we made it back in time.

Another day we were sent out wearing only T-shirts, jeans, and sneakers—and it was cool in Alabama in February—to the girls' dorm and told to kneel in front of a first-floor window. Then we had to beg for water. Loudly. A girl opened the window and another poured a bucket of water on me. Next a second-floor window opened and another cascade of water hit me. There was a lot of female laughter.

But the most trying of all the initiation rites was saved for last. I had to lower my pants and tie a long string around my dick, draw the string up inside my shirt and out the neck, and tie a pencil to the other end of the string. Then I had to go out with a notepad and get twenty-five girls to sign their autographs with the pencil dangling from the string at my waist. Every time a girl signed her name, the string yanked my dick.

One girl was hip to the deal and had a great time torturing me. First she printed her name, which had about fifteen letters in it and was of no value anyway as I needed her signature. Then she misspelled her name purposely so she had to write it over. Three times.

The A Club ring that was presented to me was real nice, but I felt it should have come with a tube of first-aid ointment.

To celebrate our letters, Dennis, myself, and three other teammates who ran around with us—David Chatwood, Charley Harris, and Terry Kilgore—went to the West Alabama Fair. We went on all the rides, played most of the games, and I almost drowned Bozo the Clown. He was seated in a chair that was suspended about four feet above a vat of water. For 25¢ you bought three chances to throw a baseball at a bull's-eye. If you hit it, the clown would fall into the water.

The bull's-eye was not very big and when we walked up to the concession nobody was hitting it. That's why the clown sat up there making faces at people, taunting them into putting up their quarters. On my first throw I hit the bull's-eye, the chair tipped forward, and the clown hit the drink. He climbed back up there, and I dumped him into the water again. He was no longer making faces.

We were all laughing, and people started feeding me quarters. I just kept throwing, and I had near-perfect control that night. Sixteen times I bought three balls, and thirteen times that clown got soaked. He must've thought someone had run in a ringer on him.

On weekends we often partied in Columbus, Mississippi, which had a bunch of really rocking joints, until I made a connection at the Smith Motel in town.

On our drives out Highway 82 I kept seeing this beautiful little Chevy street rod parked at the motel. I knew somebody at that place had the same love for cars that I had. So one day I stopped to look at the car. It was a '49 Chevy Coupé and it was *cherry*. It was painted a deep-burnished gold and had a real shiny set of mag wheels on it, a new rolled-and-pleated black leather interior, and a chrome four-speed shifter sticking up out of the floor.

A big heavyset young guy came out of the motel, Ray Smith, Jr., whose father owned the place. We started talking cars. He had an eight-cylinder 327 engine in the Chevy and he'd welded a set of traction bars to the frame in the rear to keep it from shimmying on takeoffs.

I began stopping by to bullshit with Ray Jr. and his dad, who were both Alabama fans, and we became friends. Then one day Ray Sr. said, "Ken, you got a girl sometime and want to come out here, I'll fix you up with a room back in the corner. It won't cost you anything. You can bring a few friends."

I immediately took him up on that offer, along with David Chatwood, Charley Harris, and Terry Kilgore, my center. I always took care of my centers because they always took care of me on the field. Hell, I had my hands up between my centers' legs more than I did my girlfriends'. Different strategies, but in both cases the goal was to score.

A few weeks later Ray Jr. told me he was going to sell the Chevy and that he'd let me have it for $2,000. That was a steal, given what had been spent on that car, and I wanted it the way a bear wants honey. All I had to do was convince my father to get the loan for me to buy it. He was coming up on Saturday to see me pitch in a baseball game, and I made sure he also saw the car.

I borrowed it from Ray Jr. Saturday morning and had it parked right outside the dorm when Slim pulled in. He noticed the gold Chevy right away.

"Piece of work there," he said.

"I know the guy who's selling it," I said. "He wants $2,000."

"The car's over sixteen years old. What's he got under the hood—a gold-plated engine?"

"A small-block 327, same as your SuperSport," I said.

Slim's eyes lit up. "Then that little thing'll *move.*"

"Maybe we could turn her into a drag racer this summer," I said.

That did it. I knew my father had always been interested in drag racing, that he wanted to see what he could do with the right machine. We bought the car.

I had won a couple of games pitching for the freshman baseball team and I won a couple more as a sophomore. I still loved baseball, but I was on a football scholarship. When spring football practice began, the athletic department let me know I had to take off my cap and put on a helmet.

I looked good running and passing in the spring workouts and I won the job of starting quarterback for the fall. I drove home in June feeling great. Namath and Sloan had each led Alabama to the national championship the past two years. Maybe it would be my turn. We had a hell of a team coming back in 1966.

I worked with my father at his shop that summer, and on turning my car into a racer. The Chevy's engine was fed by six carburetors. We took off the street headers and made a set that went into a collector box. That created a vacuum that helped suck the exhaust from the engine and made it breathe better for more speed. We mounted seventeen-inch power-slick tires in back and lightened the car by removing the fender wells and the backseat.

The car was fast. We won two races, picking up about $200.00 in prize money and a pair of $3.95 trophies. We could have won more if we'd had the money to build a first-class car, but racing parts were expensive.

I found out during a race in Mobile there was one part that car sorely needed, a blowproof scatter shield that covered the flywheel and clutch. On the starting line I'd have to rev the engine way up to get the maximum out of the Chevy's power curve. So I'd hold in the clutch and race the engine, then pop the clutch and the front wheels would leap off the ground. I'd cross the finish line doing over 100 m.p.h.

In this particular race in Mobile, I had pushed the r.p.m.'s up to 7,000 and was doing 110 when I hit the finish line—and the clutch blew up.

Shrapnel came flying up through the floorboards like fragments off a hand grenade. The explosion shifted the whole steering column to the right and I was dragged along with it—fortunately. Later we found a gear off the flywheel in the back of the car right behind where my head would have been if the column hadn't been blown over. The explosion also ripped the top off my left penny loafer and blackened three toes.

I soon heard from the football coaching staff at Alabama. An assistant coach phoned to tell me that racing cars really didn't fit into my athletic future. I understood. Seven-toed quarterbacks were not in high demand.

The worst thing was that the Chevy was so torn up we had to sell it. I went back to school in August, again without wheels of my own.

But I was ready for football, confident that we were going to have a big season.

Coach Bryant was tough and demanding. His drills were long on conditioning, with lots of wind sprints back and forth from sideline to sideline and plenty of stamina work. In those days, all Alabama players were lean and mean. Quickness was key and the lines averaged only 195 pounds. So we ran and ran.

We all cussed Coach Bryant under our breath: "That old sonuvabitch is gonna kill us." But that was only in the heat of practice. He'd stand up on his tower and see every little mistake you made, and when he came down he'd let you know about the errors in no soft terms.

Yet even the cussing of Coach Bryant was done affectionately. He was a hard man, but a fair man. Sometimes, in making his points, he could also be a funny man.

During a preseason scrimmage at Denny Stadium in Tuscaloosa (we also played some home games in Birmingham), I rolled out on a pass play. Ray Perkins was the intended receiver and he had flat-out lost the defensive back on him. I released the pass—and it sailed way over Perkins's head. I trotted off the field thinking, "Got to follow through better so the ball won't take off."

"Sorry, Ray," I said to Perkins at the sideline.

"Stabler," Coach Bryant said, "you throw the ball like a bush-league pitcher."

I couldn't help laughing.

In our season opener, on one play I called a pitchout. But as I rolled left, I spotted Perkins breaking clear on a crossing pattern. So I whipped the ball to him for a score. I ran to the sideline beaming.

Coach Bryant put his hand on my shoulder and I thought he was going to congratulate me for improvising and getting a touchdown. "One thing you should know, son," he said, "is you never can trust left-handed crapshooters and left-handed quarterbacks."

In our next game, needing a first down inside the ten, Coach Bryant sent in a play and I changed it. We got the first down and went in to score. Later Coach Bryant told me, "When I send in something, you don't have to call it. Run what you like—but you make goddamn sure it works!"

By the end of the 1966 season, Coach Bryant was calling our team the best he had ever fielded in his ten years at Alabama. I had a lot of help having a big year. My outside receivers were split end Ray Perkins (who went on to play for the Colts and later to succeed Bear Bryant as coach) and flanker Dennis Homan (who later played with the Cowboys and the Chiefs). We won all ten of our regular-season games, six of them by shutouts, which says something about our defense. But the offense wasn't bad. We scored at least twenty-one points in all but two of our games. I completed 64.9 percent of my passes (an SEC accuracy record) for 956 yards and ran for 397 yards as well.

Coach Bryant wasn't real happy about the way I did some of those good things. On the option pitchouts and pitchbacks, I'd roll behind moving blockers and the defense would watch my eyes. When I turned my head toward the runner I was pitching to, defenders could read me. I decided to take away that key. I knew where my runner was going to be on every play and didn't have to look at him. I'd just pitch to that spot while looking straight ahead. We picked up a lot of yardage on runs off those blind pitches, as defenders were slower getting to the ballcarriers.

But every time I made a blind pitch, no matter what we gained, Coach Bryant would be waiting for me on the sideline. "Stabler," he'd say, "you're luckier than a shithouse rat!"

I had another move in passing on a rollout that Coach Bryant was not real partial to. I liked to run along with the ball and wait until defenders drew close to me. Then I'd jump up like Harry Gilmer used to and throw a pass. In the forties Gilmer had considerable success with that maneuver at Alabama, and I completed the first five of my jump passes.

But Coach Bryant kept advising me to stop the practice without insisting that I do so. I guess he didn't feel he could, as long as my completion percentage on jump passes was 1.000. "There's only three things that can happen on the best of passes and two of them are bad," he said. "Jumping around and throwing the ball does not improve those odds."

In one game that season I connected on a couple of jump passes early, then tried another in the second half that resulted in one of those two bad things that can happen on pass plays. The ball landed in the arms of a defensive back.

"Stabler!" Coach Bryant bellowed as I came off the field. "I don't want any more of that walling your eyes back in your head and jumping up and throwing the ball. Keep your feet on the fucking ground!"

I wondered if Harry Gilmer's coach had ever talked like that?

After our final game of the season, a 31–0 win over Auburn, I went out for a few beers with Slim and two old friends from home, Billy Walker and his wife Lois Gayle. Billy said he thought sure he was going to have a fight in the stands that day.

"Somehow we ended up sitting in the middle of the Auburn fans," he said. "The guy sitting behind me was about six-six and 275 pounds, and, Kenny, he was on your ass the whole first quarter. I wasn't saying nothing, but I could see Lois Gayle was burning. Well, then you hit that long touchdown pass.

"Lois Gayle stood up, turned around, and said, 'What do you think of Kenny Stabler now, you big sonuvabitch?'

"I said to myself, 'Oh my God, that bastard's gonna hit me 'cause I know he ain't gonna hit Lois Gayle.' I was reaching for my pocket knife when that big sonuvabitch said, 'Lady, I think Ken Stabler's a damn fine ballplayer.' "

In January we went to the Sugar Bowl and beat the hell out of Nebraska, 34–7. That gave us an 11–0 record, which seemed to us hard to beat. But not to the people who vote in the final polls that rate the number one team in the country. We were ranked number three. Notre Dame, which had played a sister-kissing tie with Michigan State that season, was ranked first and M.S.U. second. But in the minds of all of us at Alabama, we were the national champions. Coach Bryant told a friend, "We would've beaten Notre Dame."

I liked to think we could have beaten the Green Bay Packers, I was so full of myself. And now I decided I was going to get myself a car. Not just any car, either. I wanted a brand-new 1967 Corvette.

I hooked a ride to Birmingham and went to Woods Chevrolet. It was a performance-type dealer, the Woods brothers having built some of the great stockcar racers. I knew the people at Woods were big fans of Alabama football. At least, that's what I'd heard. If they weren't big 'Bama fans, I had about as much chance of acquiring the car of my dreams as I had of becoming Miss America.

I walked into the showroom, my sneakers squeaking on the highly polished floor, and saw my car. It was black-and-white and beautiful, so low and sleek that it looked like it was doing 50 m.p.h. just sitting there. I rubbed my hand lightly along the Corvette's Simonized roof.

A salesman, all smiles, came over to me and said, "Beauty, isn't it?"

Before he drew close I knew I was going to own that car. Stuck in his lapel was a bright red 'Bama button.

"Yes, sir," I said, "it sure is a beauty."

He stuck out his hand and introduced himself, and I said, "How you doing? I'm Ken Stabler."

"Snake Stabler!" he yelled. "I saw you win Most Valuable Player in the Sugar Bowl. You guys just stomped the shit out of them Cornhuskers!" He gushed like a burst fuel pump, talking about that game and our team, saying there was no justice when we weren't voted number one in the final coaches' poll. Somehow, I couldn't bring myself to argue with him.

I opened the door and slid behind the wheel of the 'Vette. It felt unbelievable.

"Oh, yeah," the salesman said. "I can see this is your car, Snake. C'mon back in the office and let's you'n me work up a deal."

After we were seated in his office, and after I'd answered his questions about a scoring play in the Sugar Bowl, we got down to business. I told him I was going to be a bit short on the down payment, and that I couldn't do a whole lot about the monthly payments either. When he didn't frown at that, I was encouraged.

"You know the contract Joe Namath got when he went pro," I said. "I'm going to be a top pro pick too. When I sign, I'll have a bunch of money. You just carry me till then and I'll pay off the whole note when I get my bonus."

In Alabama, the next best thing to being Coach Bryant was being one of Coach Bryant's boys. The Bear was God, we were his disciples, and the good folks of Alabama would try to do just about anything for us.

The salesman excused himself and returned in seconds with the sales manager. I shook his hand, we talked some football, praised Coach Bryant, and I drove out of the showroom in that glistening black-and-white Corvette.

I drove the sixty miles back to Tuscaloosa humming the "Alabama Fight Song." When I pulled up outside Bryant Hall, several team-mates came running over to me. "You can touch it, but no finger-prints, please," I said. One guy brought out a six-pack to congratu-late me and I let each of the players drive the car around the area.

Then I decided to drive to Mobile, about four hours away, to see a special girl I wanted to impress with the car. I headed down University Avenue, the radio blaring, feeling like Richard Petty must feel taking a victory lap at the Daytona Speedway. Everything was just perfect: the car, the day, the girl I was going to see. And looking back, it's hard to believe the accident was my fault.

Wanting to check the mileage to Mobile and only doing 20 m.p.h., I leaned over to set the tripometer under the dash. The car came to an abrupt stop without me stepping on the brake. It turned out not to be the result of new technology, just the rear bumper of the car ahead of me that had stopped at a red light. It was true what I had heard about the effects of an impact on fiberglass. I had exactly sixty-five miles on my new car—and $2,000 in damages.

I made the same arrangement on repairs with a local dealer that I had made with Woods. Trust me.

I wasn't about to let the mishap keep me from my date in Mobile. The girl was stunning and I was in need of being stunned this eve-ning. I borrowed a friend's car and drove on down. It was an eight-hour round-trip and I had to be back for an 8 A.M. class, which only gave me ninety minutes with the girl. But it was worth it.

"Honey," I told her, "I started out today in a new Corvette that I bought without a cent down and no known credit. You don't happen to know anyone who's good with fiberglass, do you?"

She laughed and said, "No, but I'm good with some other things."

Repairs on the Corvette took a month. In February I drove it home one weekend to show the car to my father, thinking he'd love it. Instead he hardly looked at the car, wasn't interested in taking it for a spin, and didn't want to talk about it. He was real quiet around me the entire weekend, as if he wanted to avoid me.

It was very confusing. Slim attended all my games. After one of them I'd come home with Slim that Saturday night. We had a nice dinner, then I went out with some friends and hit a few honky-tonks. At ten the next morning I was still sleeping when Slim came into my room. One of my legs was hanging over the foot of the bed and my father shook it and said, "C'mon, let's go down to the Legion Post. I need a beer."

He had me sit at the bar so that all his cronies could ask me questions about yesterday's game. With each of my answers I could see my father just sitting there glowing. He was proud.

But my father's attitude toward me began changing as the season wore on. The more notoriety and acclaim I received, the more he seemed to drift away from me. The man who had always encouraged me in athletics now seemed to resent my achievements.

I wondered if he didn't feel a certain jealousy, reading about how well I had played and how bright my future looked. Some sportswriters were saying that I could become one of the richest athletes coming out of college in 1968. "Stabler will be able to name his price next year," one columnist wrote, "because he'll have both football and baseball teams bidding for his left arm."

I definitely felt my father was envious of me for owning a Corvette. Here was his son driving an automobile that was probably worth close to Slim's total assets. My father was growing increasingly self-conscious about his feeling that he wasn't doing well financially.

Slim was at the Legion Post when I got ready to drive back to school. I said to my mother, "Dad seems moodier than ever."

My sister Carolyn said, "He is. He's getting worse."

"He's been drinking real hard some nights," my mother said, shaking her head. "He gets in one of his moods and there's nothing I can do with him. He'll sit in his truck out front or in the yard and just drink till he's about ready to pass out."

"Friday night a week ago, Daddy went out drinking," said Carolyn, who was sixteen. "Momma didn't go. I heard Daddy come in about four in the morning. He woke up Momma and slapped her a couple of times."

"He slapped you?" I said, looking at my petite little mother, barely five-two and 100 pounds.

My mother nodded. "It was the whiskey."

"Daddy wanted her to fix him something to eat," Carolyn said. "Momma fixed him a plate of food, and he threw it on the floor."

A few weeks later I was in my dorm room in the early evening when Carolyn called. She was frightened and in tears. "Dad's drunk and he's pushing Momma all around the living room," Carolyn whispered. "I had to slip into the kitchen to call you. Daddy's real mean and we don't know what to do. He's wild. Please come home, Kenny."

I hurried out of the dorm and covered the four-hour trip to Foley in three and a half hours. When I got home, Slim was gone. My mother was composed, holding everything inside her, which was her way. But Carolyn was still upset. "Oh, Kenny, I was so scared," she said. "Daddy was fighting with Momma, slapping her around. It was awful."

I went out looking for my father, figuring he'd be in his favorite bar, George's. I was scared when I got there, not wanting to walk inside. If he'd slap my mother, what would he do to me? I opened the door a crack and saw my father seated at the near end of the bar in his work uniform, dark blue khaki pants and a light blue shirt with SLIM sewn over the pocket.

I walked in. There were five other people at the far end of the bar, giving Slim lots of space. He was just staring into his drink, the smoke from his cigarette curling out of an ashtray in front of him. I slid onto the stool beside him. Slim turned his head and his cold eyes bored into me. I felt my insides flinch.

"What's going on, Dad?" I asked softly.

"It ain't none of your fucking business," he said, his eyes not budging off me.

"But Mom . . . Carolyn . . ." I said, the words barely getting out. "You could hurt them."

Then he slid off the barstool and jabbed his right hand into his pants pocket. He brought out the penknife that he used to cut wire in the shop, and he opened the blade in an instant, like a man who'd had a lot of practice.

"Dad, I'm just trying to make things right!" I said.

He grabbed my shirtfront in his left hand and drove me up against the wall, putting the point of the knife in my ribs. "You just stay the hell out of it!" he said, staring rage at me. "Now get the hell out of here!"

He drew the knife back inches from my ribs and held it there. But I wasn't going to run. That's the way he was, what he'd taught me. You don't run. I just stared at him.

Then he lunged out the door and was gone.

I burst into tears and sat down on the barstool.

Wayne Mulligan, the bartender, came over and said, "What's wrong, Kenny?"

"It's none of your fucking business," I said. "Just give me a beer and a scotch on the side."

By the time I finished the drinks, my heart had stopped pounding and I drove home. "Your father's in bed," my mother said, nodding toward their bedroom. "You can go on back to school, Kenny, Slim'll be all right now. I think I know him."

I didn't know him, couldn't understand how my father could manhandle people who loved him. All I knew was that I'd been afraid of him since I was a little kid. Now I was twenty-one and even more afraid of him.

As if I didn't have enough on my mind, worrying about my family, I tore a cartilage in my left knee early in spring practice. After the knee was drained of fluid, I could walk fine but I couldn't run. The doctors said I would be all right by the fall if I laid out of the spring work. Arthroscopic surgery had not been invented in 1967 or the loose piece of cartilage would have been removed immediately. The surgery available at this time might have caused me to miss the coming season.

Coach Bryant said, "Don't do anything, Kenny. Just let that knee heal."

Wanting to practice and having to just stand around and watch my teammates having fun, I soon got bored. One sure way to relieve the boredom was to spend some time with that girl in Mobile.

I started driving down to see her three or four nights a week, leaving right after study hall ended at nine. That gave me less than two hours with the girl, as I had to be back by 8 A.M. to make my first class. So I stopped going to study hall. Then I stopped making the first class, and soon I was failing it and my second class as well. I also picked up a bunch of speeding tickets.

For some reason I just didn't give a shit. My give-a-shitter shorted out or something because I stopped showing up at practice too.

Naturally, word of my transgressions reached the athletic department. I was skipping practice, failing classes, and collecting speeding tickets as if they were chances in a raffle.

It was not easy for football players at Alabama to fail courses, particularly physical education majors. All you had to do was show up. I took such classes as audio-visual aids, where I learned how to plug in and turn on a movie projector, and industrial arts, where we were supposed to learn how to make various doodads. I took that class because the teacher was a friend of the coaching staff who got to go on trips with the team. You could go into his classroom, jack around, and still pass. I never did make a doodad. But as I said, you did have to show up.

So I kind of expected to hear from Coach Bryant—but at school, not at my home. I was visiting my parents on a weekend when the telegram arrived. "YOU HAVE BEEN INDEFINITELY SUSPENDED," it read. "COACH PAUL W. BRYANT." He didn't waste any words.

I wondered if he really meant it. I remembered when Coach Bryant had suspended Joe Namath in 1963 for some hell-raising before a game, but skipping a few classes and missing practice when I couldn't work out anyway didn't seem to be *that* serious. Hadn't I led the team to eleven victories last season?

A few hours later I received another telegram, this one from Namath. His read: "HE MEANS IT!"

I was soon notified that my grade point average had fallen below the minimum level for intercollegiate athletic eligibility. I could no longer play ball.

"To hell with all this crap," I decided, and got into some heavy-duty honky-tonking and partying with my Mobile Bay baby. I didn't care about anything but having a good time. Twice I ran into assistant coach Jimmy Sharpe in Mobile, when he was recruiting there, and he tried to talk me into coming back. I wasn't interested. I was double stupid but didn't know it.

Thank God my father did. He came up with a plan that saved me, or I probably never would have gone back to school.

Slim had a lawyer friend in Foley write a letter that appeared to be from the United States Army Draft Board, saying that if I did not return to college by the fall I would be subject to induction.

I took that letter as gospel. The Vietnam War was hot in the spring of 1967, and I had no interest in getting shot. In June I went back to school and got a part-time job loading trucks. And I enrolled in summer school to regain my eligibility, signing up for five credits, one more than I needed. The mind-taxing courses were "Modern Dance" and "Marriage and the Family."

I had to move out of the athletic dorm into another one, and the day I did so I happened to pass Coach Bryant. I told him I was going to summer school and that I was sorry I'd messed up.

"Son, you're crazy," he said. "I think you might as well go on off and play baseball." Then he walked on by.

He was tough, but I felt I could show him. Summer school, only six weeks, wasn't bad at all. I met another girl, did a little partying on campus, and did Mobile on weekends.

The day I regained my eligibility to play football, I went to see Coach Bryant in his office. Even without his hat on and sitting down behind his desk, the man looked tall and massive. He looked like he weighed four hundred pounds as he stared at me. He had the loudest stare I've ever encountered. Then he took a drag on his Chesterfield and spit tobacco into the paper cup in his hand.

"Coach," I said finally, "I've made myself eligible to play again and I want to come out and get back on the team."

He stared at me through his expressionless, half-lidded eyes and said, "Stabler, you don't deserve to be on my football team." He spit in the cup.

I stood there shifting my feet, not knowing what to say. "Well, Coach," I heard myself telling him in a loud voice, "I'm coming out anyway."

He didn't say a word. He just spit once more.

"I guess that's it for me at Alabama," I thought, going back to my room. "Football practice starts in two weeks for everyone but me."

I was angry, depressed, totally confused as I packed. I was determined to show Coach Bryant I could play football under his rules if he would just give me a chance, but he'd written me off.

As I snapped my suitcase and turned to leave, assistant coach Jimmy Sharpe came bursting into my room. "He's letting you come back!" he yelled. "That thing you said to him sold him!" He clapped me on the back.

I let out a whoop and cried, "Jimmy, I love you!"

I ran to my car and headed for the nearest 7-Eleven store to buy a six-pack of beer. Then I drove home, smiling and hook-shooting the empty cans over the roof at road signs all along the way.

I wasn't so happy when I reported to the first practice. Coach Bryant had not finished punishing me. At Alabama you get your workout uniforms in a wire basket that's handed to you through a window. In it are socks, a jock, a T-shirt, and a jersey. The color of the jersey designates which team you are on. Red jersey is first team, white is second team, blue is third team, green is fourth team, orange is fifth team, and the sixth-team jersey is brown, which is appropriate.

Coach Bryant's favorite word for anyone who screwed up was "turd." More than once he had said to me, "What was *that* supposed to be, Turd?" I guess everyone who played for him got the turd call at least once. And the sixth-team jersey was turd brown. That was the color of the jersey in my basket that first day of practice.

I was a senior, coming off MVP of the Sugar Bowl, and I had to wear a turd-brown jersey. I also had to begin practice with the sixth team. Then I had to work my way up through all those different-colored jerseys during the next four weeks. I felt like one of those multicolored packages of Life Savers.

Our opening game of the season was against Florida State in Birmingham and it was on national television. By then I was wearing a red jersey again, but that did not mean I would start. On game days all the players wore crimson. I did not start.

Coach Bryant started junior Joe Kelley at quarterback. Kelley ran three plays, we punted, and the offense came off the field.

"Stabler," Coach Bryant said, "let's see what you can do next series."

We were two-touchdown favorites in that game, but the odds-makers were way off. Florida State had a fine quarterback in Kim Hammond and a top receiver in six-five Ron Sellers. F.S.U. scored thirty-seven points against us. We also put thirty-seven points on the board.

That was the most points we scored in a game in 1967. With the loss of Ray Perkins and five starting offensive linemen to graduation, we weren't the team we had been the year before. I passed for over 1,200 yards and nine touchdowns, but my knee had to be drained a lot and I couldn't run well. But we battled and finished with an 8–1–1 record, which wasn't too shabby.

My proudest moment came after the Auburn game. It was played in the rain and the footing was so bad nobody could move. That was probably why, with us trailing 3–0 in the fourth quarter, nobody could tackle me when I got off a forty-seven-yard run to win the game.

And afterward Coach Bryant came to me and said, "Son, I am as proud of you as I am of anybody who's ever been here. You've done a great job for me on and off the field."

We planned to start the new year with a win over Texas A&M in the Cotton Bowl, but we lost, 20–16. That disappointment faded a few days later, though, as I had to worry about my family again. Carolyn called me at the dorm and there was terror in her whisper: "Kenny, Daddy's got his shotgun . . . he says he's gonna kill us and then kill himself!"

I jumped in the Corvette and raced home as fast as I could go. I wasn't going to stop for any police. Let them follow me right into Foley if need be, and that might not be a bad idea. I didn't know what I was going to face at home, but I was afraid my father was capable of anything. It was a cool late-January night, and I was just pouring sweat.

When I walked into the living room about midnight, my mother was sitting on the couch, my sister in a chair, their faces flushed with fear, eyes red from crying. No one spoke.

My father looked up from his chair by the window. A bottle of Early Times was on the table next to him, a couple of inches of bourbon left in the bottom. His shotgun rested across his thighs, one hand on the pump, the other on the trigger grip of the stock.

"Mom . . . Carolyn . . ." I said. "I think it's best if you leave."

They stood up and moved toward me, but I never took my eyes off my father. I said, "Dad, I'm gonna go too, as long as you're like this."

"Nobody's leaving," he said, turning the shotgun on us. "I'm gonna kill everybody and then kill myself." He stood up.

"Dad, you can't do that!" I said.

I took a quick step toward him and grabbed the shotgun by the barrel and by the pump grip just below his hand. I tried to wrestle the gun away from him, struggling desperately. "You just can't do this sorta thing!" I yelled.

He had forty pounds on me and I couldn't break his grip as we pushed and pulled. Then he stopped struggling, just held fast, staring into my eyes from two feet away. I thought the anger in them would burn through me.

I glanced over to see that my mother and sister had gone outside. When I looked back at my father, he suddenly released the gun, stepped around me, and went into his bedroom, closing the door behind him.

I was so scared, it felt like my heart would pound through my chest.

I had to get back to school, but my mother told me later that my father never mentioned the incident. In fact, he didn't speak to my mother or sister—not a word—for three days. That was his pattern whenever he messed up. It was as if by not commenting on the incident, he felt maybe we would forget it ever happened. But there was no way any of us could ever forget that night. We all lived in fear that Slim could go off again any time he drank heavily.

After that I always let my mother and sister know where I could be reached, day or night, though the days weren't scary. Some weeks later I was in Mobile between semesters visiting friends when Carolyn called me. Our father was like a stick of dynamite, his drinking the match that might set him off at any moment.

"He was sitting in his truck out front drinking for about four hours," Carolyn said. "Then he came in, loaded his shotgun, and said he was gonna kill us all. He had us hysterical again, then he took the gun and went back out to the truck, I guess because his bottle's there. He's still sitting in the truck with a loaded shotgun."

The question was: What would Slim do when he came back into the house?

I made it home in about thirty-five minutes and I could see him in the truck. I got out of the Corvette wishing I'd come in another car. "He might just blow me away," I thought as I approached the truck, fear rising in me like a massive bruise.

"Dad, what's the matter?" I said.

"Nothin'."

The shotgun was propped against the seat, butt on the floor, beside him. The bourbon bottle was in his hand, resting on the steering wheel.

"You sure you're okay?" I asked.

He refused to look at me or answer.

"Dad, something's wrong or you wouldn't—"

"It's none of your goddamn business!" he roared, starting the engine. He jammed the truck in gear and took off.

I was too full of apprehension and confusion to sleep. I finally went to bed at about 4 A.M. and heard him come in an hour later. But I just lay there until morning, trying to figure out what made my father the way he was. He was such a good man most of the time. His friends won't believe what I'm writing about Slim Stabler. But when he drank that bourbon hard, he got depressed—about his circumstances, the fact that he couldn't give us more—and he felt miserable. Then he got mean, wanted to kill himself and his family, put us out of what he must have seen, somewhere near the bottom of the bourbon bottle, as *our* misery.

Thank God he never did it. Thank God he never acted on that demonic thought that was buried in him and given expression only by the booze. I have thought about this through all the years since the incidents occurred. I know my father loved us all. And I believe that it was his love that prevailed against his demons.

I also knew that I was basically made up of Slim Stabler's genes, that I had his temper, and that I had to guard against ever losing control the way he did. When he wasn't occupied, my father was always thinking, something grinding away in his mind that he never let loose. Every woman I've had a long relationship with has said the same thing about me. My wife Molly tells me now, "You're always preoccupied and I never know what you're thinking."

Still, my father was so much fun generally, and he was never visited by his demons when he was having fun. Maybe that's why, from way back, going for the good times became such an important part of my life. Having fun, I could not be set upon by anything like Slim's demons.

Football was fun. I was always higher on the field than any glow alcohol could ever produce. But off the field the party glow wasn't half bad either. Just stay in the fast lane and keep moving.

4

~~~~~~~~~~~~~~~~~~~~~~~~

Breaking In
Was Fun to Do

Soon after we lost the 1968 Cotton Bowl, I was surprised that the Houston Astros selected me in the second round of baseball's winter free-agent draft. I was the twenty-fourth player picked, even though I hadn't pitched the past two years. When Spec Richardson, the Astros' general manager, phoned to see if I wanted to talk about a contract, I told him I wanted to wait a few days and see how I did in the NFL draft. "I'll probably sign with whoever offers me the most money," I said.

I was hoping the high baseball pick would increase my football value. I wasn't interested in spending years in the minor leagues, as most pitchers do, before getting my shot at the majors. I was confident I would be a starting quarterback in the NFL sooner.

My father pointed out that young baseball pitchers, especially lefties, tend to get sore arms. "But quarterbacks and prostitutes make their living a lot alike," he said. "Most of the time they're on their backs."

In the NFL draft I was happy for my roomie Dennis Homan, who was taken by Dallas in the first round, but I was disappointed for myself. I was the last pick of the second round, number fifty-two overall. The only good thing about it was that I was picked by the Raiders, who drafted quarterback Eldridge Dickey of Tennessee A&I

number one. The AFL champions were an exciting team with a reputation of having a great organization.

The press offered three reasons why I wasn't drafted in round one: because the Astros would come after me strong, because I was a left-hander, and because Coach Bryant had been quoted as saying I would be a $200,000 bonus baby. I don't know if the coach said that. But baseball scouts kept telling me back in high school that left-handed pitchers were in far greater demand than left-handed quarterbacks. The only southpaw to have had much success in the pros was Frankie Albert of the 49ers in the forties and fifties.

Lawyer Jack Propst of Foley, whose son Eddie had played football with me in high school, represented me in the negotiations with Oakland. I signed a four-year contract that called for salaries of $16,000, $18,000, $20,000, and $22,000. The salaries wouldn't make me rich, but the $50,000 bonus I got up front sure made me *feel* rich.

I bought a few things for my family: window air conditioners, a color TV, a refrigerator for my mom, a stereo for my sister, and I paid off a $2,000 car note for my father. It was no big outlay of money, but I felt good. My family had done so much for me and now I could do a little for them.

Everyone thanked me except my father. He seemed to be offended that I had been able to do the things he wanted to do and couldn't. He was a proud man—too proud. I felt sad for him.

Although I continued to live at the dorm that spring of 1968, I dropped all my classes. I hadn't gone to college to earn a degree. My goal had always been to use college as a stepping-stone to pro ball. Now that I had achieved my goal, I had to get ready for my career.

When I signed with the Raiders in March, I stayed in Oakland for the weekend to participate in a minicamp: twenty-eight hours of meetings with coaches and workouts on the field. The head coach then was John Rauch, the former Georgia quarterback, and he worked me out with veteran end Bill Miller. I realized immediately that I didn't have a strong enough arm—not for the Oakland passing game.

The Raider receivers ran real deep cuts then. I would drop back ten yards and Miller would run downfield seventeen yards, break—and the ball had to be there. Now, that was a twenty-four-yard pass minimum. But if you're throwing from one hashmark across the field, it becomes a forty- to fifty-yard pass.

And in the pros, the ball needs to be on a line, a rope to the receiver. I didn't have that kind of arm strength. Every one of my throws on a deep cut was low. I'd crank up and heave the ball, and Miller would catch it at his knees or shoetops—if the ball didn't hit the turf in front of him.

I went back to Alabama with a series of weight-lifting exercises and began working out to strengthen my arm. But only for a few days. In between the bench-pressing, curling, and so on, I played basketball, thinking it would build up the muscles around my left knee. Instead I damaged it more.

The Raiders flew me back to Oakland, where team orthopedist Dr. Charles Rowe removed the loose cartilage. I came back to Tuscaloosa a week later on crutches.

I had been having my first serious relationship with a girl since I'd been at Alabama. Isabel Clarke was a real cute junior with a bubbly personality, a girl who liked good times, as I did, and we'd been having fun running around together for months. That wasn't going to stop just because I was on crutches. I had Isabel drive me around in the Corvette, even though she wasn't real comfortable in that high-powered car with the standard transmission. Sometimes she forgot the clutch.

One evening we decided to play shuffleboard and have a few beers at The Tide, where we could usually find some of my former team-mates and their girlfriends. There was a parking space right in front of the place and Isabel pulled into the curb nose-first. She braked to a stop, but didn't shift into neutral or turn off the engine. Then she took her feet off the brake and the clutch—and the 'Vette hopped the curb, its front smashing through The Tide window. Eight feet of glass fell on the car.

I panicked out of embarrassment, saying, "Let's get outta here!"

We drove to Smith's Motel and hid out. But Sergeant Green of the campus police force quickly tracked us down. He phoned me and said, "Kenny, did you run your car into The Tide?"

"No, I didn't," I said. "But the car did hit the window."

After paying for the damages, I sold the Corvette and paid off my note on it. In June I bought a 1968 Buick Riviera. I was going to drive to training camp and knew that would be a better car for the cross-country trip. I was also going to take Isabel.

I thought I was in love and didn't want to leave her. But I'm sure I didn't know what love was about then. I think I felt I'd be lonesome, going off alone to a whole new environment. I hadn't been out of Alabama for any extended period of time, and now I was going for six months. Isabel looked forward to going to California. She had lived all over the country, as her father was a career military man who was then commander of Luke Air Force Base in Phoenix, Arizona.

So we married, drove to Alameda, California, and rented an apartment. Then I went up to camp in Santa Rosa. The doctor found my knee fully recovered from surgery, but it was weak. I exercised it daily in the weight room. But I had little mobility on the practice field and couldn't get in much work. Eldridge Dickey was very mobile at quarterback. He was so quick, Dickey was also being tried at receiver. He showed a lot of moves.

I didn't show much of anything. At Alabama I had been able to move around behind the line and avoid pass rushers. Now, after dropping back into the pocket, I should have been able to do the same thing. My knee was supposedly healed, but my left leg just wasn't strong.

The Raiders sent me to play for the Shockers of Spokane, Washington, in the Continental League. They wanted to see how my knee would hold up under fire. It would not have held up long with the Shockers. I played one game and completed twenty passes, seventeen to my teammates, almost got killed, and returned to Oakland. The Raiders placed me on the injured reserve list, which meant I could not work out or travel with the team. On the taxi squad I felt like a lost soul. A wasted season.

The next year was worse. At this time it wasn't emphasized that rehabilitating an injured knee was as much a psychological as a physical problem. The knee still bothered me and I was afraid to push it. I could see why I was playing behind Eldridge Dickey in camp.

We each played a half in a scrimmage against the Dallas rookies, who had a twenty-seven-year-old rookie quarterback named Roger Staubach. Dickey and I both moved the team. I managed to throw two touchdown passes as we won, 33–0. But I didn't feel right, physically or mentally. I was not the player I had been, and I felt like I never would be again. For the first time in my life, I lost my confidence as an athlete.

A few days later, totally frustrated, I asked Dan Birdwell if I could borrow his car for about thirty minutes. I drove it to San Francisco International Airport, and left the ignition key under the mat. I phoned the Raider office and told the girl who answered where Birdwell's car was and that I was going home.

My decision to take Birdwell's car showed where my mind was. He was not a guy to mess with. He was such an awesome physical specimen that guys kept saying, "Dan, you're so big we're gonna get you a job at Disneyland—as a ride." An All-AFC defensive tackle, Dan had told me, "The name of this game on defense is to hurt people. Every time I hit a guy, I aim to punish him. I beat 'em up so bad in the first half, I own 'em in the last quarter."

I guess I borrowed Birdwell's car simply because it was a wreck, one he brought to camp just to rebuild and sell. The big man from Big Springs, Texas, was a good mechanic and a good guy off the field. He tore up his knee in 1969 and had to retire at age twenty-nine. The last time I saw him—years later—he was running his own garage in Fairmont, California. He just laughed about my leaving his car at the airport.

I joined Isabel in Tuscaloosa, where she was completing work on her degree. Obviously I was all screwed up mentally, and that didn't help the marriage. About all I did was drink and fight with my wife. I was annoyed, and everyone was annoyed with me. My father kept saying, "You're throwing away a helluva opportunity, Bud."

In the spring of 1970, Sonny Rittenberry, who lived in the same apartment complex we did, introduced me to a young lawyer. Henry Pitts said he could help me get another chance with the Raiders. Henry phoned John Madden, who had been in his first year as head coach when I walked out of camp. Madden was not real enthusiastic about me, but he told Pitts to bring me to his office for a talk. We flew to Oakland and I convinced John that I sincerely wanted to play, saying the knee that had bummed me out was now fine. The Raiders were probably the one NFL club that would have given a guy like me another shot.

I was the only quarterback at the spring workouts and again when training camp opened. The NFL Players Association was negotiating a new contract with the owners and threatening to strike if demands weren't met. So the owners barred the veterans from camp. For two weeks I got all the work and I took advantage of it.

John Madden would stand behind me when I dropped into the pocket during all the passing drills and scrimmages. That is the only way to tell which receiver is open from the quarterback's point of view.

"Ken, I don't know how you spot the open receivers and get the ball to them so fast," John told me. "You're hitting people I can't even find looking over your shoulder. You're getting the receiver the ball when he's being pinched by two defenders and you're hitting guys on the dead run when they're shoulder-to-shoulder with a cornerback. You've got the touch."

I had always been blessed with the ability to read defenses quickly and release the ball quickly. I don't think I had any special vision, but I did have a special feel for what was going on in front of me. My confidence was definitely back.

Madden warned me that I couldn't always trust the receiver who comes back to the huddle and says he was open on the last play. He demonstrated this when we viewed films of a scrimmage. Just as I was about to release the ball on film, John would stop the projector and ask, "Okay, who's the open man on this play?" A receiver would say he was open, then John would roll the film again. We'd see that the man had come open only *after* his coverage had reacted away from him.

There was pressure on me from the start of camp to walk out with the veterans. Technically I was a rookie, but I had been with the team, though nonrostered, in 1968. Guard Gene Upshaw and cornerback Willie Brown were the representatives to the union. They had set up a strike headquarters in a wing of The El Rancho Motel away from the Raider rooms. Gene and Willie kept after me to come out with them.

I didn't know what the strike was all about. I just wanted to play football. I thought if the veterans stayed on strike, the owners would field teams of us hopefuls, maybes, and has-beens. But fearing I would lose the respect of the veterans, I finally moved to the other wing of the motel with them until the strike was settled.

We had to play our first exhibition game shortly thereafter and, as I was the only quarterback who was at all ready, I stayed in for three quarters against the Colts. They played like they were still pissed off over having been upset by the seventeen-point underdog Jets in the last Super Bowl. In the first half the Colts came at me in squads and I threw two interceptions, muffed one center snap, and was sacked in the end zone for a safety. But I didn't get upset, I just wanted to go back out there.

John Madden complimented me on my coolness under pressure, and in the third quarter I threw some good passes and took the team to a couple of scores. We lost, 33–21, but afterward our injured defensive tackle Tom Keating came up to me and said, "Listen, Ken, after getting the shit knocked out of you in the first half, you stood in there and did a helluva job." I appreciated that.

The following week I threw three touchdown passes in a win over the Eagles and I felt real good. Our veterans were getting their timing down, the offensive line gave me great protection, and I was certain that I could play in the NFL.

But I had to leave camp again the next week. We were in a meeting, preparing to play the Rams that afternoon, when our team doctor came up behind me and whispered, "Can I see you outside?" When we went out into the corridor, he closed the door and said, "I'm sorry to have to bring you this news, Ken, but your father died."

I was shocked. That big strapping man who had never missed a day's work due to illness, that man who had seemed immortal to me, was dead at the age of forty-seven. I felt like my life was just starting, and my father's was over.

Flying home to help with the funeral arrangements and to make sure my family's financial situation was all right, I got depressed thinking about my mother and sister. Slim had cut down on his drinking and caused no real scenes of late. How would they fare without him?

I found out why Slim had been feeling better about himself when I reached Foley. He'd had migraine headaches for years, sometimes so intense they would bring tears to his eyes. I suspect they stemmed from the tension within him that he couldn't release, that ongoing feeling that he wasn't accomplishing enough.

But just a few weeks before he died, Slim had finally bought the house he'd always wanted and his migraines had disappeared. His property was on the water in a place called Fish Trap up on Wolf Creek, about fifteen miles from Foley, and it had a little cottage on it.

"You should have seen the difference in him, Kenny," my mother said. "We were fixing it up on weekends and going to move in, then build a bigger house. Your uncle Harold had built us some nice big kitchen cabinets. We already moved some furniture to the cottage. We'll have to give up the place. Slim was going down today to get insurance on the property."

"Daddy was supposed to go fishing with Cotton Blackwell out on Willis Hancock's boat Saturday," Carolyn said. "But Daddy told him the night before that he'd decided to go to Fish Trap and cut the grass on his property. I heard him tell Momma he'd be back to pick her up at Dr. Foster's when she got off at noon."

Slim had a massive coronary. The doctor said later his heart had just exploded. But he still managed to pick up the lawnmower, load it into the back of his truck, and drive fifteen miles to Dr. Foster's. He went to the back door of the office, slumped over, his face grayish-white, his polo shirt wringing wet with sweat. My mother screamed for the doctor and ran to Slim. Without a word, he reached in his back pocket and pulled out his wallet, handing it and his truck keys to her, the possessions he had with him. He knew he wouldn't be needing them.

Slim collapsed and was rushed to the hospital, just two blocks away, but he was dead on arrival. My mother kept saying, "If I'd just been there with him."

"Sally, even if I'd been there nothing could have been done," Dr. Foster said.

"Momma was fixing to quit work," Carolyn told me, "and that would have been like a feather in Daddy's hat. You know how bad he felt about her having to work all these years."

I knew it had hurt him. I knew he lived with a lot of hurt inside. I was damn sorry that, when he finally had things coming together, he had to go like that. But at least he had briefly felt he was succeeding. That had changed him for the better, but not enough to save him.

"He had bad indigestion for two weeks before he died," my mother said. "I think that was the heart attack coming. I tried to get him to see the doctor, but he wouldn't. He just wouldn't go to a doctor."

The only time I can ever remember my father seeing a doctor was when I was in my late teens and he'd been having stomach or chest pains. It may have been a very bad case of indigestion from all the cigarettes Slim smoked and whiskey he drank. The doctor told him he would have to quit drinking.

My father said later, "I told him I'd have to get a second opinion." Which, of course, he never did, just as he never stopped drinking.

But Slim Stabler was loved. There were 125 sprays of flowers at his funeral and twice that many mourners. My mother took the loss hard for over a month, Carolyn told me when I phoned from training camp. "Kenny, I thought the world had about ended for her. But I finally said, 'Momma, he's gone and there's nothing can be done. At least you won't have to go through what you've been through again.' People kept coming up to her and saying, 'I just don't know who I'm gonna take my car to now.' At first Momma wouldn't say much. But now she smiles and says, 'Well, I don't know nothing about no car either. I just know to put gas in it and mash that pedal.' She's gonna be fine."

During the 1970 season, I threw exactly seven passes. If starting quarterback Daryle Lamonica got hurt or was ineffective, George Blanda played. Brilliantly, at age forty-three. In one five-week stretch, Blanda won four games, tied another, and earned himself AFC Player of the Year honors. In a 7–7 tie with the Steelers, Lamonica went down, so George went in and threw three touchdown passes and we won the game, 31–14. The next week, trailing the Chiefs, 17–14, George kicked a forty-eight-yard field goal to tie the game as time ran out. The next week he kicked a fifty-two-yard field goal with three seconds on the clock to beat Cleveland, 23–20. Then he beat the Broncos with a twenty-yard touchdown pass with less than three minutes left to play. There were four seconds remaining in the game against the Chargers when George kicked a sixteen-yard field goal for the victory.

I learned a lot from Professor Blanda. We would stand together on the sidelines and analyze the offense when Daryle was in. I'd watch Daryle's attack and tell George what I would've done. Then he would advise me, tell me whether he agreed with my plan or not and why. He kept pointing out that it was just as important knowing what *not* to do as knowing what to do. His message was: Don't worry about interceptions and don't be conservative, but never force a pass. Instead, take the hit and get up to throw again. Forced passes led to foolish interceptions. Blanda was a big, big factor in my development as a pro.

I became pretty good friends with George and loved listening to his war stories. I was three years old when he left Coach Bryant at Kentucky and joined the Chicago Bears in 1949. Sid Luckman and Johnny Lujack were ahead of him at quarterback, but George could kick. "I even played linebacker in 1950 and 1951," George said. "We only had thirty-three-man rosters then." At six-two, 215 pounds, George wasn't the smallest linebacker of that time, and I'll bet he was tough. He was tough in everything he did, and I have never met a more intense competitor.

A guy would give him a hard time at practice, and George would fix the guy with his steely gray eyes and say, "Listen, son, I was here when you got here and I'll be here when you're gone."

In over twenty years of pro football, he'd seen hundreds of players come and go, he was still winning games with his arm and foot and making a great living. After his performance in 1970, George told me he made as much from off-season speaking fees and endorsements as he had playing the previous three years—over $300,000. I understand that George still makes a fortune giving motivational speeches for corporations.

Anything George Blanda wanted to do he could do well. The card games we played—gin, crazy eights, any kind of poker—George almost never lost. He was a real good pool shooter who could just make that cue ball talk. After he'd sink a shot, the cue ball would roll around the table and line up in perfect position for his next shot. If you challenged him in basketball, bowling, or golf, George would always beat you.

He asked me to play gin with him on our plane trips. I knew he'd beaten everybody he'd played and that he just wanted some new competition. George also liked me and I enjoyed his company, his intensity. I played everything to win, too. I didn't expect to have much success against him, but I thought it would be fun to watch him work. Hell, it was always fun to watch George's mind in action on the football field, the way he called a play here to set up a big gain later, the way he waited to the last second for the wide receiver to clear out the middle, then hit the tight end underneath.

George played gin the way you should, counting the cards, knowing exactly what was still available to draw, reading your hand and knowing what you likely needed to fill. He'd change his hand completely in midgame. He had played a lot of gin on a lot of airplanes, on prop planes, fan jets, and now jets. And he beat me on trip after trip through the season.

But during our gin marathon on the last road trip of 1970, a six-hour flight to New York, I caught all the right cards. We played for a penny a point, and there wasn't much money involved, about $5. But I won all the way cross-country. When we landed, George stood up, angrily threw his cards down, and walked away. He wouldn't speak to me the rest of the trip, or sit with me on the plane ride home. That's the kind of competitor he was. Tough as leather.

He could be just as tough with the public, downright cranky. One night George, Pete Banaszak, Freddy Biletnikoff, and I were all having dinner at The Grotto in San Francisco with our wives. It was a real nice place, crowded as usual. A woman in her forties kind of tiptoed over as we were eating and said, "Mr. Blanda, I hate to disturb you—"

"Well, you already *have,*" George said. "What do you want?"

I couldn't understand that. I always enjoyed people coming over to me in public. I'd sign an autograph, exchange a few words, and everyone would be happy.

Maybe George had had too much of it. He hadn't hesitated to give me an autograph when I was a kid, but that was a long time ago.

A few years later a group of Raider players, George and myself among them, were invited to the New Orleans Fairgrounds horse races during Mardi Gras. Freddy, Pete, and I were betting casually and just enjoying ourselves, laughing and jacking around. Not George. He was a serious horseplayer, betting about $500 a race. Of course, George was serious about everything he did—from kicking a football to rolling out his toothpaste so perfectly that the bottom of the tube never creased and went off at an angle like it did with every other human being.

George was standing up in the aisle off the row where we were sitting. He was watching the race through binoculars. Two couples came up behind him. The lead man said, "Mr. Blanda, Mr. Blanda." George kept watching the horses sweep around the oval. "Mr. Blanda, would you mind signing this?"

"Hey, sonuvabitch!" George said, eyes glued to his glasses. "Can't you see I'm watching the race!"

The man slunk off and I was embarrassed for him.

George threw his hand into the air and, turning to us, said, "Another winner!" He had already forgotten that there had been a man bothering him.

George Blanda could be gruff and hard, but he was a man's man and everybody respected him. Daryle Lamonica was not as popular with his teammates. He was aggressive, had a tremendous ego, and was always talking about how well his outside business deals were going. His personality did not sit well with some of his teammates. I liked him because he always took time to answer any questions I had. But we had different styles of play.

Daryle was "The Mad Bomber," a big, strong guy who would throw the ball long and throw it often. He had come to Oakland from Buffalo in 1967, led the AFL in passing, and took the Raiders to the second Super Bowl. He played behind a good offensive line and had excellent receivers in speedy Warren Wells, elusive Freddy B., and hard-nosed Billy Cannon at tight end.

Lamonica led the AFC in passing in 1970, then went out with a groin injury in the championship game against Baltimore and never returned to the game. While some Raiders felt he could have come back, I don't think anyone had the right to say that. But he hadn't returned to the 1969 playoff game against the Chiefs after suffering a hand injury, and Daryle had a reputation as being a little gun-shy after a hard lick. I would never question his courage because everybody has a different threshold of pain. Besides, I've been popped around out there at times, and whenever I heard the telephone ring, I flinched.

In my opinion, Lamonica was a good thrower, not a good passer. Up until 1970, most teams stayed in man-to-man defenses. A guy with a powerful arm like Daryle's could go deep. But as more teams began mixing in zone coverages, Daryle could not adjust because he was not a touch passer. He could not hit the seams of a zone by feathering a ball over a linebacker and between a deeper halfback. He was aptly named "The Mad Bomber" and was a very good one until the zone defenses defused his bombs. He just didn't seem to try to read defenses better and change. He kept going with his strength after it had become a weakness.

Another error that Lamonica made was in not establishing a good rapport with his teammates. It's not enough that a quarterback be respected by the men who block for him, run for him, and catch his passes. A quarterback has to be liked by his teammates. From the beginning, I went out of my way to make everyone like me. If you're liked, players will put out that little extra for you. A quarterback often needs that little extra protection, that little extra drive from his ballcarrier, that little extra concentration from a pass catcher to keep those chains moving downfield.

But Lamonica was the starting quarterback, Blanda was the backup, and I accepted the role of third-stringer. The 1970 season was devoted to learning, having a good time as a charter member of The Santa Rosa Five, and getting to know my teammates.

I also got to know the legendary Al Davis a little bit by observing him and listening to the veterans talk about him. Al made sure nobody got to know him well. But it was apparent that everyone was more than a bit afraid of him. Nobody wanted to mess with the guy whose name was on the bottom of that piece of paper you cashed to make your car payment.

Al liked to promote the image that he was a street tough from a poor family in Brooklyn, though we later found out his parents were actually well-off. He tried to dress like the boss in an old gangster movie, wearing nothing but black-and-silver or black-and-white outfits. Some said that was because he's color-blind. The truth was, he liked the Raider colors and the tough look.

"I'll bet even his pajamas have the team logo on them," Pete Banaszak said.

"He loves that pirate wearing an eyepatch," Freddy Biletnikoff said.

"Al would wear an eyepatch if it wouldn't ruin his peripheral vision," Pete said. "He's always afraid someone's trying to spy on us."

"When I came here in 1965," Freddy said, "one of the veterans told me he saw Al throw a rock at a plane that flew low over the practice field. He thought it was a spy plane."

He didn't like strangers at practice. One day two young kids were hanging on the fence watching us work out. Al sent a ball boy over to chase them. "Lucky they're not bigger," I said to George Blanda, "or Al might send a defensive tackle to stomp on their toes."

Al also loved to wear dark glasses. The first time I saw him wearing shades and his white trench coat with the collar turned up, I thought he looked like the cartoon character in "Spy vs. Spy."

To make himself look bigger, Al wore padded shoulders in his jackets, though he wouldn't admit it. Someone once asked him if he didn't think those padded jackets were out of style.

"What padded jackets?" Al said. "I don't wear padded shoulders. Don't need them."

We often saw him pumping iron in the weight room and eyeing himself in the mirror, trying to build up his deltoid muscles so he could stop wearing those padded jackets that he denied wearing.

One thing that Al could do nothing about in the weight room was the fact that his pants bagged in the seat. There was enough fabric hanging there to clothe a midget. But even Al wouldn't wear cheek pads. He looked like a man who had gone to the track and literally lost his ass.

Pete Banaszak did the greatest imitation of Al Davis, who had a habit of sucking his teeth and admiring his diamond ring. He would stand at practice cupping an elbow at his waist with his other hand at his chin. Then he would suck his teeth, roll his wrist up, cock his pinkie, and admire the ring he had on it bearing a diamond about the size of a shot glass. He was always bareheaded, proud of his pompadoured hair that he greased and combed straight back on the sides like Bowser of Sha Na Na. I guess Al favored the greaser look from his tough youth in Brooklyn.

In the locker room Banaszak would lower his pants around the cheeks of his ass, stuff towels in the shoulders of his jacket, slip the tab from a beer can on his pinkie, soak his hair and comb it straight back on the sides. He never could fashion a pompadour. Then Pete would walk around sucking his teeth, rolling his wrist, and admiring his ring. He'd say, "Anybody know who this is?" and guys would break up.

One day at practice Pete walked up about five feet behind Al and stood there in the same pose, elbow cupped at his waist, his other hand on his chin. Freddy noticed the scene as those of us on the field huddled up. "Sneak a peek at Pete standing back of Al," he said. We all started laughing.

Al yelled, "What the hell's wrong with you guys?"

Then he looked behind him, but Pete quickly turned his back.

"Nothing, Al," someone said as we got control of ourselves.

I called a play and ended it with tooth-sucking sounds, and everyone broke the huddle holding in laughter.

I enjoyed practice and would always stay out late with anyone who wanted extra work, and I also enjoyed going out with the guys at night. Some of those evenings ran late, too, if I connected with some talent. My wife and I hadn't gotten along from day one, so I wasn't real anxious to get home.

One of our favorite hangouts in Oakland was Al's Cactus Room, the best sports bar in town. That was where the players stopped for drinks after home games. Everybody kidded Al about his last name, which was Polish and had a mess of letters in it that looked like an eye chart. He was a good guy, a real fan who never charged us for drinks. And every Wednesday after practice Al would cook a big meal for all the players.

He had more sports photos and memorabilia than I've ever seen anywhere else in a bar. In glass cases behind the bar he displayed jerseys belonging to Freddy and Billy Cannon from the Raiders, Rick Barry of the NBA Warriors, plus a couple from the short-lived California Seals of the NHL. And he had all kinds of bats, balls, and artifacts from the Oakland A's championship teams, everything but Reggie Jackson's jock.

After I'd gotten to know Al, he told me, "In a couple of years, I'll want one of your shirts for the glass case."

"As soon as I'm starting, you got it, Al," I said.

I liked to drop by Al's Cactus Room because I could usually find teammates there that I didn't mix with that much at practice, like the defensive players. One night I got talking to a fellow rookie named Carl Weathers, a linebacker from San Diego State. He was a tad short for that position at five-eleven, but he was 220 pounds of sculptured muscle. Carl, a reserve linebacker, was real quick and a double-tough hitter on special teams.

"Carl, you're doing a helluva job on kick coverage," I said.

"That's my game for now," he said. "I like to be the first one downfield."

"A tough job."

"Yeah, and I'm only gonna do it one more year if I can't play linebacker, too," he said. "This game is not my life's work. I'm gonna be an actor."

Carl Weathers gave us one more year, then went into acting and finally hit it big playing Apollo Creed in the *Rocky* series. His height hurt him in football but no doubt helped him win the role opposite Sylvester Stallone, who's only five-eight or so. Carl has his own company now, Stormy Weathers Productions. I just wish he'd had a better shot at linebacker with us because he had the mean.

Probably our meanest defender in 1970 was strong safety George Atkinson, who was downright surly with tight ends. They usually outweighed him by fifty pounds, but the 170-pound George applied a lot of hurt on them. He liked to hit receivers in the head from the blindside with a blow he called "The Hook," catching them in the crook of his right arm and ringing their bell. When I met George in Al's, I told him I liked his "Flipper" better. A receiver would go up high for a pass and George would dive at his ankles and flip him so that he landed on his head.

"That's just timing and doesn't sting like 'The Hook,' " George said. "The goal is to get the receiver to flinch every time he hears you coming. I try to discourage them from even coming *near* me."

One reason the Raider defense always featured a gang of punishing, intimidating players was those were the kind of individuals Al Davis looked for, the kind of guys who helped you win ball games. Another reason Raider defenders were so aggressive is they tended to take speed. By the handful.

Up until there was reported drug abuse on the San Diego Chargers in the early seventies and the league tried to cut back on the use of amphetamines, there was always a big jar of them in the Raider dressing room. Players who wanted some extra energy could just dip in. I understand this was the situation on every pro football, baseball, and basketball team then. Hell, one study found that 50 percent of the women in the country were taking diet pills—spelled "amphetamines"—seven days a week. If little ladies could take seven uppers a week, the thinking seemed to be that big football players could take a bunch in a day without harm.

The big Raiders jar contained gray-colored amphetamine capsules that the players called "rat turds." I had taken some speed in college when I was seeing that girl in Mobile and staying up all night. Typically, it would make my brain race and my mouth so dry I couldn't even spit. I'd feel like I was so wired with energy that I could go forever without sleep and do anything. As I was a hyper, high-energy guy anyway, I had to be careful with speed.

I tried a rat turd before a scrimmage one day in camp just to check it out, and it made my mind too busy. As a quarterback, I had to be as clearheaded as possible because there were so many things to remember, so many variables that came into play on each down, I had to think quickly but calmly, not with a mind that was racing.

I hadn't seen myself on speed, but I saw my teammates on the sidelines before and during games. Their eyes would get real big and they'd have a kind of wild, distant look in them. They would be so wired they couldn't stop moving their jaws and grinding their teeth. I was standing next to Blanda before one early 1970 game watching guys seemingly grinding their teeth down to nothing, and I said, "They're gonna have to wear a mouthpiece out to dinner."

"Yeah, I wouldn't take that shit," George said.

The guys also kept reaching for the Gatorade to get some moisture in mouths that felt like they'd just crawled across the Mojave Desert. They would slake their thirst, and five minutes later toss down more Gatorade.

Everywhere you looked you'd see wild-eyed guys slurping Gatorade and moving their jaws like an old man gumming food—and you knew they were ready to play.

It was all part of the game. If it made a guy play better, or made him think he played better, fine. The team owners and the league itself didn't care how much speed was taken until the Charger headlines appeared. Then there was an outcry in the media, public opinion turned against the league, and that worried the TV networks that paid the NFL millions of dollars every year. The networks feared advertisers would withdraw from NFL telecasts if the drug situation wasn't cleared up. So the NFL said it was policing the situation and that henceforth only team doctors could dispense amphetamines and other medications.

But I played over ten years after the so-called NFL crackdown on speed, and it was always readily available to players. Guys took it for diet reasons, for hangovers, and for that extra jolt they like to bring with them into games. But in fifteen years in the NFL, I never heard of a player becoming addicted to amphetamines.

Warren Wells was the only player I knew personally who reportedly had serious problems with drugs. At least, I was told that drugs were behind the problems he had with women that eventually landed him in jail. When I watched him in 1968 and 1970, on the field and on films, he was a great, great receiver. He was just as smooth as silk, a guy who could glide down the field and pass everybody. Wells played only four seasons, but he averaged 23.3 yards for *each* of his 156 catches and 42 of them went for touchdowns.

After getting in trouble, he tried to come back in 1971, but he just wasn't the same guy. He was someplace else, not on the football field. He walked around in a kind of daze, by himself, not saying much. I said something to him one day and he looked right through me, no longer the open, good-natured person I'd known before.

And running routes on the field, Wells was not a burner any more. He ran like a guy who was trying to get his legs loose, as if they were tight and he couldn't stretch them out. He would run out, cut at three-quarter speed—which was slow motion for the old Warren Wells—and when he'd turn the ball would be by him. It was sad to see a man who should have played a long time be finished so soon. It was a great loss for the Raiders.

The day Wells was cut, Freddy and I went out after practice for a few drinks.

"As soon as Warren got here, I got better," Freddy said. "They had to double him, and I increased my pass catches from seventeen to forty."

"You'll miss him."

"Everyone on this team will miss that guy," Freddy said. "He was some weapon. Hell, every pass he caught was like two first downs."

"Drugs are scary," I said. "I get high enough on this." I held up my scotch on the rocks. "But, you know, Freddy, there's nothing like that adrenaline high you get in a big game when you're playing good and the crowd's roaring. That juice starts pumping in you, you just can't beat that high."

"Adrenaline's some powerful drug," Freddy said. "But we can handle that."

5

~~~~~~~~~~~~~~~~~~~~~~

Winning the Job with a Little Light Surgery

The next two seasons, 1971 and 1972, were totally frustrating. I thought I should be the starting quarterback. I went to Al Davis and told him I wanted to go somewhere else where I could play. Good old Al said, "Stabler, go stand on your head."

I played most of the preseason in 1971 when Lamonica was hurt and we won five of six games. During the regular season, with Daryle again sidelined, I went all the way in a 27–16 victory over Denver. I played another half against Philadelphia and moved the team well, but not into the end zone. A fumble and an interception killed drives.

I still thought I was ready to start and should be playing. I told George Blanda I really wanted to be traded. George had been through it all and was very wise. He'd spent ten years with the Bears and had gotten all too few chances to start. Then in 1959 George Halas had released him, saying, "You're too old." Blanda was then thirty-one. George is one of the few players ever to play for George Halas who didn't say nice things about him. In fact, Blanda hated Halas the way he hated a blown center snap on a field goal attempt.

"Just be patient," George told me. "I had to wait ten years, sit out a year, and wait for a new league to start before I got a chance to play. Just keep yourself ready to play when you get your chance. You're young and your career's still ahead of you. And you're fortunate to be with a real good football team that's gonna be good for a long time.

"You're better off here," George said. "You go someplace else where you'll get a chance to play, it'll be with a lesser ball club and you'll probably get the hell beat out of you. Look at the other good young quarterbacks playing with weak clubs. Archie Manning with New Orleans, Jim Plunkett with New England, they win two or three games a year and get their asses kicked. So be patient, you'll get the opportunity to play here. When you get it, make the most of it."

George kept preaching that to me every time I got down. But my friends thought I should be playing. I thought I should be playing, even though, looking back, I may not have been ready. But Daryle Lamonica was having more and more trouble with the zone defenses. Wells was gone. Three men were being used in his place on the left side: Rod Sherman, Drew Buie, and Eldridge Dickey. I thought Dickey, who came out of college with the nickname "The Lord's Prayer," had some nice wrinkles as a receiver. But I had the feeling he had lost some of his heart for the game once he was no longer given the chance to play quarterback. As it turned out, 1971 was Dickey's last season with the Raiders.

At least I got into every game in 1971 as the holder for Blanda's placekicks. George wore a big old square-toed shoe that was not hard in front, as it was on most kickers' shoes. Before every kick George would reach his right foot behind him and tap the front of that shoe on the ground to push his toes forward. "I like to feel my toes hit the ball," he said. "I can tell if I hit it right." He had kicked 201 consecutive extra points from 1967 until he finally missed one in 1971.

I went to camp in 1972 all excited. My divorce from Isabel had gone through in the off-season and I devoted myself to a weight-lifting program to increase my endurance and strengthen my throwing arm. With my stronger arm and a lot of determination, I beat out Lamonica for the starting job during the preseason.

We opened the season in Pittsburgh against "The Steel Curtain" and, man, did it clang down on me. I was awful. I completed five of twelve passes for fifty-four yards and gave up three interceptions in fifteen minutes. We also had a punt blocked for a Steeler touchdown and trailed 17–0 when Blanda replaced me.

I kept thinking of what George kept telling me: "When you get your chance, make the most of it." I had flat-out blown it, and didn't know when I'd get another chance.

But I bounced back and gradually eased past Blanda as the number two quarterback in relief of Lamonica. Overall I hit on 59.5 percent of my passes for 524 yards and four touchdowns, and I had no interceptions after the opener. Football was fun again.

I played the second half of the season's final game against the Bears. We had a lead and I kept it by completing ten of eleven passes as we won, 28–21. But what was memorable about that game was I had my first and only encounter with Hall of Fame linebacker Dick Butkus.

We were ahead by a touchdown in the fourth quarter and driving for another score that would lock up the win. This was only a year before Butkus's bad knees forced him to retire and he could no longer move around much, but he still hit like a tank. I had heard he was ornery. But it seemed like the more mobility he lost, the meaner he got.

We got a first down on the Bear five-yard line. I handed off to Pete Banaszak up the middle, and he banged down to the three. Center Jim Otto came back to the huddle looking a little woozy after his collision with Butkus. So I handed off to Pete over left guard Gene Upshaw to about the one. Pete Banaszak had the best nose for the end zone of any back I ever played with. On third down I gave him the ball again over the right side and he drove in there as Butkus charged. We all thought Pete had crossed the goal line.

The referee came in and placed the ball down inches shy of the goal line. I ran over to him. "Hey, ref, what the hell are you doing?" I said. "He was in. What the hell's he gotta do?"

From behind me came a voice that sounded like it was talking into a drum: "HE'S GOT TO GET ACROSS THE GODDAMN GOAL LINE!"

I looked around and Butkus was standing right behind me, looking like Conan the Barbarian, wearing Bear jersey number 51.

"GET BACK TO THE HUDDLE!" Butkus said, and that's what

I did. I got my ass back behind the safety of my teammates *real* quick.

We went to Pittsburgh for the playoff game in brand-new Three Rivers Stadium, and neither team could score a touchdown going into the fourth quarter. The Steelers led 6–0 when Madden sent me in with six minutes left to play. We moved the ball fifty yards in eleven plays down to the Steeler thirty. I called a pass play, the Steelers came on an all-out blitz, my blockers picked up everyone, my receivers ran off all the defensive backs, and I raced down the sideline for a touchdown. There was 1:13 on the clock, and I thought we had won the game, 7–6.

The Steelers gained eighteen yards after the kickoff, then Terry Bradshaw threw three incompletes. With only seconds left to play, Bradshaw's final pass was to halfback Frenchy Fuqua curling over the middle. Free safety Jack Tatum nailed Fuqua in the back, and the ball went sailing toward the line of scrimmage. Franco Harris of the Steelers grabbed the ricochet at his knees and ran sixty yards for the game-winning score. His catch became known as "The Immaculate Reception," one of the most stunning finishes in NFL history. But to this day there is no certainty that it was a legal catch—that the ball bounced from Fuqua to Tatum to Harris—but that was the official ruling.

A photo in the papers the next day showed me standing on the sidelines with my head in my hands, revealing just how I felt. But I decided that for me to run thirty yards for a touchdown against the Steeler defense was a miracle, so I guessed Pittsburgh deserved one too.

In the off-season I again worked out and partied in Gulf Shores, and once again I met a girl I married. I dated Debbie Fitzsimmons for about three months and when it was time to return to California I decided I wanted her with me. I guess I always felt a need to have somebody at home for me. Again I married for the wrong reason. I wanted a wife and I also wanted to go off on my own, a combination that does not make for marital bliss.

My main interest was looking toward the next season. I had been lifting weights steadily for two years now and my arm and upper body had never been stronger. Many people believed that a quarterback should not lift weights, that the muscles in his passing arm would bind up. But John Madden didn't believe that. Certainly I couldn't throw hard after pumping iron, but the following day I'd feel stronger, my spirals would be tighter, and my velocity would be better.

I knew I would never be a Terry Bradshaw or a Joe Namath. Only God gives out those kind of passing arms. But I dramatically improved what I had and I felt confident I knew how to win with it.

Toward the end of the 1972 season, a writer had congratulated me on my having established myself as the quarterback behind Lamonica. "As far as I'm concerned," I told him, "being number two is like being number twenty-two. I want to start."

From what the veterans told me, the reason why I wasn't starting had less to do with my abilities than it did with Al Davis's views. Al had traded for Lamonica in 1967 and he had taken the Raiders into the playoffs for the first time ever, then into the Super Bowl. The next year Daryle led the team into the playoffs again. But some veterans said he blew the game against the Jets by throwing a backward lateral in the fourth quarter that cost them the game. In the playoff game against Kansas City in 1969, he insisted he could play with a bad hand and he played so badly that George Blanda publicly blasted him. In 1970 he ignored the running game in the playoff loss to Baltimore, continually throwing the bomb against a deep-zone defense that could not be beat, while the middle was wide open to middle-distance passes. Al Davis was quoted in the press after that game: "Honestly, I don't know what gets into Daryle's head sometimes."

After we had missed the playoffs in 1971 and been knocked out in round one by Pittsburgh in 1972, some of my teammates and members of the media were saying that I should replace Lamonica in 1973. There were those who believe John Madden felt that way, too, but that Al Davis did not. I don't know.

All I know is that I thought I won the starting job in the preseason of 1973, but Lamonica opened the season at quarterback. We lost to Minnesota, 24–16. Daryle didn't throw a touchdown pass in that game or in the next one against Miami. But George Blanda kicked four field goals in the 12–7 victory. Everyone was elated because the Raiders had broken Miami's eighteen-game winning streak. Everyone except me. I had done nothing but hold for placekicks.

I commiserated with Tony Cline. Looking for more size at defensive end, Al Davis had traded our outstanding tight end Raymond Chester to the Colts in July for big Bubba Smith. Tony had been a starter and our best pass rusher for three years until Bubba was given his job at left end. Before the third game, Tony bitched to the coaches and returned to the starting lineup. He made eleven tackles that day against Kansas City.

I watched Daryle and our offense struggle in that game against the Chiefs, scoring only three points. With six minutes left to play, Madden sent me in, saying, "Okay, Kenny, all we need are a couple of touchdowns."

"Sure, John," I thought running on the field, "and all I need is for the Chiefs' secondary to be struck by sleeping sickness."

The Chiefs knew we had to pass and we did. My first throw missed. My second hit Pete Banaszak right in the numbers and, God bless him, bounced off. Middle linebacker Willie Lanier intercepted. We lost, 16–3.

I was so frustrated that I went in to see John Madden early Tuesday morning. I was always one of the first people at practice and there was no one else in his office.

"John, that situation you sent me into on Sunday, down by thirteen with just a few minutes left to play, I don't want to go into one of those again," I said. "Start me and I'll go all the way. But you can't count on me to go into situations like that again. I think I'm playing well enough to start and I want to."

"I hate to hear you say I can't count on you in those situations," John said, running a hand through his floppy hair.

"You can count on me, John," I said. "But you can count on me to play regular and do the job. I just don't want to go in and mop up somebody else's mess."

"Well, I'm sorry you feel that way, Ken," he said. "But we haven't decided to change our starter. That's the way it is right now. What you have to do is go out there in practice and just keep working hard."

I went to the workout totally pissed off. I had to put on the red jersey and play quarterback Jim Hart of the Cardinals, our next opponents, who were running Don Coryell's wide-open offense. And I threw the hell out of the ball and we moved at will, up and down the field. I just did light surgery on our defense.

The next morning I was again the first at my dressing cubicle. John called me into his office. "Uh-oh," I thought. "Maybe I went too far, telling him he couldn't count on me as a backup."

"You're gonna start this week in St. Louis," John said. "And win or lose, you're gonna play. It's your ball, Kenny."

I kept it for seven years in Oakland.

We beat the Cardinals and the Chargers, tied the Broncos, and then I had my best passing game against Baltimore. Even though the Colts had a strong pass rush and sacked me six times, our great offensive line gave me time to complete twenty-five of twenty-nine passes for 304 yards and two touchdowns. At one point I completed fourteen passes in a row. In the locker room after our 34–21 victory, a writer said, "You just set an NFL record."

But the game was closer than the final score. We were leading by only seven points in the last quarter when we clinched the game on a great thirty-four-yard run by halfback Clarence Davis. He broke several tackles and dove into the end zone. Still, when offensive captain Gene Upshaw announced the game ball was awarded to Davis, I did a double take at Gene. Having set a league record, I really thought I'd get the game ball. I'd gotten it against St. Louis and I'd played better here. Later I found out that Joe Namath and Len Dawson shared the record for consecutive pass completions with fifteen.

Ironically, Madden had called for a pass play on Davis's run. But I saw that the Colt defensive alignment was ripe for a sweep, and that's what Clarence scored on. When I came off the field, Madden gave me a big smile. He seldom sent in plays, but even when he did I was under no obligation to use them. Even if I passed up one of his calls and mine did not succeed, he realized that I might have used that one simply to set up a later play.

Writers asked Madden after the Colt game, "How do you account for Ken Stabler's accuracy?"

"He has a feeling for finding the open man," John said. "He's just a natural quarterback."

"What took him so long to find out?" I wondered then. Now I see that maybe I needed those three years.

Fullback Marv Hubbard said to me in the visitors' dressing room:

"You know, Ken, there's nothing that makes a club go to hell faster than a quarterback who loses his cool. And you are one cool country boy."

I think what Madden liked best about me was that I stayed relaxed in games, refusing to get rattled, because that was my nature. John, on the other hand, would often go berserk on the sidelines. He would hoot and holler at officials, slobbering at the mouth, pulling at his hair, and waving his big splay-fingered hands all around. All the while his face would get pinker and pinker until we sometimes thought it would burst. Some of the guys called him "Pinky."

In the Baltimore game I play-faked a handoff at the Colt thirteen and dropped back looking to pass over the middle to tight end Bob Moore, a good possession-type receiver. Moore got knocked down getting off the line, but the play fake was so good it held the rush and I just waited until Bob got up and then hit him for the touchdown.

Freddy Biletnikoff, who caught six passes for ninety-six yards in that game, told the press afterward, "Kenny sits back there and waits for someone to get open. He doesn't try and rush a pass. He's willing to take a good shot."

I had been tackled for losses six times in two of my starts. Sometimes receivers were not open quick enough, sometimes I probably didn't see them, and sometimes the blocking couldn't hold. It didn't matter. I didn't give up any foolish interceptions.

Getting close to all my teammates helped my quarterbacking. The best part of the game was the brotherhood, laughing and working together. It was my personality to be part of all that, to go out for drinks with the guys, jack around, chase and carouse with those who wanted to. I asked everyone about their injuries, their families, whatever they wanted to talk about. I made sure that everyone knew that I was interested in them not just as players but as people. Again, it was important for me to be liked and it was important that my teammates knew I liked them.

As soon as Bubba Smith arrived in training camp, I welcomed him to the club and we became friends. Bubba, Freddy, and I would get a couple of six-packs after dinner and go drive around and sip before the evening meeting. Santa Rosa is beautiful rolling land, farm country, and we'd just drive the back roads and build a buzz and talk. One

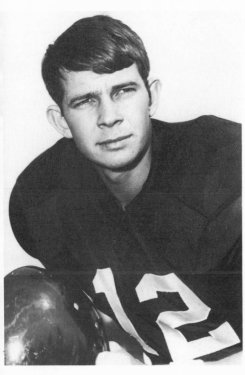

I was all ears in this picture—and when Coach Bryant, Dennis Homan, and I met Mickey Mantle just before the 1968 Cotton Bowl Game. (Photo: University of Alabama)

At the end of my senior year in high school, I played in the statewide All-Star Game and was named MVP. (Photo: Bobby McCrory)

Most of my early plays with the Raiders consisted of holding for George Blanda's placekicks. (Photo: Los Angeles Raiders)

The guys I roomed with in train ing camp as long as they were Raiders: middle linebacker Dan Conners (number 55), defensive end Tony Cline (number 84), re ceiver Fred Biletnikoff (number 25), and running back Pete Bana szak (number 40). I called us "The Santa Rosa Five." (Photo Los Angeles Raiders)

Dave Casper was just the best tight end I've ever seen. (Photo: Los Angeles Raiders)

Somehow I stayed up all night before this game played in a Denver snow-
storm, but I still managed to throw four touchdown passes that afternoon.
(Photo: Los Angeles Raiders)

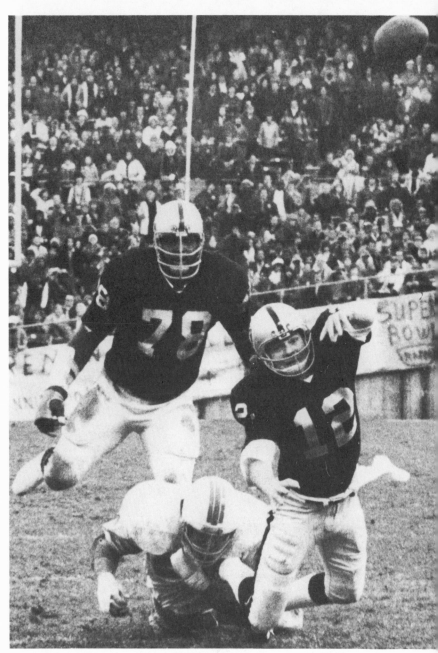

With twenty-six seconds left in the 1974 AFC playoffs against Miami, I was in trouble when Vern Den Herder hit me. But I managed to get off this pass to Clarence Davis, who outwrestled two defenders for the winning touchdown. (Photo: UPI/Bettmann Newsphotos)

day Bubba spotted several peacocks strutting around a farm and had us stop there. He got out of the car and tried to call the birds.

Freddy and I just laughed, watching this six-foot-seven man stand there with his hands to his mouth calling, "Whaooa! Whaooa!" at those delicate peacocks.

"Bubba," I said, "I'll bet those peacocks are saying, 'What the hell's that big bird want with us?'"

"I can get 'em to come to me down in Texas," he said.

"You got to learn to speak California peacock, I guess."

The guys I always spent a lot of time with before games were the offensive linemen. I wanted to know how they were feeling, if they had nagging injuries that might prevent them from making a certain kind of block, if there was anything that I could do to help their game. Their game was my game.

Our offensive line was easily one of the best in the league. Everybody we played said, "Christ, you guys got a big fucking offensive line!" It averaged almost 270 pounds per man, and that was much heavier than any other line in the NFC. But our guys weren't just big, they were quick and agile.

Three of the starters had made All-Pro, right tackle Bob Brown, center Jim Otto, and left guard Gene Upshaw. Left tackle Art Shell, 290, made the Pro Bowl in 1973 and for years thereafter. Right guard George Buehler could have made it, too, as he was a huge slab of a man at 270 pounds, strong, smart, and a very good pulling guard. But Buehler's mind tended to drift during games and someone would have to slap him to get his attention. I remember a scene late in a close game when we were in the huddle trying to figure out what to do, and George suddenly said to Pete Banaszak, "Where'd you get those shoes?"

"What?" Pete blurted, looking down at his new football shoes without having any idea why Buehler was asking about them in the midst of a ball game.

"I just wondered where you got those shoes because I'm thinking of changing mine," George said.

Pete slapped him.

Upshaw, six-five, 265, was quite simply All-World, and Otto, a Hall of Famer, used to be. Jim had played every game in Raider history, and while age and bad knees had slowed him some he could still do a good job. The middle linebackers he couldn't go out and block he sure could tackle. And he was so slick about it officials seldom caught him.

Bob Brown was the most intriguing character up front. A six-five, 285-pounder, with a massive upper body and little bitty calves, Brown could run with some backs. And he was mean. He wrapped his forearms from wrist to elbow—over lengths of hard molded plastic. It was like he carried two clubs. He just hated defensive linemen and was devoted to making them pay for troubling him, particularly those who used the head slap. Bob punched back, right in the solar plexus.

He was the only offensive lineman I ever heard say things like this: "I try to punish defensive ends. My game is based on an attack formula. I use a 'Two-Hand Rip-Up' to attack soft spots like the spleen, the liver, and the solar plexus. I think the universal quotient for this particular occupation is pain, and I attempt to apply pain. Constantly."

Bob Brown was different and he was proud of it. He did things his way, and if anybody didn't like it . . . well, he did not send sympathy cards.

He was always weight lifting. We had a lot of guys who regularly pumped iron, but Bob was the only one who ever pumped in the dining hall. He carried a dumbbell to lunch and did curls with one hand while he ate. An ambidextrous eater, he would then switch his fork and dumbbell into the other hand and continue. Dumbbells looked like cuff links in Bob's hands.

On his first day in training camp after coming over from the Rams in 1971, guys were just jacking around on the practice field. Bob Brown lined up in his stance in front of one of our wooden goalposts. Then he fired out and laid a forearm smash on the upright. The post shattered and toppled over, dragging the crossbar to the ground.

"Can you believe that big fucker?" I said to Banaszak. "Breaking a damn goalpost with his forearm!"

"He's in the room next to ours," Pete said. "I hope he doesn't slam the wall."

I think everyone was about half scared of Bob Brown, including his roommate Upshaw. One night I heard six or seven gunshots go off in rapid fire right outside my room. Freddy came in and I asked him what was going on.

"Bob Brown brought some pieces from his handgun collection to camp," Freddy said. "He's out back firing into the air to check the gun's action or something."

" 'Or something,' " I said. "Did you tell him that might not be the best idea?"

"Would you tell him that?" Freddy said.

"No."

The Raiders got the reputation in 1973 of being a left-handed team. The media kept reporting that we ran mostly to the left side because I was left-handed. We did run left more, even without the tight end set over there, but it had nothing to do with me. We had Shell and Upshaw over there and they buried people.

Bob Brown didn't like to be thought of as a player on the weaker side of the line, and he kept complaining in practice that we didn't run off right tackle enough. The next thing I knew, we went to the line of scrimmage in a game and Bob registered his complaint so that all could hear.

"Can I please get a few fucking plays run to *my* side?" he said in his booming voice.

I looked over at that small mountain glaring at me and I nodded. The next play went right over the top of him, as everyone on the opposing line knew it would. All Bob did was drive his defensive end about four yards off the line and tie up the linebacker too.

If Bob Brown hadn't been forced by an injury to retire early, I think he might have played until he was forty. He kept himself in great shape, loved to play, and he was that rare offensive lineman who played football mad. All the time.

After beating the Giants, 42–0, to make our record 5–2–1, we hosted the Steelers. They beat us, 17–9, for the third time in a row. Defensive tackle Joe Greene knocked me out of the game on the second play of the second quarter. He fell on my left knee just after I threw an incompletion, and it was real sore. I probably could have gone back in, but I was doing a certain amount of rolling out, play-passing, and scrambling at this time, not by design, just to counter the pressure and gain a couple of records. But I couldn't do that on one leg against the best pass rush in the league.

Mean Joe Greene, Dwight White, and L. C. Greenwood were joined in this game by former Raider defensive tackle Tom Keating, who had been traded in the off-season. It was interesting seeing Tom work against our great guard Gene Upshaw. It was a war in the trenches. I said to Gene on the sideline after one series, "Tom seems to know when you're going to pull, when you're going to pass block."

"He does," Gene said. "Hell, we practiced against one another for six years. This is homecoming for him."

On a later series I saw Upshaw and Keating jawing at one another after a play. Gene turned away and Tom rapped him in the back of the head. On the next play they got into it and our center, Jim Otto, jumped in between them.

When I asked Upshaw about that incident, he smiled. "I grabbed his jersey a little bit, and Tom started cussing me. I cussed him back and walked away—and the sonuvabitch hit me in the back of the head. So on the next play I blocked him and punched him in the mouth. It was an emotional thing. Keats went all out and I respect him. We're still friends."

A writer said, "I heard they gave Keating the game ball. Any comment, Gene?"

"I don't mind them giving him the game ball," Upshaw said. "I just wish we hadn't given them the game."

Raider trainer George Anderson designed and built a lightweight brace for my left knee. He called it a "Knee-Stablerizer" and later began selling the brace to college teams. It was simply two pieces of aluminum, hinged on each side, with padding underneath and Velcro secures. The brace provided real good support to the knee on blows from the side.

George Anderson was a real good guy who's still the Raiders' head trainer. We used to bet every year on who would lose the most weight during training camp. I'd usually want to lose 10 or 12 pounds to play at 215. George would say, "Well, I'm going from 200 to 175." The bet was $5 a pound. George would starve himself, take amphetamines to cut his appetite, and I'd drink every night, eat anything I wanted. Yet we always came out even because weight just fell off me in the workouts when I was young.

George was in his forties, but he had a lot of miles on his face from all the drinking he'd done over the years. I never once ever saw him drunk, but he liked to keep a little steady glow going—except on game days. He would rinse out a number of empty Maalox bottles and fill them with premixed Mai Tais. He kept them on a shelf in the trainer's room with the Maalox. I found out that the Maalox was on the right and the similarly labeled Mai Tais were on the left. I found out the hard way.

For all his own sipping, George was not sympathetic to anyone who came in to him seeking help for a hangover. You were a football player and he expected you to be tough. The first time I went in to ask George for help after a night of heavy drinking, I said, "I'm hurting. I really need something for my stomach."

"You pussy," he said. "Go get a bottle of Maalox and leave me alone."

I grabbed a bottle off the shelf, took a long swallow, and wondered what the hell it was. It tasted kind of familiar, but nothing like Maalox. I took another hit and realized I'd found out where George stored his Mai Tais. I jogged slowly out to practice, feeling the buzz of the night before come scudding back.

The brace helped my left knee in the next game against Cleveland, but I didn't have much mobility. Then my right knee got hurt when Upshaw blocked Browns' defensive tackle Jerry Sherk and he fell on my leg. It wasn't a hard lick, it was just his weight landing on my leg when it was extended after a pass. I was able to go back in the game later, but the Browns caught us on one of those hopelessly bad days, winning by a baseball score, 7–3.

After the game a writer said, "Ken, did you know you guys converted just one out of fourteen third-down situations all day?"

"I'm surprised at that," I said. "I didn't think we made any."

I really wasn't discouraged. The media pointed out that those two straight losses at the Coliseum were a first for the Raiders since 1966, and that our 5–4–1 record dropped us to third place. But I felt we would finish strong. We had scored only twelve points in the last two games, and we had too much offense to keep that up. And the defense had played good all along.

We needed to win the last four games to make the playoffs. The opposition included Kansas City, which had beaten us, and Denver, which had tied us. We won all four games.

At halftime of the season finale in Oakland, the Raiders Booster Club presented me with the annual Gorman Award as the "player who best exemplifies the pride and spirit of the Oakland Raiders." I was tremendously proud of it because it was voted on by my teammates, who were saying I was their MVP. I was to win this award two more times. But having begun the season on the bench, the first award gave me the biggest thrill, as I received it at midfield before 52,000 cheering fans.

The Raider fans were wonderful. They were my kind of folks: hardworking people who arrived at the Oakland–Alameda County Coliseum three hours before game time. They would park their recreational vehicles of every size, shape, and description, then pull out tables and chairs, television sets, well-stocked bars, and barbecue grills. They partied in the parking lot before and after every game, waving their Raider pennants, wearing their Raider rooter caps, and drinking from their Raider mugs.

After games I usually tarried in the dressing room to let the traffic thin out. But when I finally walked into the parking lot, I had to move through dozens of parties that were still perking along. I enjoyed visiting with the fans, wending my way from vehicle to vehicle, signing autographs, talking football, and accepting with thanks some of the food and drink that was thrust upon me. By the time I reached my car, I was often pretty drunk.

The fans were kind of another special team for us during the games themselves. Particularly those in the lower right-field bleachers that came down right behind the visiting team's bench. There were a slew of very tough individuals who always had those seats, everyone from bikers to longshoremen. They wore the wildest outfits and loved to harass the opposition any way they could. Players from other teams told me they just hated to play us in Oakland.

"Playing in front of those madmen in the bleachers was as tough as playing you guys on the field, and you had enough madmen," Ed Podolak, the all-purpose running back of the Chiefs, told me years later. "We'd get hit in the back with all kinds of shit. I'd stand on the sideline and keep my helmet on."

When we made the playoffs, I remember thinking that had solidified my position as the starting quarterback. If we hadn't made the playoffs, the job would surely be up for grabs next year. Daryle was still there, and there was nothing wrong with his arm. But I had a couple of advantages over him now. My teammates had complete confidence in me, and even with sore knees I had more mobility than Lamonica and could buy a little more time to throw under pressure.

Gene Upshaw told a writer, "You can be losing your block, and the Snake will still make you look good. He's mobile. He doesn't cling to a pattern. He moves here, there—he's a snake, man. Daryle drops back ten yards and he stays there. He can't move."

The Raider offense had changed since my takeover. We went to a short-to-intermediate passing game, going deep only enough to keep defenses honest. I dropped back seven yards instead of ten and got rid of the ball quicker. I also changed the pass patterns on my own. I told the receivers to make their cuts a little shallower than they had before. If we needed ten yards for a first down, there was no point in running seventeen-yard routes. Twelve- and thirteen-yard cuts would do just fine.

Besides, we had no Warren Wells to go deep. Freddy Biletnikoff was a possession receiver and a great one, but he had little speed. Mike Siani on the other side had a longer stride and was faster than Freddy, but he was no burner. Neither was tight end Bob Moore. Raymond Chester, who had been, was in Baltimore.

Our playoff opponent was our nemesis, the Pittsburgh Steelers, and this time we were on our home field. But it wouldn't have mattered where we played. Our entire team was so fired up that everyone played a near-perfect game and we won, 33–14. As Mean Joe Greene said afterward, "They just beat the hell out of us."

I threw only seventeen passes all day, completing fourteen for 142 yards. You don't have to throw when your running game gains 232 yards. Our offensive linemen loved it, firing out and taking it to the Steelers. In pass blocking the linemen played a more passive game, absorbing a beating to keep the rushers off me. In a running game they could all be Bob Browns.

After one series I went to the sideline with Upshaw, and the coaches put up a play on the blackboard. "Hey, John," Upshaw said, "leave the Snake alone. Let him call his own plays. He's calling a great game."

Charlie Smith and Clarence Davis combined to run for 121 yards out of the halfback slot that day. But fullback Marv Hubbard had the biggest day, rushing twenty times for 91 yards and two touchdowns. He was our grinder, a six-two, 230-pounder with no speed and no moves, just pure bludgeon power. Running low, legs driving, he just loved to take on linebackers with his helmet and shoulder pads and knees. He didn't run over many backers, but he punished all of them.

Hubbard was an eleventh-round draft choice out of Colgate in 1968, a halfback the Raiders tried to turn into a tight end. But he was too light and not a good blocker, so he was cut. When the Broncos also cut him, he went to play for the Hartford Knights of the Continental League for $225 a week. He put on ten pounds, learned to block, and made the Raiders in 1969. Marv worked like hell for two years before he became a regular. In the last two seasons he had rushed for over 2,000 yards and averaged close to 5 yards per carry.

And he loved to block. Marv, a real innocent-looking guy, liked to say, "I get this nasty little thrill out of sticking my helmet into somebody's stomach." Then he'd chuckle. "Heh, heh, heh."

Marv Hubbard was just an old-fashioned fullback who never gave up. That's why I was surprised to hear, after we'd beaten the Steelers, that "The Immaculate Reception" loss the year before had almost caused him to give up football. "I was so broken up and disappointed over the defeat that I thought seriously about quitting," he told a writer. "When you devote your life to the game and come so close, it really gets to you when you lose."

He was an emotional player who took losses harder than most. Marv had gone out with Freddy, Pete, and me a number of times. When we won, he always had a good time. When we lost, he was liable to give anyone he met a bad time. If he fumbled and we lost, it was worse. He would get real deep into bourbon whiskey, and at some point in the evening you knew he was going to break something. A glass, a bottle, a window—something had to shatter.

One night after a loss, the group of us were heading for Clancy's, a restaurant in Jack London Square. We had started at Al's Cactus Room and hit another bar or two before reaching San Francisco, and Marv was ready to break something. Loud music was pouring out of the open doors of a rock 'n' roll club in the square, and Marv hollered, "Turn that shit down!"

The rest of us kept walking, thinking nothing of it. Then someone yelled, "Fuck you!" and went at Marv. A mistake on that man's part. Marv grabbed him by the throat, threw him up against the wall, and popped him. Another guy tried to sucker-punch Marv, missed, and also got himself punched out.

After that, his aggressions apparently all out, the man who had gone to Colgate on an academic scholarship joined us in Clancy's for a nice dinner.

But Marv Hubbard could get a little crazed on the field, too, particularly when we played the Chiefs. Kansas City was always the toughest competition in our division until the late 1970s when Denver came on. Kansas City also had the best middle linebacker in the AFC, if not in the entire league. Willie Lanier weighed about 240 and hit like he weighed 260. Marv went to war with Lanier every time we played Kansas City because our fullback plays were all off-tackle and up the middle.

Marv would take a rat turd, get that jaw working, get that glazed look in his eyes, and just hammer away at Willie Lanier. And late in the games, when our running attack picked up a lot of yards because defenses tended to be beaten down from all the pounding by then, Marv would start yelling at Lanier.

We'd break the huddle and Marv would point at Willie and yell, "Here I come! I'm coming right at you, Willie!"

And that's where the play would be going!

I'd scream, "Shut the fuck up, Marv!"

The Kansas City fans hated Hubbard. They'd boo him during the introductions and boo everything he did, yelling for Lanier and the big nose tackle Buck Buchanan to kill that Raider fullback. I don't think Marv heard a single boo. When he stepped on a football field, the only thing he heard was the play called, the sound of him banging into someone, and maybe he heard some of the words he hurled at opponents. Maybe not.

Marv got into it with another middle linebacker in one game after receiving a couple of cheap shots in pileups. He stood up and yelled, "I'm gonna get you if I have to bomb the bus you leave on!"

Marv ran well in the AFC Championship Game, gaining 54 yards on ten carries, but the Dolphins ran us into the ground. Bob Griese passed six times and handed off fifty-three times as Larry Csonka, Mercury Morris, and company piled up 266 yards on the ground.

But well into the fourth quarter I still felt we would win. After the Dolphins kicked a field goal at the 9:42 mark to move ahead, 20–10, we drove back to our forty-five-yard line. On third and one, I thought Pete Banaszak picked up the yard. But when the officials spotted the ball we were about six inches short. No problem for Hubbard, who might even bust a good gain with the Dolphin defense packed in on fourth down. Marv banged in there and got a yard, but when he got hit by a linebacker, safetyman Dick Anderson followed and his helmet speared the ball loose. I grabbed the fumble and tried to go around left end, but got tackled for a loss. That was the game.

Marv was furious afterward. But there's very little a ballcarrier can do when he's stopped and held up, then a second defender drives his helmet into the ball. The fumble wasn't why we lost anyway. We had won all season by getting ahead and dictating the game, which is what the Dolphins had done to us. We couldn't stay with the run and we couldn't stop the run, which was no knock on a Raider defense that had played exceptionally all year.

The Dolphins ran mostly to our left side, against tackle Otis Sistrunk and end Tony Cline. I felt real bad for Tony, the quickest pass rusher on the team. But at 235 pounds he gave up over 20 pounds to tackle Norm Evans, and Sistrunk did the same against guard Larry Little. Tony also was constantly double-teamed by the tight end or cut by a back. My friend just wasn't strong enough to fight off all that. Tony was finally replaced by Bubba Smith, six-seven, 265, and he didn't fare any better, so maybe it just wasn't our day.

My own personal opinion of why we lost is because we got too high the week before, wanting so bad to beat the Steelers, and we just couldn't bring ourselves back to that level of intensity. We would get them next year; that's how all the Raiders felt. The only problem was, we had to wait six months to get started.

6

Awards Don't Mean Much When You Don't Win the Championship

The World Football league was formed in the spring of 1974 and began making big offers to NFL players, which excited all of us. The average NFL salary in 1973 was $29,000. One NFL team had reportedly offered Larry Csonka, Jim Kiick, and Paul Warfield of the Super Bowl champion Dolphins six-figure contracts for the 1975 season. I had already signed a new contract with the Raiders that would pay me $37,500 for 1974, so I wasn't complaining.

But the Birmingham franchise of the WFL saw me as a hot property. I had a lot of fans in Alabama from my college days, and I had just led the AFC in passing, completing 62.7 percent of my passes. Bill Putnam, chairman of the board of the Birmingham Americans, got in touch with my lawyer, Harry Pitts, and made me an offer I couldn't refuse. A $50,000 bonus and salaries totaling $825,000 over seven years, plus an attendance clause in the contract that would pay me a fortune if the team drew well.

Equally important was the chance to return to the South to play at Legion Field. I would be helping a new league and working for a seemingly strong owner in Bill Putnam. And I wouldn't be leaving the Raiders for two years because the option year on my contract carried through the 1975 season. I would have time to win a couple of NFL titles before going for one in the WFL in 1976. All I wanted was everything.

I was a little concerned that some of my teammates might be upset with me for jumping ship, but they were all for me. Our player representative Gene Upshaw said, "Blame Snake? I think what he did is super. I'd sign with the WFL too, except I'm on a multiyear contract. But this is gonna stir things up. There's no way I play for less than what a rookie wants to sign. They give him $90,000, I want that or I'll sit out."

I made a mistake, though, in not telling Al Davis about the Birmingham offer before I signed. I didn't want it to seem like I was using the WFL to get more money out of the Raiders, and I didn't think he could've changed my decision. I wanted to get back to the South because that's where I felt my future lay. But I knew Al Davis would be upset with me. Maybe that's why I didn't get in touch with him. Like everyone else, I was always a little afraid of the man.

I received a lot of nasty letters from people who said things like, "Now that you've got yours by jumping to the WFL, you won't give a damn about the Raiders."

So I went up to the El Rancho Motel several days before training camp officially opened. Then the Players Association voted to strike, which put me in a real no-win situation. After pretty much sitting on my ass four years, I had finally become the starting quarterback and leader of the Raiders, and I still couldn't play football. I booked a room, along with the other veterans who showed up. I supported the union and didn't want to let down my teammates who were on the picket line. Gene Upshaw told us every day to stay out of camp, that we'd force the owners to give us what we deserved.

Again, I didn't even know what the issues were. All I knew was that I thought we could win on the field this year, not on strike. I hated to cross a picket line that 80 percent of my teammates were for, but winning was more important to me. First Freddy Biletnikoff crossed the line, and the next day Tony Cline, Pete Banaszak, and I went to work. We only had ten days before our first preseason game.

We had a bunch of work to do because the coaches were instituting a new style of passing. Instead of throwing timing passes, releasing the ball either before or on the break, they wanted me to hold the ball a bit longer and throw quickly *after* the receiver had made his cut. Our receivers would go out, break, and come straight back to the ball. Timing passes have a much greater chance of being intercepted. But when your receiver cuts away from the defender and comes back to you, shielding the ball from the defender, there is little possibility of an interception. Unless the receiver doesn't pull in the ball and it ricochets into the air, or you simply throw a bad pass. I've been known to throw a few of those, passes that the moment I released them I wanted to yell, "Come back here!"

My having to wait before throwing meant that our blockers had to keep their men off me even longer, four to five seconds. We had lost tackle Bob Brown, but third-year man John Vella, a six-four, 260-pounder, stepped in and did a fine job. He was tough and tenacious and had a real short fuse. Big John won my heart after the Steelers' middle linebacker, Jack Lambert, did something that pissed him off. John just slapped Lambert about five times real quick and backed him up to the Steeler huddle.

One reason why the Raiders didn't have a breakaway-type running back was because all of our backs had to block for the quarterback *and* for our power running game. We always kept one back—and usually two—in on pass plays. The halfback could not flare out for a pass until he had checked that there was no blitz. If the linebackers didn't come, the fullback would slip over the middle for a five-yard pass.

Our backs were all strong blockers. My favorite was Clarence Davis, who was only five-eleven and 200 pounds. But he was just devastating. Clarence, firing out of a low stance, had a way of driving his helmet and shoulders into a blitzing linebacker that would just stun him. I've seen him nail blitzing safetymen and knock them three feet backward right on their asses. He was also a quick, slashing runner. And while he had the worst hands on the team, pure wood, that didn't keep him from making some crucial catches for us.

We were going to throw longer passes this season, which was another reason why the blocks would have to be held longer. We were going deep because we again had a bomb threat in Cliff Branch. A 9.3 sprinter out of Colorado, he was even faster than Warren Wells. Primarily a track man and a kick returner in college—where he had scored eight touchdowns—Cliff came to us in 1972 without much experience as a receiver. He had to work hard on his concentration, on looking the ball into his hands. Freddy Biletnikoff helped him a lot on that and on reading coverages.

And I would stay after practice and throw again and again to Cliff, who learned to catch the ball with his hands, not his body. I'd release the ball when his back was turned so that he had to react quickly. "I'm even working at home, Snake," he said to me one day. "I walk around dropping the ball on the floor and trying to catch it as it bounces up."

Cliff's catches had increased from three in 1972 to nineteen in 1973, and this season we all knew he was going to really open up our offense. Cornerbacks had to set up at least twenty yards off him to even have a chance of being near Branch when a long pass arrived. My only problem, not being a real long thrower, was worrying about underthrowing Cliff. He's one receiver I can safely say I *never* overthrew on a deep pass.

I don't know how many times over the years I heaved the ball as hard as I could to Branch flying down the left sideline and knew as I was hit and falling down that the goddamn pass was short. "Shit," I'd think. Then I'd get up to find that Cliff had adjusted to the ball and come back for it as the defender kept going. Touchdown. I had to practice clapping my hands together as if I'd planned the pass that way.

With Branch on the left and Freddy on the right, one of them had to be double-teamed. Freddy had so many moves, ran such precise routes, and read coverages so well, he could get open against two men as easily as one. He was a perfectionist. I can't remember Freddy ever dropping a pass he should have caught. He even practiced, regularly, catching the ball with one hand. He must've caught a dozen of mine that way in games.

Of course, Freddy wore so much stickum on his hands that it was hard for him to get the ball out of his hands after a catch. He kept a big glob of Hold-tite on the inside of his socks, then he got Cliff doing the same thing, and soon that shit was all over the ball. Our towel boy got a lot of work running on the field and doing wipe offs.

Freddy was an intense competitor. I've seen him drop a pass in practice and get so angry he'd throw his helmet over the fence. He bit his fingernails down to the quick, had ulcers, and threw up before every game. We got used to him moving into the bathroom just before we were to take the field and going, "Earl, earl, earl" as he up-chucked. A rookie would say, "What's that?" Someone would reply, "That's just Freddy calling his Earl."

So I had a bomb threat on one side and a top possession receiver on the other. When defenses doubled both of them, I'd go to tight end Bob Moore, a solid short- to medium-range receiver who was real good against zones. He'd find the seams, and I'd find him.

We were halfway through the exhibition season before the strike was settled and all the veterans joined us. I don't know if that was a factor in our opening loss to Buffalo, 21–20. That was the fifth year in a row we'd lost the first game of the season. "Maybe next year," I told Pete, "we ought to start with the second game."

Then we went on a four-game winning streak that included a 27–7 beating of Kansas City and a 17–0 shutout of the Steelers in Pittsburgh. The next game was one of those I just loved to play in. Behind by four points with no time-outs left, we beat the Bengals in the last ninety-six seconds.

We opened the scoring on Blanda's longest field goal of the season, a forty-nine-yarder. Then the Bengals went ahead 14–3. We made it 20–14. They went ahead 21–20. We added three to make it 23–21. They scored six to go ahead 27–23.

The clock showed 1:36 to play when we got the ball a last time, needing to gain fifty-two yards for the winning touchdown. With no time-outs left, we went into what we call our "clutch" offense, using no huddle and calling all plays at the line of scrimmage. I hit Freddy on the right sideline for twelve yards, using up only four seconds. Figuring the Bengals would expect more sideline passes to stop the clock, I had Freddy and Cliff run out-patterns to pull the secondary away, then hit Bob Moore on consecutive passes up the middle for fourteen and twelve yards. First down on the Cincinnati fourteen-yard line.

Mike Siani replaced Branch because, being six-two and a good leaper, Siani was a better target in congestion, and it gets awfully crowded near the end zone. Siani had been the starter the previous two years, catching forty-five passes in 1973. He'd lost the job to Branch's afterburners, but down close there's no room for speed to maneuver in.

I missed my next two passes. There were thirty-three seconds on the clock. The Bengal defense was dropping deep, expecting me to go for the end zone with time running out. I was looking for Moore and Biletnikoff over the middle, then I saw Siani at the five on the right sideline. I spotted him because he was standing there all alone, waving his arms. He caught the ball and got knocked out of bounds at the one.

Hubbard lost a yard, I threw an incompletion, and halfback Charlie Smith came running in with a play from Madden. Charlie was to carry on a power sweep to the right, led by Gene Upshaw pulling from left guard. I liked the play. The Bengals had six men stacked in the middle. If Charlie couldn't get in on the sweep, he could get out of bounds and stop the clock. It showed thirteen seconds. Charlie ran behind the power blocking, then bounced off a safetyman and into the end zone.

Bob Moore and Cliff Branch each caught seven passes for almost 100 yards in this game. Charlie Smith had carried only one other time this day, gaining 3 yards. But Charlie got the game ball and I was glad. He had rushed for over 3,000 yards for the Raiders in five seasons and had taken a beating that was slowing him now. He wouldn't have many more opportunities for heroics, and if Charlie had gotten stopped on that play we would have lost.

The writers were shocked when it was announced that Charlie Smith had received the game ball. "Charlie got the game ball," Madden explained, "for not being tackled. That's why."

That game was played October 20, shortly after the A's won the World Series, and the infield had been sodded, which made it tough to run on. It was also wet, which made it even harder for visiting teams. Our guys got used to the field. We were always hearing complaints that our field was overwatered to slow down opponents. Management denied that the field was watered excessively, and I don't know that it was done purposely. But I do know that field was just soggy as hell. A swamp.

We beat the 49ers, 35–24, then flew to Denver, looking for our seventh win in a row. In Denver we stayed at an old, cold, ratty hotel called the Continental. Everyone hated it, except Al Davis, who apparently kept the team at the Continental because the Raiders had always been successful while staying there. Al, of course, denied that he was superstitious.

Freddy and I checked into our room and saw a roach had a mouse backed up into a corner. Neither of the lamps on the night tables had shades on them. The bare bulbs poked out of them like lights in a flophouse.

Some of us never worried about our accommodations on the road. We came to town to have a little fun and win a football game. The fun was aided by the endless number of women we got to know in every town we played in. They all enjoyed coming out and playing with us. You had to watch the partying the night before a game a little bit, not wanting it to run too late. But as I didn't need a lot of sleep, I didn't worry about the good times too much.

And sometimes the pregame partying would make you feel loose the next day and you'd come up with a real good game. I know a lot of players who would agree with that. Bobby Layne always did. They used to say that if Bobby didn't go out and get plowed the night before he played, he wasn't going to have a big game. I loved his style.

I remember having a drink with my writer friend Jack Smith one night and saying, "You know, I'd like to be like those quarterbacks who could drink and hell around all night and then go out there with no sleep, like Bobby Layne, and throw me about four touches. But me, I'd probably just throw up."

Of course, I was kidding Jack. I hadn't thrown up since high school.

Anyway, in Denver Freddy and I called a couple of girls we knew after dinner and asked them to come over and bring four bottles of wine. Freddy was between marriages at the time, so what the hell? We already had a nice glow from our dinner wine and wanted to keep it alive. No problem. We got so ripped that by 4 A.M. we were all sitting around nude, making shadow puppets on the walls using the harsh light cast by the bare bulbs. And laughing like there was no tomorrow.

There was, and we finally went to bed at about five. Up at eight-thirty for the pregame meal, I opened the blinds and it was snowing like hell.

"Look at this shit, Freddy," I said. "And we gotta play today!"

We went down to breakfast and got a bunch of cold drinks to put out the fire, had coffee, then went out and had a big day. I threw four touchdown passes, Freddy and Cliff each catching two. They received game balls. I thought a third should go to Bobby Layne.

I had a little scare just before the first half, though. I threw off-balance, twisted my right knee, and had to limp off the field. It hurt, but I didn't think it was serious and I told Madden, "I'll be okay for the second half." Dr. Rosenfeld worked on it at halftime. He was more concerned about my left knee, which had some loose particles floating around in it that he would remove at season's end. But not now. I could still move around in the pocket and duck under rushers, and we were going for a championship.

We won five of our last six games, the lone loss to Denver at home, 20–17. Our 12–2 record meant that both of our playoff games would be at home, beginning with the Dolphins. Veteran TV broadcaster Curt Gowdy later called this "the greatest pro football game I've ever seen."

It started with a bang as Nat Moore of the Dolphins ran back the opening kickoff eighty-nine yards for a touchdown. We tied it when Charlie Smith came in on a third-down play at the Miami thirty-one and outran middle linebacker Nick Buoniconti right down the middle of the zone defense and caught a touchdown pass. After a Miami field goal, Freddy made one of his patented one-handed catches in the corner of the end zone with Tim Foley pinning his right arm behind him. Freddy reached up and pulled in the ball lefty. "Look, Ma, one hand!"

The Dolphins came back with nine points to go ahead 19–14, then it was Branch's turn for a big play. He made a forty-three-yard reception on which he turned around Henry Stuckey, fell down, got up, and ran past the defensive back to score on a seventy-two-yard play. We led 21–19. Two minutes later the Dolphins made it 26–21. The clock showed 2:08 and we had to pick up sixty-eight yards.

"We can do it," Upshaw said, "we can do it."

That became the chant after every gain. A run and five straight pass completions took us to the fourteen, with Freddy's eighteen- and twenty-yard catches the longest gainers. Clarence Davis drove six yards off-tackle for a first down at the eight. There were thirty-five seconds on the clock and we had used all of our time-outs.

On the next play our line gave me about five seconds, but Freddy, Cliff, and Bob Moore were covered on a right-side flood. I moved to the left to avoid pressure. Just as I felt someone hit me from behind at the ankles, I saw Clarence Davis run into the end zone and threw as I fell forward. The looping pass reached Clarence between two Miami defenders. The guy with bad hands won the wrestling match for the ball and the game.

The championship game was against Pittsburgh in a season when Terry Bradshaw finally established himself as the starting quarterback and Lynn Swann had a fine rookie season. Our defense held the Steelers to three points going into the fourth quarter, and we had ten. But once again we couldn't stop the run in the big game, giving up 210 yards. Even worse, we couldn't run the ball ourselves, gaining only 29 yards in twenty-one attempts. But the Steelers scored twenty-one points in the fourth quarter and won, 24–13.

The Steeler defense was the most complex I'd seen. They mixed their coverages on every play, which was one reason why I had two interceptions in the fourth quarter. You needed time to read the defense, and L. C. Greenwood, Fats Holmes, Joe Greene, and Dwight White did not give you a lot of time. They gave you a lot of hurry.

But I think our defensive end Horace Jones best summed up our performance in the dressing room. He smacked his taped right hand into a locker and said, "When we were beaten last year by Miami, we broke down and cried. But nobody in this dressing room's crying now because we didn't deserve to win. We have people here who made the same mistakes."

I had a good year, leading the league in touchdown passes with twenty-six, half of which went to Branch, won the Gorman Award again, was named AFC Player of the Year, made the Pro Bowl team again, and All-Pro unanimously for the first time. But it didn't mean all that much when you don't win the championship.

George Blanda had been saying nice things about me to the press.

"Stabler is a great passer," George said. "He has accuracy, great timing, great touch. He can throw the ball through a linebacker or over a linebacker. He has a good touch on the long pass or he can drive it in there. But his greatest knack is being able to read defenses. He knows where to go with a pass."

Most of the time, he might have added. Bob Griese of the Dolphins and I were the AFC quarterbacks in the Pro Bowl, against John Hadl of the Rams and Roman Gabriel of the Eagles. Griese set up five field goals as the AFC won, 15–13 on a frozen field. I threw four interceptions.

Afterward I went back to the hotel and John Hadl saw me in the lobby. He started laughing his ass off, and I had to laugh too. "Let me tell you something, son," he said. "Those won't be the last four you throw. Just keep on throwing."

The Birmingham Americans, having financial problems, defaulted on two payments due me and the courts ruled my contract was void. I wished the WFL well because it was certainly giving a lot of good football players work. But I was happy to remain a Raider. Al Davis gave me a three-year contract at $200,000 per year. Daryle Lamonica went to the WFL in 1975, and Jim Otto finally retired after starting 210 consecutive games over fifteen years.

Jim didn't want to quit, so management retired him to a job in the front office. He came to camp and tried to do it one more time. But he had a terrible limp. His knee was ruined and he could hardly run. We all knew he couldn't get it done any more, and we felt for him. He kept lining up in practice and trying so hard. Jim played one series in an exhibition game in San Francisco, then started back on the field the next time we got the ball. But the coaches called him back and sent in Dave Dalby, our great young center. And that was it. Looking back now, I understand even more what Jim Otto was going through.

Middle linebacker Dan Conners also retired after eleven years. He wasn't real big and he didn't have a lot of range, but he was smart and an overachiever who was always around the ball. His career interceptions and fumble recoveries totaled over thirty, five of them for touchdowns. Dan was the guy who could handle the linemen and linebackers who got too emotional in games and wanted to maim people. He had also been a tremendous help to left linebacker Phil Villapiano during his rookie year.

Phil had played defensive end at Bowling Green and he had to learn his new position as he went. As the opposing quarterback called signals, Phil would look over at Conners and say, "Where do I go?" Dan would tell him, and Phil would go to it. In between getting burned, he just knocked the shit out of people. He was one tough wild man from the beginning.

Late one night, Freddy and I walked into Al's Cactus Room and found Phil standing up on the bar. Then he dropped his pants and danced down the bar, carefully avoiding kicking over anyone's drink. People applauded, so he danced back the other way.

That wasn't the last time Villapiano performed that little skit at Al's. Center Dave Dalby thought it was so entertaining that he climbed up on the bar, dropped his pants, and did a lineman's version of "The Villapiano Boogie." Phil was a laugher and a kidder and if you went out drinking in Oakland or San Francisco, you were going to run into him.

We acquired another outside linebacker in 1975, six-seven Ted Hendricks, probably the best I ever played with. He had been called "The Mad Stork" in college, but with us he became known as "Kick 'em in the Head Ted." When he blitzed, blockers tried to cut him and he'd leap over them, occasionally kicking them in the head. Sometimes scoring knockouts.

Hendricks was a full-blown free spirit and off-the-wall individual who would do just about anything for a laugh. During one of our Monday night games, a camera moved in on Ted seated on the bench. He reached behind him and put on a mask with a false nose.

We had a linebacker coach, Myrel Moore, come in one year bearing a huge medicine ball, one that weighed about forty pounds. The coach had his guys pushing that ball all over the field to teach them how to fend off low blocks. After one day on that little exercise, Ted said, "Enough of that beach ball shit."

That evening he stole the ball, threw it in his truck, and deposited it in Al's Cactus Room.

When Myrel Moore started the linebackers working on a special weight machine, Hendricks built his own weights. He mounted two empty five-gallon cans on a bar and painted 500 LBS. on each. One

Halloween Ted hollowed out a pumpkin and came to practice wearing it squashed down on his head as a helmet. Most Raiders loved to party, but Ted Hendricks was a party all by himself.

You would expect to find a team's most ferocious defenders among the down linemen or the linebackers. The meanest critters on the Raiders in the seventies were the defensive backs. They definitely got the attention of anyone who entered their territory.

The left cornerback, Skip Thomas, was nicknamed "Dr. Death." The free safety, Jack Tatum, was known as "The Assassin." The strong-side safety, George Atkinson, did not need a nickname to behave on a football field in a way that some might call "felonious." In charge of all these rowdies, the man who kept them from going too far was defensive captain and right cornerback Willie Brown. He kept the others from killing.

Willie had been a pro since 1963 and he had covered all the great receivers with distinction, one-on-one. He was big for a cornerback, six-one and 210 pounds, with a very strong upper body that gave him an edge in holding up receivers at the line of scrimmage. He'd hit his man and stand him up at the line, then hit him again. I've watched quarterbacks look left for their split end down the field, only to see him blocked three yards from the line by Willie Brown.

Skip Thomas was as big as Willie, but quicker and very physical. He liked to bang his man at the line, then turn and run with him, and Skip usually led the club in interceptions. If the end caught the ball on him, Skip liked to knock his head off. He also loved the name "Dr. Death" so much that he had it painted on the doors of his white Corvette, in gold-leaf letters about a foot high, right over the Raider skull and crossbones he had on the doors.

George Atkinson heard a lot of complaints about his roughhouse style of play, and he ignored all of them. "I treat receivers the way I would treat a burglar in my house," George said. "Don't nobody mess with my things."

I thought George was going to get killed early in Jack Tatum's rookie year, 1971—by Jack. As the free safety, he seldom had a man to cover, so he roamed around and helped the other backs or linebackers who were on a runner coming out of the backfield. What Jack did mainly was let the others play the ball while he punished the receiver. He went for knockouts. He went so hard that twice he knocked out George. He'd hit the receiver and his teammate at the same time. He also KO'd Willie Brown and Nemiah Wilson, who was the left corner in 1971.

Jack was real nice off the field: quiet, intense, hardly ever smiled. But nobody fucked with Jack. I don't care if you were six-eight and weighed 300 pounds. Jack wore a kind of permanent scowl on his face and kept a hangman's look in his eyes, and that's how he played. There was nothing dirty about his game—he stayed within the rules. He occasionally used "The Hook" that Atkinson taught him, but usually he just hit with his helmet and his shoulders, a five-eleven, 205-pound missile. He'd run into guys with his eyes and never blink.

Tatum hit Broncos' tight end Riley Odoms, a six-four, 240-pounder, with a shot in Mile High Stadium that sounded like a cannon went off in that thin air. It was a stalemate, as somehow Odoms held the ball. But he was the only player I ever saw take a Tatum blow like that and not be carried off the field. Odoms just staggered off.

Intimidation was Jack's game, and he was the champion. In one of our games with Miami, Paul Warfield tried to run a crossing pattern on Tatum and he had to be helped off the field. Later in that game Warfield was open down the sideline. He heard Tatum coming, took his eye off the ball, and it went through his hands. Jack did that to a lot of receivers. His footsteps broke up more passes than his hands did.

"They're not really bad fellows," Kansas City Coach Paul Wiggin once said of our defensive players. "It's just that they're trained to kill."

In 1975 our defense ranked third in the league, had forty-five sacks and thirty-five interceptions. The offense was not as consistent early, due largely, I felt, to my right knee. I'd had the loose particles removed and felt good as we won five out of six preseason games and scored thirty-one points in each of our first two games, wins in Miami and Baltimore. But during practice for the next game in San Diego, I twisted my right knee and couldn't pass on Sunday.

Backup quarterback Larry Lawrence started. He had made the team in 1974 after playing two seasons in Canada and spending the next two years touring the country on a motorcycle. When he arrived in camp with a pharaoh hound, a tiger tattooed on his calf, and a red beard, we knew he was one of us. He had a decent arm, ran the ball well, and he could make things happen. In one preseason game he made up a play in the huddle, and called himself on an option. When Larry was hit behind the line, he tossed the ball to a trailing back who went in and scored. Madden laughed like hell on the sideline.

But we only scored three points in the first half against the Chargers, and Lawrence hurt a knee that needed surgery. So I played the second half and took the club down for another field goal. Luckily, the defense pitched a shutout.

George Blanda, who dressed next to me, was angry after the game, I guess because he hadn't gotten a shot at quarterback at the age of forty-eight. He was such a competitor that he refused to accept the fact that he was now strictly a kicker. I was being interviewed by a group of writers, one of whom was leaning in George's locker.

"Get the hell out of there," George growled.

"Sorry, George," the writer said. "But that's what you get for having a locker next to Ken's."

"I don't get nothing," Blanda said angrily. "You're the one who will get it if you don't get the fuck out of my fucking locker. I'll kick the shit out of you."

I loved the man, but he could be a tad testy.

The following week I thought my knee was better until I threw on the artificial turf at Arrowhead Stadium in Kansas City. I couldn't plant my right leg and follow through properly and I was intercepted three times.

It was a real windy day and my receivers tried to defend me. They said I hadn't thrown that badly and claimed two of the interceptions had been caused by the wind. I appreciated their support, but the other team got a bunch of TDs throwing in that wind. The Chiefs had a pretty little girl gallop a painted horse around the field every time they scored a touchdown. They got six that day and by the end the horse looked so tired I thought they'd have to shoot him.

A week later, in Cincinnati, we lost, 14–10, in the rain. Four interceptions. I was glad Lamonica was gone because I was throwing the ball like George Plimpton.

After five games on the road, we went home and beat San Diego, 25–0. Thank God I finally hit on a bomb. Cliff Branch told me they'd given him single coverage on a corner pattern, and I hit him on it in the second half. I had to be careful with Cliff. He had so much confidence now that he was always telling me he was open. We'd be coming out of the tunnel to start the game and Cliff would start claiming he was open.

But I really needed that long one. I could have connected with Cliff about five times earlier. I'd see him open and say to myself, "I'll hit this fucker." Then I'd release the ball and watch it fall yards short of Cliff. I was not stepping and planting right because of the knee, so I didn't have the balance or strength to throw deep. My throws were all arm and it just wasn't strong enough.

That shutout of the Chargers was the beginning of a seven-game winning streak. My knees continued to bother me, the left one getting sore from favoring the right. I wrapped them in Ace bandages and took painkillers—Darvon and codeine—but I never took a shot of Novocain. I knew guys who had taken that stuff to play and, because they couldn't feel the joint, they'd done more damage to the injured area. I had a fairly high threshold of pain.

Another thing that helped was knowing how to take a hit. I instinctively relaxed and went with the blow. Our blocking was generally excellent. But because I was immobile and we held the ball till the last second, I took a lot of hits just after releasing the ball. Usually the rushers' momentum would carry them into me. I didn't believe in complaining. I think that's why very few guys tried to hurt me. When they did, my guys took care of the cheap-shot artists.

In the 38–17 win over Cleveland, I took several late hits from defensive ends Earl Edwards and Turkey Jones. On one play I rolled out to the left and threw a twenty-five-yard pass to Branch. I was standing there watching the ball in flight when Jones came running at me from about ten yards away on the blind side and hit me in the back of the head. Gene Upshaw always arranged for turkeys like Turkey Jones to receive a message about their deportment, usually from a double-team.

"Look, this guy took a cheap shot at Snake. Let's take care of him," Upshaw said in the huddle. On the next play Vella and Buehler dropped Jones. As he was getting up, Upshaw ran over and leveled him, and Turkey was carried off the field.

We gained 427 yards against the Browns, and afterward Coach Forrest Gregg said, "The Raiders remind me of the old Packers—

nothing fancy. They just take a football and drive it down your throat the way we did in Green Bay." I liked that.

The Raiders had never played an overtime game, but during the streak we played two in a row. The first was in Washington, which had lost only one game at home in four years. It only took us three hours and thirty-five minutes to beat the Redskins, 26–23. After missing an extra point and a thirty-five-yard field goal near the end of regulation play, Blanda kicked a twenty-seven-yard field goal to win the game in overtime. "Just didn't do my job earlier," George said. "But I've missed before and I'll miss again."

As we figured they would going in, the Redskins put two backs on Branch and left Pat Fischer alone on Biletnikoff most of the time. Fischer was a tough little cornerback, but no match for Freddy, who just ate his lunch, catching nine passes. When the 'Skins also doubled Freddy, I went to Bob Moore over the middle four times for ninety-two yards.

Pete Banaszak had a great game. He scored three touchdowns, one on a beautiful twenty-nine-yard run behind an Upshaw block, increasing his career total to thirty-two to pass Clem Daniels's team record. "I'm not the ballplayer he was," Pete said. True. All Pete was was a big old heart wearing football gear.

Gene Upshaw, who tended to get up in the morning talking and go to bed at night still talking because he had an awful lot to say, was bellowing in the dressing room afterward. Some of the Redskin players had popped off about us in the Washington papers that week, and the clippings had been posted on our bulletin board in Oakland. Defensive tackle Diron Talbert, who played opposite Upshaw, paid for his words.

"Talbert might want to see some guys, but he doesn't want to see me again," Upshaw roared. "Talbert mouthed off all week, saying we were the team of grab and they're the team of gab. But he didn't say much once the game started."

Surprisingly, even Willie Brown sounded off. "Charley Taylor said we were good, but that we hadn't seen receivers like they have," Willie said. "When I read that, I just thought, 'We'll see.' Charley caught one pass against me for two yards." Willie smiled.

Fullback Marv Hubbard busted the longest run of his career in the Redskin game, a fifty-three-yarder. But later he dislocated his left shoulder for the second time that season. Reserve fullback Mark van Eeghen, who was faster than Hubbard but who was only in his second season, would fill in.

We beat Atlanta the next week in overtime, 37–34, as Blanda kicked three field goals and four extra points. The Falcons had what they called the "Grits Blitz" defense in which they were sending everybody at me, including assistant coaches and ball boys, it seemed like. So we ran at them for 286 yards, Banaszak getting 116 and Van Eeghen 82. The victory clinched the division title for us.

Although we finished with an 11–3 record and were at home for the playoff, the Bengals were favored. Critics said the Bengals had played a tougher schedule. Critics also said that we were a team that couldn't win the big one. They said that because we got into the championship game every year but we didn't get into the Super Bowl. We hadn't won the big one.

But we beat Cincinnati, 31–28, as Ted Hendricks pressured quarterback Ken Anderson all day and sacked him four times. Banaszak scored his seventeenth touchdown of the year, and Bob Moore, Mike Siani, and Dave Casper caught touchdown passes.

Once again, though, we lost the big one in Pittsburgh. The wind-chill factor that day was minus twelve, so cold that even the stickum froze. The tarp on the field the night before had either blown off or been pulled off the sidelines. There was little footing anywhere in Three Rivers Stadium, but the sidelines were solid ice and we couldn't run our out-patterns. The hitting was vicious, and there were eight fumbles and five interceptions in the game. George Atkinson laid his "Hook" on Lynn Swann and sent him to the hospital with a concussion.

The only thing good about this game was the emergence of Dave Casper. The six-four, 245-pound tight end kept getting hamstring pulls for two seasons and had caught exactly nine passes in that time. He made five tough catches in traffic this day. Three came in a sixty-seven-yard drive when we drew within nine points of the Steelers. Siani caught a touchdown pass that made it 16–7. Then, with seventeen seconds left in the game, Blanda kicked his longest field goal of the year, forty-one yards, to bring us within six. Marv Hubbard recovered a Steeler fumble of our onside kick and we got the ball back. I hit Branch with a pass at the Steeler fifteen-yard line, but he couldn't get out of bounds and the clock ran out. One more play, I swear that's all we needed. I kept telling myself, "We didn't lose. Time just ran out on us. Again."

Mean Joe Greene said after the game, "The only thing wrong with the Raiders is that they've always been so good they've never been able to sneak up on anyone."

That about said it.

7

Winning the Big One

For about two weeks after the loss in Pittsburgh, I'd wake up every morning and replay the game in my mind. I tried to figure out what I could have done differently that would have changed the outcome—my play calling, my passing. I just focused on myself because the only thing I could worry about was what I personally controlled.

I wanted to be remembered, and I knew the only way that was going to happen was to win the Super Bowl. When people sit around in bars and talk about the quarterbacks who excelled, the names that come up are guys who won that game. I was obsessed with winning it all in 1976. The thing that tormented me most was coming so close four years in a row, and never even getting into the big game.

"We didn't get in because we lost to great teams," John Madden said when I called him. "Kenny, for two years Miami was a great team, so were the Raiders. The Dolphins beat us. Then Pittsburgh had great teams and beat us. In all four of those years, the teams that beat us were the world champs."

"Well, we're gonna win it all this year, John," I said.

At the end of the 1975 season, Al Davis had told a writer, "I never said this before, but I think Ken Stabler might be the most accurate passer in football today. Other than that, the only thing I can say about him is that he is a winner."

He never said anything like that to me. Al didn't say much of anything to the players. What he did say was rarely a compliment. No matter how well anyone performed, Al's words always seemed designed to motivate us to do better. In one game I hit Freddy with a touchdown pass. Afterward Al said, "You know, Clifford was wide open on that play, nobody near him."

I couldn't see what difference it made if I'd had three other receivers wide open. You can only score one touchdown per pass. But Al liked to nudge you.

I didn't know if my lifetime completion percentage of 58.7 through 1975 was actually tops in the league among active players, but for Al Davis to call me the game's most accurate passer, well, I regarded that as a breakthrough. He expressed more confidence in me than he had before.

After I became the starting quarterback and had a few good games, Al said to me at practice one day, "Young man, do you know what you're doing this week?"

"Well, if I don't, we're in a helluva shape," I said, "because I understand I am playing quarterback."

Later on, during one of our winning streaks, I said something about how nice it was to be putting a lot of points on the board.

Al looked at me and said, "Well, you should. You're driving a Cadillac."

"Al," I said, "even a Cadillac needs somebody to steer it in the right direction."

Al Davis had been a successful coach, the commissioner of the AFL who had forced the merger with the NFL, and the shrewdest owner in the game, a man who put together teams that had won more games in the last nine years than any other club. In my mind Al was the biggest man in football. And as a guy who worked for him, I kept wishing he would loosen up a bit and be more like John Madden.

Big John could be tough, especially during practice. If plays weren't running smoothly, he would keep us out on the field until the offense was tuned like a racing engine. We just kept working until we got it right, with John standing there hollering, waving his hands in the air, and cussing.

He was real excitable and emotional, a man who lived with ulcers and demanded perfection of himself and his players. A certain amount of his ranting and raving was designed to put fear into players and get them to do the job. Coaches have always used fear as the main motivational force in football. Players are afraid of coaches because they are afraid of losing their jobs. That's why everybody plays hurt, fearing that if they sit out a game and allow an injury to heal, a replacement would take their job. Coaches can't use players who can't be out there on Sunday.

But a certain amount of John's motivational raving was an act. He would come to practice with a player in mind who had been fouling up. At a certain point John would burst into the huddle, get right in that player's face, and hoot and holler and scream, just go on and on. His arms would be moving, his hair would be flopping around, and his face would get so flushed you were afraid he was going to have a heart attack. Abruptly, though, John would pivot and walk away. Then, as he headed off to the side, he'd look over his shoulder at me. And wink.

John Madden plays a funny character on the Miller Lite commercials. You see him waving his hands around with the fingers spread wide apart, his jaw working, and his hair bouncing. I watched him do that stuff for years, so he just looks like John to me.

He was a good guy, the ideal coach for the renegade Raiders. Everybody liked John and got along well with him. I never heard one player ever cuss him seriously. Guys would bitch and moan when he kept us out for an extra hour of practice, but it was soon forgotten.

In training camp, John would come into your room, sit down, and chat. He liked to talk, he liked to get to know all his players and to let them get to know him off the field. I was always among the first guys to come into the dressing room before home games (on the road we all bused in together). John would come by and drop down on the stool next to me, and we'd sit and talk about anything but football.

John showed everyone that he cared, and I think that set a tone among the Raider players that brought everyone closer. Pro football teams are made up of competitors, guys who have already been starring in the game for ten years—in junior high school, high school, and college. In the pros not everyone is a star; almost half the players are not even starters. For the first time in their lives, they back up someone else and work like hell hoping to get some playing time, to prove that they are good enough to be regulars. The reserves are often unhappy. I know how they feel because I was one of them for over three years. But there were always guys on the Raiders who encouraged me. George, Freddy, Pete, Tony, and others believed in my ability and helped me to hang in there. Many of the veterans on the Raiders did that with other younger players. And John Madden was the man who fostered that attitude.

Pete Banaszak told me he'd heard guys complain about having to play on special teams, covering kicks in the open field—and those guys didn't get help. They also didn't last long as Raiders. "I love to play on special teams," he said, "because more games are decided by teams play than by offense and defense."

Pete had played on all the special teams throughout the 1975 season when he had rushed for 672 yards, scored sixteen touchdowns, and won the Gorman Award. That was his tenth season on special teams, and in 1976 Pete would be busting his ass on them again.

Some other veterans would not be, including our good friend Tony Cline, whose knee was still hurting. He was waived. Tony managed to hook on with the 49ers as a spot player for another year or so. I missed him and his sense of humor. He used to rag me to the press and whenever we attended Booster Club lunches together.

"This guy Snake makes me sick," Tony would say. "You'd think he was a Pollyanna or something, always saying nice things about everybody. He's really just a kiss-ass and a company man. The truth is, that he's overrated, overpaid, and way past his prime. In fact, he only started throwing left-handed just recently. When I first met him, he was right-handed."

Tony Cline and I had put down a lot of drinks together and had a bunch of fun for six years, and it was sad to see him go. I think that's why some football players wouldn't get too close to other players. Guys were always coming and going, stars one day, injured and gone the next. We all knew it could happen to any of us at any time. Nobody wanted to think of that.

It was also sad to lose George Blanda. Everyone knew that management was looking for a guy who could kick longer than George. He was still accurate short, hitting on thirteen of twenty-one in 1975, but he'd kicked only one over forty yards and had been replaced on kickoffs by punter Ray Guy. Rookie Fred Steinfort, a left-footed soccer-style kicker from Boston College, was the competition. George wouldn't even speak to the kid. Steinfort, who had a tiger tattooed on his hip, just shrugged and beat him out.

One day George was there, and the next day his locker had been cleaned out. George was annoyed that he hadn't been asked to quit in the off-season. He said he'd told the front office that he didn't want to keep his job only if Steinfort failed. "They told me not to worry. 'You'll be here,' " George related. "I'm just disappointed at the way it was handled. But I'm not bitter. Hell, Al Davis gave me nine extra years in the game."

George only played twenty-six years.

Marv Hubbard played just seven years. The left shoulder he had dislocated twice in 1975 popped out again. Marv had averaged almost 5 yards a carry in rushing for some 4,400 yards, but he wouldn't gain any more. Most guys left with a knee, but Marv's shoulder took the beating. You wouldn't think it possible if you saw the lineman's shoulder pads he wore that came down below his sternum. Yet he wore a helmet that he said the manufacturer guaranteed would withstand 200 *g*'s of force before it would break. "I busted about a dozen of those helmets," he added. In football, everything was subject to break.

We also lost defensive end Horace Jones and defensive tackle Art Thoms during the preseason, with knee injuries they couldn't come back from. Otis Sistrunk was the lone starter left among our rush men. Thoms was a bit of a character who had his own fan club in Oakland called "Art's Army." The first time I saw him on a road trip he boarded the airplane carrying his personal gear in a Mickey Mouse lunch box. But he was a good player. Thoms, playing nose tackle, had jammed up the middle all day in the championship game against Pittsburgh.

With three quarters of our rush line gone, we were going to have problems stopping opponents. Injuries the year before had forced Madden to play a lot of our "Orange" defense, using three down linemen and four linebackers. That became our full-time defense in 1976. Dave Rowe was the nose tackle, Otis Sistrunk the right end, and rookie Charles Philyaw the left end. Philyaw was a six-eight, 285-pounder, but blockers kept cutting him and he didn't adjust. He kept charging in, getting hit below the knees, and falling down. We got the impression he was a tad slow upstairs when he kept sitting in on the wrong meetings.

Defensive line coach Tom Dahms was in charge of "Large Charles." Tom would get so excited during games that he'd run up and down the sideline yelling and only realize he was wearing a headset when he outran the cord and the phones were yanked off him. Finally Tom was sent upstairs during games. He didn't have a lot of patience with Philyaw.

One day as the defense moved into a meeting room and the offense into another, someone told Dahms that Philyaw was going with the offense. "Let him stay there," Tom said.

One day at practice I said something to fullback Mark van Eeghen. "Why'd you call him Mark?" Philyaw asked.

"That's his name," I said.

"I thought his name was Van," he said.

That was a good sign—Charles could read the names on the back of jerseys. But he was different. One day he asked Freddy if he could borrow a pair of shoes. We were in Houston and Charles had forgotten to pack his shoes. Freddy looked up from the stool by his cubicle and said, "What size do you wear?"

"Sixteens," Charles said.

"Figures," Freddy said. "I wear elevens."

It became apparent as we went 5–1 in preseason games that Large Charles was not the answer at left end. It took a couple of weeks for Al Davis to come up with John Matuszak for the position. The six-eight, 280-pound Tooz had had problems elsewhere, but he was a player for us.

Madden had come to me earlier and told me what we had to do this season. "You'll have to throw the ball more, Ken," he said. "We want to establish the passing game and have it dominate, just mix in the running game. But we'll have to control the ball and put a lot of points on the board until the Orange defense meshes."

"John, I love to throw the ball," I said. "If the defense gives us the run, of course we'll take it. I like Van Eeghen and think he's gonna have a big year."

I felt I was ready to have my best year, too. I think my bad knees had actually made me a better passer. Not being mobile, I had to drop back and stand there and the blockers knew they had to hold longer. Particularly on the deeper cuts that Branch ran. Also, I seldom decided in the huddle who I was going to throw to, as most quarterbacks did. I waited to see what the defense was giving us.

Another reason I expected to do well was a healthy Dave Casper at tight end. Bob Moore had been a good one, but we had lost him in the expansion draft to Tampa Bay. I thought in the preseason that big Dave could be all-league. He was a crushing blocker, having gotten All-America honorable mention at Notre Dame when he played tackle during his junior year. As a receiver, he was real smart reading coverages, knew how to get open, and, like Freddy, he could catch any pass. Dave could make diving catches, go way up for the ball, reach behind him, whatever—he'd bring it in. He beat out the veteran Ted Kwalick as the starter.

"In the preseason most people thought Ted had the job," Casper told the press. "I thought he would have to beat me out."

Dave Casper was not shy about speaking out, and you never knew what he was going to say or do. He was extremely intelligent, an academic All-American who graduated cum laude from Notre Dame with a degree in economics. But he had a strange attitude for a great athlete.

From the time he joined the Raiders, he said he could take football or leave it. And it took him two years to earn the respect of his teammates. He appeared to be lazy because of his lackadaisical attitude. His thighs were so muscular that he kept pulling hamstrings and couldn't play. He wouldn't even try to practice. That didn't keep Dave from being one of the first players to speak to the press, and some veterans resented his open-mouth, no-play posture.

But once Casper started playing, he was just incredible on the football field. Off of it, I've seen him walk by a water cooler in training camp and turn it over, or go into a meeting and kick chairs across the room. I didn't ask why because I didn't care. What mattered was that Casper was a powerful weapon, quick and strong enough to outmuscle any defensive back.

He was always thinking, his mind just motoring. I'd be talking to him about lifting weights or something. Freddy would come by, and Dave would say something to him about fishing. While Freddy was answering him, Dave would make another comment to me on weights, then Pete would appear and Dave would ask him about his new car. Dave would go on like that, talking to all three of us at once as long as we could stand it. That usually wasn't too long.

One day, out of nowhere, Dave said, "I wouldn't mind putting on about thirty-five pounds and playing guard."

"We've got guards," I said. "We don't have any other tight end like you. In fact, there isn't another tight end in the world like you."

I think Dave was also a frustrated quarterback. He'd walk back to the huddle with me in games and come up with the most off-the-wall plays for me to call. One time we were backed up at our ten-yard line and he said, "Snake, I got it."

"What?"

"Let's run a double reverse."

I looked at him, thinking about all that ball handling near the goal line, and just shook my head.

"Nobody will ever expect it," he said.

"No shit, Dave. Nobody else on this team will expect me to call it either. And if I did, they'd kill me."

In another game we were leading with about a minute to play. We took possession at about our forty and I was just going to fall on the ball and kill the clock in two plays. As we went on the field, Dave said, "Listen, Snake, instead of falling on the ball, just duck down like you're falling. Then raise up and throw me a long one."

"Dave, did you really graduate cum laude?"

"Aw, come on," he said, nudging me with his elbow. "It'll work."

"Get in the huddle and shut up," I said.

We opened the 1976 season at home against Pittsburgh. We didn't have to worry about a frozen field, just a soggy one. That was probably good because the hitting in this game was even more ferocious than in our last meeting. First George Atkinson applied his "Hook" to the back of Lynn Swann's helmet and put him in the hospital with another concussion. Then Branch caught a pass, Mel Blount grabbed him low, picked him up, and dropped Cliff on his head. Jack Tatum was not pleased when tight end Randy Grossman hit him after the whistle. Jack threw Grossman to the ground and punched him. It went on like that. The fact was, the Raiders hated the Steelers and the Steelers hated us.

If I'm not mistaken, this was also the game against Pittsburgh that opened with a little levity. Dick Romansky, our equipment man, had come up with a plan to keep Raider players from stealing footballs. Our guys must have walked off with more footballs than players did on any other five teams combined. The thinking was that, historically, Raiders were supposed to steal. Romansky decided to put a stop to this by painting FUCK in big letters on about two dozen of our practice balls. Those were not balls that anyone would give away, as most of the stolen footballs ended up being presented to kids.

But one of the FUCK balls ended up in the game. The Steeler center looked down, saw the inscription, and demanded a new ball. It came out in the Pittsburgh papers that the Raiders were a low-class outfit that wrote obscenities on game balls to annoy opponents. That the practice ball got in the game was accidental. At least, that's what I was told.

It was no accident that George Buehler came out that day with Vaseline smeared all over the shoulders and upper sleeves of his jersey. George had to block Joe Greene, who lined up on an angle between center Dave Dalby and Buehler. Among "Mean Joe's" pass-rushing techniques was a move called a "Grab and Jerk." Others used it, but few as successfully as Joe. He would grab the blocker's jersey, jerk him to the side, throw his other arm over the guard's inside, and surge by him. Joe didn't get a good grip on George this day—thankfully.

Al Davis once called Joe Greene "the most dominant force in football," and George Buehler always got steamed up to play against Joe. "I like to play against him, but I wouldn't want to do it every week," George said. After one of their battles, Joe told Upshaw that Buehler was one of the strongest blockers he faced. George walked around smiling for a week after that.

Dave Casper caught a touchdown pass to open the scoring against Pittsburgh. But the Steelers came back with twenty-one points before Freddy made a diving catch in the end zone to bring us within seven. The Steelers went ahead 28–14, with only three minutes to play. Then Casper caught another touchdown pass. We got the ball back with 1:47 on the clock. After three successive incompletions, I hit Branch at the two. On a rollout to the left Casper was doubled, and I ran in to score the tying touchdown, 28–28, with 1:05 to play.

On Bradshaw's first pass, Dave Rowe tipped the ball to linebacker Willie Hall on Pittsburgh's thirteen-yard line. Then Fred Steinfort kicked a twenty-one-yard field goal. We had scored seventeen points in three minutes to win the game.

And I felt like we'd just won the championship. Hell, we'd just beaten the team that kept beating us in championship games, and it had looked like they'd had us again. But we came back and defeated the goddamn world champions!

It was such an emotional high and I was so drained in the dressing room after that game that I walked around in a daze. But I knew that night I was going to celebrate. Some of us did that whether we won or lost. But when we lost the drinking could get a little depressing and the hangovers were always worse, double-dose headachers.

That night Pete and I took our wives out to The Grotto, a seafood restaurant in San Francisco, ate a pound of shrimp, and drank about a bottle of Johnnie Walker Red apiece. Everywhere we went that night we laughed and danced and had a hell of a time, and not surprisingly we attracted a crowd. I loved it. Part of the reason I played football was for the recognition it brought me. I liked to be recognized every night I was out, which was most nights—but I particularly wanted to mix with folks after we beat Pittsburgh.

Winning just cuts you loose. It cures the common cold, the uncommon injury, whatever's been ailing you. You're on top and you don't mind who shares in the celebration. Some nights you just had to fight off the women and get it down to one, which was another part of the fun.

We won another close one in Kansas City, 24–21, after leading 24–7. In the first half we were almost perfect, rolling up 288 yards to K.C.'s 37. At one point I completed nine passes in a row, and Freddy caught career reception number 500 in his twelfth year. Casper, Branch, and Mike Siani caught touchdown passes. On Mike's catch, he drove the cornerback to the middle, cut back like he was going to the corner to yank the cornerback over there, then ducked back underneath him to the post. Chiefs' linebacker Jimbo Elrod came on a blitz that I didn't even see and hit me as I released the ball. My right knee bent as I went down under him. Backup Mike Rae finished the game at quarterback.

Tackle Art Shell was asked about his three holding penalties in the first half. "On two of those penalties I told the ref he made good calls," Art said. "Wilbur Young is a good defensive end, and he has a move where he gets his arm under you and you almost have to hold or he gets a free shot at the quarterback. I'd rather take the ten yards than let him come in for a clear shot on Snake."

All of our down linemen felt that way, and it made sense to Madden and me. We could get the ten-yard penalty back, but we couldn't get me new knees.

The next week I missed an entire game for the first time since I'd been a regular. My right knee was strained and painful. Joining me on the sidelines were Freddy, Clarence Davis, Skip Thomas, and Carl Garrett. A feisty running back and kick returner, Garrett—five-ten, 205 pounds—was known as "The Militant Midget." He had been a tough player and a pop-off with the Patriots, Bears, and Jets before Davis traded for him during the preseason. Carl promptly ran back a kickoff ninety-six yards for a touchdown. The Davis touch for acquiring malcontent veterans had struck again.

In game three against Houston, Mike Rae hit Branch with two touchdown passes and we held on for a 14–13 win. Matuszak proved his value by leading a goal line stand that kept the Oilers out of the end zone. Large Charles Philyaw also had a big game after avoiding jail when we arrived in Houston. He was arrested for not paying a fine he'd incurred while attending Texas Southern. The Raiders paid the fine, and Charles was so happy that he made two sacks, five other tackles, and blocked four passes against the Oilers. "If I'd known he was going to cause so much trouble," said the judge who released Philyaw, "I wouldn't have let him off."

Matuszak became the regular left end when Philyaw got hurt in the New England game. I was just happy we got out of Foxboro Stadium alive that day, as the Patriots kicked our ass to the tune of 48–17. They controlled the ball, running for almost 300 yards, and shut down our wide receivers. The only thing we got going for us was Dave Casper down the middle. He caught twelve passes, a Raider record, for 136 yards. We knew the Pats would be tough because they had already beaten Miami and Pittsburgh. What we didn't know was that we should have stayed on the bus that Sunday.

Several of us partied pretty good before the next game in San Diego. We had some girls there who just wouldn't quit, and nobody likes a quitter. We all realized that football was a serious business and that our performance affected a lot of other people. If I went out on

Sunday half-assed and didn't do my job the way I was capable of doing it, I would be letting down forty or more teammates. But I knew what I could do in the pregame hours and still perform at a peak on the field.

I also knew that if I let football totally dominate my existence it would overwhelm me. If I didn't stretch the rules and dodge a few curfews, I would have been bored stiff and distracted from the real task at hand. I felt the need for diversions because, having so much energy and needing so little sleep, what else could I do with the empty hours? The partying relieved the pressure and kept the tension at bay. I was always "Cool Hand Ken" during games. It was the night before them when time moved so slowly that I felt the tension building. But I never had trouble pitching it away.

I think the quarterbacks I admired most after Bobby Layne— Sonny Jurgensen, Joe Namath, and Billy Kilmer—all followed a similar pregame plan to prepare for games. I had to love Kilmer, who won a championship and led his team to the Super Bowl playing with one leg shorter than the other.

We got the deep passing game going again in San Diego, as Branch caught forty-one- and seventy-four-yard touchdown passes, and Casper pulled in a twenty-eight-yarder. Freddy picked up four first downs in as many catches for forty-seven yards. For years defenses knew that when we needed an eight- to twelve-yard first-down play we often went to Freddy, yet he kept getting open. Now that defenses had Branch *and* Casper, Freddy got open even more. We beat the Chargers, 27–17.

As the Oakland A's controlled our home field, we were still on the road in game six, our fifth straight game out of town. We went into Denver concerned about stopping Rick Upchurch, who had already returned three punts for touchdowns. But we needn't have been. Ray Guy's five-second hang-time punts and our coverage men—led by reserve end Morris Bradshaw—got themselves to Upchurch on time.

Still, we came out in the second half behind 3–10. We tied the game on a nice adjustment by Branch. He went deep down the sideline and bent toward the middle, beating corner Calvin Jones. But I saw the free safety coming over, so I threw toward the sideline, Cliff read the pass, reached to his outside, brought it in, and scored. Later Pete

Banaszak dove over from the one for the winning touchdown: Raiders 17, Broncos 10.

The following week Branch made his longest catch of the season, an 88-yard touchdown against Green Bay. I passed for 220 yards and three touchdowns all told in this game, but we missed all three extra points and were lucky the defense saved us late in the 18–14 victory. Placekicker Fred Steinfort tore a groin muscle and was lost for the year.

Guys wondered afterward if Blanda would be brought back. "I don't think he'd come," I said. "George has too much pride."

"I think he would if Al asked him," Freddy said.

"I hope Al asks him and that George comes back," I said. "We're gonna win that ring this year. I'd like to see George wearing one."

"I wonder if he could help us," Pete said. "He's been away from football for three months."

"George could fly in here tomorrow and kick field goals," I said. "He could kick inside the forty until he's sixty."

That week Davis signed Errol Mann, the eight-year veteran who had been dropped by the Lions after hitting on only four of ten field goal attempts. With us he would kick four of eleven, which led to more comments like: "Al should have brought back George." The grumbling stopped in the playoff and championship games as Errol went two-for-two on field goals.

In game eight we knocked Denver out of contention, 19–6, then squeaked by the Bears, 28–27, as I got knocked unconscious and had to be helped off the field. I went back in because we were trailing by seven in the fourth quarter. On the first play I got creamed again and fumbled. The Bears recovered and ran the ball into the end zone. We got a break when the referee mistakenly blew his whistle and the Bears were given the ball at our thirty-nine-yard line. I was so wobbly I didn't know what was going on. I was still in a daze when Hendricks intercepted a pass and we went back in.

The Bears had an excellent cornerback in Virgil Livers, who hadn't given up a touchdown all season until Branch beat him on a seventy-five-yard pass play earlier. Now Cliff said he could beat Livers again and he did. Livers tipped the ball, but Branch still caught it and scored on a forty-nine-yard play. To this day, I don't know how I threw that pass.

But it won the game when, with fifteen seconds left to play, a Bear field goal attempt hit the upright and caromed off. Another lucky break. This definitely felt like our year.

Of course, I didn't understand all this until the game was over. The concussion had made me so fuzzy that I don't even know what plays I called. I had just played on instinct. Tackle John Vella had done the same thing earlier in the season after being kicked in the head. In the huddle I could tell from his eyes that he wasn't all there, but he was still able to block the defensive end. Even semiconscious, football players are so well trained they're like field-trained hunting dogs—just turn 'em loose.

After beating Kansas City, 21–10, we clinched the division title in game eleven with a 26–7 win over Philadelphia. Then we blew away the expansion Tampa Bay Buccaneers, 49–16.

Our next game was against Cincinnati on Monday night. There was talk in the papers that the Raiders might lie down in that game because if the Bengals won, Pittsburgh would be eliminated from the playoffs. That was the dumbest thing I ever heard. The Raiders tried to beat the shit out of whoever we played. And we were all hoping we'd play the Steelers again. We owed them.

We made sure the Steelers could have a shot at us by beating the Bengals, 35–20, as I hit on four touchdown passes. Hell, it was a Monday night game on national television when you played with all your peers watching, and we never lost those. The Raiders kind of liked to show their wares. We always thought we were the best, and this season we planned to prove it.

I wasn't missed in the final game, as Madden held out several other regulars and myself to get younger players work. Mike Rae passed for three touchdowns and Van Eeghen went over the 1,000-yard mark rushing in the 24–0 win over San Diego. We finished with a 13–1 record. The last Raider team to do that, in 1967, was also the last to go to the Super Bowl.

Those Raiders lost to the Packers, 33–14. Gene Upshaw told me that after that game the great Packer defensive tackle Henry Jordan had tried to console him by saying, "Don't take this too hard. You guys are gonna be in a lot of these games." And Gene was saying now, "My worry then was if I had enough fingers for all them Super Bowl rings."

The Raiders were given a ring for playing in that game. Willie Brown, Upshaw, Pete, and Freddy all have those rings, but I never saw them wear one. "That ring was for the losers," Freddy said. "You don't wear something that says you finished second."

Our playoff opponents were the Patriots, the only team to beat us, and they came close to beating us again. George Atkinson announced early in the game that we had come to play. As the Pats drove for a score, tight end Russ Francis caught a forty-yard pass. George, running hard, made the tackle with a forearm that drove between Francis's two-bar face guard and broke his nose. Blood just poured out. It was a legal hit and no penalty was called, though many people weren't sure that the blow was necessary.

But if I was a six-one defensive back like George who had to cover a six-six end like Francis who outweighed me by over sixty pounds and I couldn't carry a concealed weapon, I'd probably do what I had to do to balance the odds a bit. Besides, Francis came back and caught a touchdown pass in the third quarter. The big SOB was so tough, if he couldn't breathe through his broken nose he probably breathed through an ear.

We went into the last sixteen minutes down 21–10, and I told myself, "I should have been more wary of these guys. Maybe all our work this season is going down the tube again."

But John Madden said, "Get one touchdown back at a time, Ken. Don't rush anything. We've got plenty of time."

Upshaw said later, "Snake came into the huddle and he had ice water in his veins. I thought to myself, 'This is why we do it all the time because he is like that.' I felt right then we were going to do it."

We moved right down the field in eleven plays—six runs and five pass completions. Mark van Eeghen scored from the one: 21–17. Then the Pats missed a fifty-yard field goal at the 4:12 mark. I told the guys, "Okay, this may be the last time we get the ball this season. Let's get it done."

I was going to throw on every down, as we had in the opening game comeback against Pittsburgh. I hit four out of five, got sacked for a nine-yard loss, and missed on a pass. We had a third-and-eighteen with a minute to go. I called a sideline pass to Carl Garrett, who was covered, but I threw anyway because the rush was on me. Just as

I released the ball, Ray Hamilton's momentum threw his arm into my face.

Christmas came a week early! The officials called roughing the passer and we had a first on the thirteen. I hit Casper for five, Clarence Davis gained four on a delay up the middle, and Banaszak got one. It was going to be a close measurement for the first down, but one of the Pats started yelling at the officials and was called for unsportsmanlike conduct. We had a first down at the one.

They stopped Pete. Then I rolled left behind Gene Upshaw, looking for Casper, but Gene cleared the way and I dove in for the winning score: 24–21. "Bring on the Steelers!" was the cry in the dressing room.

I liked to play against the Steelers because they were the best, winners of the last two Super Bowls. Their defense was a wild bunch, just like ours. I remember games we were winning when those guys would be fighting among themselves, arguing and cussing each other. It would look like they were about to come to blows. Joe Greene would be yelling at somebody, Jack Lambert would be cutting up one of his teammates. They were emotional players, the best kind.

Joe Greene was "The Man" of that group. He could be the nicest guy when they were two touches ahead. He'd run in there, knock me down, then help me up. When we were ahead, he'd run in there, knock me on my ass, and growl. I always said, "Nice play, Joe."

I remember completing a pass in the season opener and Joe Greene's big right paw swiped at me just as I released the ball. We were standing together watching as the catch was made. I said, "How'd you like that one?" Joe just smiled.

Later in that game I ran a sprint-out to the left, chased by Joe and L. C. Greenwood, and I was right on the line of scrimmage when I threw the ball to Casper. Joe and L.C. screamed at the officials, "He was over the line! He crossed the goddamn line of scrimmage!"

The referee spotted the ball and cried, "First down!"

"Close, wasn't it," I said to Joe and winked.

"Close, shit!" he said. "The goddamn ref needs a seein'-eye dog!"

But Joe Greene had never given me a cheap shot. I don't think any of the Steelers did. They just hit me as hard as they could. That was enough, thank you.

In the championship game both defenses excelled early on. Steeler running backs Franco Harris and Rocky Bleier were sidelined with injuries, but I don't know if they would have been able to run against our three-four that day. I didn't see many holes to run through. By this point in the year, our Orange defense that had started slowly was playing great.

Leading 10–7, we put together a sixty-five-yard drive just before the half that gave us a first down on the Steeler four. We brought in our three-tight-end offense that we used in short-yardage situations. Two of the ends were on the line and Warren Bankston set in the slot. Those three big ends gave us a lot of power blocking on running plays, which we usually called. But on our first-down play we faked a handoff to Van Eeghen and Bankston faked a block, slipping into the end zone all alone. I hit him for the touchdown.

In the third quarter we got another drive going to the Steeler twenty-four. On fourth-and-one, Bankston caught a seven-yard pass for the first down. From the five I sent Pete into the end zone, knowing linebacker Andy Russell would have to cover him. Russell was a smart twelve-year veteran, but I knew he couldn't stay with Pete. He caught the pass and we were up 24–7. I didn't see linebacker Jack Ham coming on a blitz from the blind side and he put a double-duty lick on me, bruising my ribs and knocking the cap off a tooth. That was okay, as 24–7 proved to be the final score. We were the AFC champions!

Naturally, we went out and celebrated that night. All night. The win and the scotch made those sore ribs feel just fine. Around about dawn, I didn't feel anything.

A few days later the UPI and AP news services named Bert Jones of the Colts as the best quarterback in the NFL. I wasn't in full agreement with that, but I wasn't about to say anything.

Freddy did. It wasn't like him to sound off, but Freddy told a writer, "Kenny got fucked. Bert Jones couldn't wash Kenny's jockstrap. When you are picking the best quarterback, you have to go over what he means to his team and what situations he's been through. You also have to figure what the guy has done against good teams in critical situations. If you take all that into consideration, I think Kenny has contributed more to our team than Bert has to Baltimore. Everybody really has a lot of confidence in Stabler."

The following day, when the Pro Bowl starters were chosen by the fourteen AFC coaches, I was picked number one and Bert Jones was number two. "The news services don't know shit," I thought. "Except in the other years when they picked me first."

I still phoned Freddy and said, "How'd you like to be my press agent?"

Freddy's locker was next to mine in the Coliseum and he was always a mess before games—nervous, hyper. He'd smoke a pack of cigarettes in the locker room and drink four or five Cokes. And he had a whole elaborate program for getting dressed to play. It would sometimes draw a crowd.

First he'd take a pair of scissors and snip off every little thread hanging from his pants. The threads could be so minute that most naked eyes couldn't detect them, but Freddy twisted and turned those pants in the light till he got them all. His pants had to come just over his knees, and he'd cut them in back for more freedom. He wore his black undersocks just over his calves so the flesh was bare to the knee.

Then he'd go through the ceremony of what shoes to wear. Receivers tend to be real picky about their shoes, depending on the field conditions and the weather. Even on perfect days Freddy was picky. He might put on a pair of Riddells, then go to a pair of Spot-Bilts, then pull on a pair of Converse. One day I saw him put on one Riddell and one Spot-Bilt. I guess one cut better to the left and the other to the right.

He was so superstitious he'd put a dime in one shoe and two nickels in the other. He literally turned on a dime. And he always taped a crucifix under his shoulder pads, flimsy little things that looked like they were made out of a couple of Kotex.

Once he finally decided on his shoes, Freddy would tie them about twenty-five times to get them just right. Whatever that was. Pete and I would drive him crazy. Sometimes we'd hide a shoe, or lace up a pair and skip an eyelet near the bottom.

Freddy would tape over his shoes up to the ankle, which was called "spatting." He'd tape his arms from just below the elbow to the wrist, then take a can of stickum and spray the tape. Finally he'd pull on his helmet and adjust the chin strap.

Then Pete would walk over, wink at me, and say, "Goddamn, Freddy, your uniform looks like shit today!"

So Freddy would take the whole sonuvabitching thing off and start all over.

"Be a little more careful," I'd say.

Freddy chewed gum throughout games. He liked Doublemint, which came in a white wrapper, and Juicy Fruit, which came in a yellow wrapper. Every time we came off the field Freddy would go to equipment manager Dick Romansky holding his hands away from him because they were full of stickum. "Dick," he'd say, "give me two yellows and a white." Or: "Give me two whites and a yellow." At first, people thought he was taking pills. Freddy was taking gum.

Pete, Freddy, and I had adjoining rooms at the Marriott Hotel in Newport Beach where we stayed the week before the Super Bowl against the Minnesota Vikings. We prepared for the game as we would for any opponent: off Monday, the day we arrived, then workouts Tuesday through Saturday. John Madden, bless his heart, didn't give us a curfew until Thursday night. We took full advantage of that.

Freddy and I had become friends with the actor James Caan and we called him to get into some action the first night. Jimmy was on location, but his brother Ronnie picked us up in a Rolls and took us to the Playboy Mansion. It was full of beautiful women who gave us a tour of the place. We had so much fun that we didn't leave until about 4 A.M.

The next night, after a short, crisp meeting, I went to the condo of a girl I'd met at the Playboy Mansion. I stayed with her till morning. On Wednesday, Freddy, Pete, and I just barhopped in Newport Beach. That ended the partying, except for a little scotch sipping in my room to relax. I never get to sleep before two.

Our workouts were all loose. The Super Bowl wasn't just another football game, but that's the way we practiced. Serious work got done, with a lot of laughing and grab-assing in between.

We had seen on the Viking game films that we had a tremendous mismatch up front on offense. Center Dave Dalby was our lightest offensive lineman at 255 pounds. The heaviest Viking pass rusher was tackle Doug Sutherland at 250. Art Shell, 290, would be blocking end Jim Marshall, who could not have weighed over 225. Upshaw, 265, would be on tackle Alan Page, 235. Buehler and Vella, both 270, would be on Sutherland and end Carl Eller, 245.

"Pete," I said, "I'd say we're gonna do some running on these guys."

The Vikings' pass defense was rated best in the NFL, having given up only eight touchdowns all season and an average of just 4.3 yards per completion. But it didn't look that tough to me. The secondary played all zone defense, and that was my game. My line gave me the time to read and slice up zones.

I had to tell myself not to lose sight of the fact that the Vikings had put together a 13–2–1 record. They had to have done an awful lot of things well to get here.

But I still remember a funny column Jim Murray wrote about the difference between the Vikings and the Raiders. "The Vikings play football like a guy laying carpet," he wrote. "The Raiders play like a guy jumping through a skylight with a machine gun."

That is kind of the way the game went. Playing before 100,421 people in the Rose Bowl, we took the opening kickoff right down into field goal range. The big gains were a 25-yard pass to Casper and a 20-yard run by Clarence Davis, a play we put in for this game. Casper lined up next to Shell and they double-teamed the end. Van Eeghen hit the linebacker. Buehler pulled and led Davis around end. He would gain 35 yards on the same play later, and 137 on the day as our offensive line did what we expected. Although we missed the field goal, I had read every Viking defense correctly and I went off the field superconfident in the Super Bowl.

Our next series began on our three, and we again marched down the field. This time Mann kicked a twenty-four-yard field goal. John Madden was storming around on the sideline when I came off, feeling we should have had two touchdowns. "John, don't worry," I said. "There's a lot more where those points came from."

We scored touchdowns on the next two drives to help John relax a bit. On the first, Casper ran a little eight-yard catch into a nineteen-yard gain, shrugging off tacklers. Freddy leaped high and caught a sideline pass at the one, then I play-faked and hit Dave for the TD. Freddy set up the next score, too. He ran a seventeen-yard post pattern and made a great catch between two defenders at the one. Pete scored, and Clarence Davis ran to him and said, "Do something with the ball!" So Pete heaved it into the stands. He had never done that before. But he had never scored in the Super Bowl before either.

After Mann kicked a forty-yard field goal in the third quarter to put us ahead 19–0, Fran Tarkenton finally got the Vikings going, completing five passes in a sixty-eight-yard drive. The last pass was an eight-yarder to Sammy White for the touchdown at the end of the quarter. The next time Minnesota got the ball, Tarkenton completed an eighteen-yard pass to White, who made a nice catch between Skip Thomas and Jack Tatum. But he paid for it.

Tatum hit him so hard that White's chin strap popped and his helmet flew ten feet away from him. That was the only time I ever saw Tatum look disappointed after a good hit. I guess he'd hoped White's head was still in his hat. Jack stood over White lying on the ground like a lion stands over its prey. When he saw White had held the ball, Jack just shook his head.

A few plays later Hendricks put a hard rush on Tarkenton, who forced a throw that linebacker Willie Hall intercepted. We took over at our forty-six and picked up four yards on two runs. Then I went to Freddy again on a fifteen-yard post pattern. The Viking safety blew the coverage and Freddy caught the ball with nobody near him. He turned up field and ran thirty-three yards before he was pulled down from behind at the two. That was Freddy's longest run in years, and as he loped back to the huddle he said, "I was looking for a gas station along the way."

Pete Banaszak, following Buehler and Vella, scored on the next play and again threw the ball into the stands. It had become a tradition.

The score was now 26–7, seven minutes into the fourth quarter. And as I ran off the field, I said to myself, "We just beat their ass. We just beat their ass good and plenty."

But the Raiders weren't through. Minutes later Willie Brown, thirty-six years old and a fourteen-year veteran, intercepted a Tarkenton pass intended for White and ran seventy-five yards down the sideline for a touchdown. For the second time in the game, Mann missed the extra-point kick. It didn't matter. The final score was 32–14. No one could say we couldn't win the big one any more. That was like getting a piano off my back. We had won the big one *big*.

With about two minutes left to play, it was announced on the PA system that Freddy had been named Most Valuable Player in the game. He had caught four passes for seventy-nine yards and set up three touchdowns. We had a whole team of MVPs this day, but if you had to pick one, there was no better choice than Freddy. When the announcement was made, Freddy, standing on the sideline, just burst into tears. I went over and hugged him. There were a lot of watery eyes on that sideline.

I looked around at the four guys who had played in this game before and lost, and thought about how great they had played today. Freddy was the MVP. Pete scored two touchdowns. Willie scored one. Upshaw blocked Alan Page right into the ground. God, I felt so good! I remember thinking, "This is one of the greatest moments in my life, and it always will be."

I met Al Davis walking into the dressing room, and he had on a smile you couldn't break with a stick. We hugged and I said, "I told you that I'd win it for you."

Freddy was seated by his locker hugging his ten-year-old son, Freddy Jr., who looked just like his dad with the same white-blond hair. They were both bawling. It was one of the most touching scenes I'd ever witnessed, big old tears of joy streaming down their faces.

When the press came in, Freddy's tears had dragged his under-eye blackener down his cheeks and he looked like he'd been hit in the face with a handful of mud. He didn't care, didn't even bother to wash up. He just sat there chain-smoking cigarettes and answering questions.

"I wish every guy on this team could get the award," he said, "because every guy deserves it. I honestly feel guilty winning MVP. To accomplish this with a group of guys you see every day, a group of guys you love, well, it feels like someone stuck a needle in my arm and pumped me full of warm blood. It's like someone gave you a very special present. It hits your heart."

I heard Upshaw's booming voice: "We knew that if we could get through the front four it would be for big yardage because their secondary is not known for making too many tackles. Their secondary isn't like Pittsburgh's. The Steelers have no guests back there. Everybody's a player."

Then he smiled and said, "We've done it all. There are no more football teams to beat. So where are the world champion Cincinnati Reds?" He laughed.

The only thing wrong with the whole scene was that Tony Cline and George Blanda weren't there. They'd given this ball club so much, and it was a shame they missed the big one.

I also felt kind of bad for Fran Tarkenton. He was an amazing player, just amazing. Not only had he passed for a ton of yardage in sixteen years, he was a quarterback who had gained over 4,000 yards *running* the football. And he had been to the Super Bowl three times, and three times he had failed to win. Goddamn, that had to hurt.

I got to know Fran a bit after this game. We spent a week together making television appearances: "Dinah!", "Donny and Marie," a Bob Hope special, and "Hollywood Squares." Inevitably, when two quarterbacks get together over dinner and drinks, they talk shop. And when we talked about the Super Bowl, Fran laid the loss off on his teammates. He said the secondary didn't tackle, the offensive line didn't block for the run or give him enough time to pass. I respect him as a player, but I lost a little respect for him as a person when he knocked his teammates. I always felt that when you lose, you lose. You take your lumps and that's it.

When the TV week ended and I went home, I thought about the quarterbacks who had won the Super Bowl. Bart Starr, Joe Namath, Len Dawson, Johnny Unitas, Roger Staubach, Bob Griese, Terry Bradshaw. That was a pretty good group to be in.

8

~~~~~~~~~~~~~~~~~~~~

Cooling Out on the Redneck Riviera

At the end of the NFL season, most football players take a little vacation and then go to work at their other profession. As the average pro career lasts less than five years, players feel the wise thing to do is to begin preparing for their future. I never thought much about the future. It wasn't going anywhere. And there was so damn much to do in the present.

At the close of each season, what I thought about was getting back to L.A.—Lower Alabama. Back to my roots. After six months of dealing with pressure and accumulating bruises, it was nice to do little more than cool out and play with folks I'd known since childhood. No worries about curfews, bed checks, or guys like Mean Joe Greene falling on my sore knees, nothing to focus on but simple pleasures.

I've always had a house near or in Gulf Shores, Alabama, which is only ten miles south of my hometown, Foley. Gulf Shores features miles of sugar-white beach that fronts on the Gulf of Mexico and is separated from the mainland and a group of small islands by the

Intracoastal Waterway. It was an obscure, unpretentious resort community until a 1979 hurricane leveled most of the modest structures along the shore. A subsequent building boom has dotted the area with $200,000 condominiums on the beach and $500,000 homes on the islands. But the place is still known affectionately as the "Redneck Riviera."

The year-round residents are mostly farmers and fishermen, hard-working—usually hard-drinking—men. The tourists who flock in range from bikers to bankers, from yahoos to yuppies, everyone looking to have a good time.

A whole lot of good times were had in the array of roadhouses and honky-tonks I love in Gulf Shores, places with names like The L.A. Pub & Grub, The Pink Pony, and The Seagull Lounge, which we called "The Dirty Bird." We often ended up at The Bird after everything else shut down around 2 A.M. The Dirty Bird didn't spread its wings until the evening, but it flew into the dawn.

The honky-tonks offered some of my favorite things, like shooting pool and listening to music, either on the jukebox or live. Or you could get a big plate of boiled shrimp or crawfish in garlic sauce and wash them down with Johnnie Walker Red on the rocks, a tall Jack Daniel's in a short glass, or a sweating-cold bottle of Bud. And, of course, you could happen upon the fine-looking young women who had wandered off the crackling-hot beach into the air-conditioned honky-tonks.

One of the best roadhouses is The Flora-Bama Lounge, which is just inside Florida near the Alabama line. "Do it on the line" is its slogan. A sign behind the bandstand proclaims, not SAVE THE WHALES but SAVE THE BALES.

There are so many places to bring in good-sized boats from the Gulf of Mexico, entrances to the Intracoastal Waterway, that marijuana importers have been fond of the Shores. Many have been busted, including one shrimp boat that was reportedly nabbed carrying ten tons of grass. Often when patrol boats approach the importers, they hurriedly dump the bales of pot into the drink and they wash up on shore. The next morning there are so many boats chugging around the area that you'd think an endless school of fish had appeared. But those boats wouldn't be after fish. They would be bale-hunting. Jamaican ganja can make for some awfully mellow toking, though I happened to prefer sipping.

Gulf Shores is also a boatman's paradise, particularly if you like speed. You can run a speedboat flat-out on the Intracoastal Waterway because the barrier islands generally fend off the winds from the Gulf and leave the water mirror-smooth. A group of us, including my closest friend, Randall Watson, and I really got into boats. Just about every year we bought new boats with bigger motors, always going faster and faster.

I started with a sixteen-foot Checkmate and hung a 140 h.p. Mercury outboard on it. We all rerouted the fuel line on our boats and bolted an accelerator on the floor like a car's. We mounted the electric trim switches on the steering wheel, so that with a touch we could tilt the motor to keep it parallel with the water's surface as the boat rose up on its tail. When it was opened up, the boat only had eighteen inches of its tail in the water. That made for maximum speed and maximum danger if you were running into the wind. A sudden gust could throw you straight up into the air and knock you over. You had to hang in there on that ragged edge that all racers must straddle—the edge of total success and total disaster. I loved it.

If I had a boat that would do 70 m.p.h. and I only made it run 65, that wasn't good enough. I had to make that machine perform to its maximum capability. And when I did, it gave me that same feeling I had in driving a team down the field, all the parts meshing, the yardage chains dancing along on the sideline until you scored. Getting it all on the water, it was like winning on the field.

The boating bunch usually met at the Bear Point Marina around nine each morning. If you hadn't had at least two beers by then, you were behind everyone else. None of us wanted to be behind in anything.

We'd drop our boats in the water and race around the winding channels of the Intracoastal, jumping each other's wakes, looking like so many waterbugs, darting about and getting nowhere fast.

Getting nowhere fast, that was my off-season philosophy. I figured it wasn't where you were going that counted because we all end up the same place anyway. What really counts is *how* you get there. Was the trip fun?

Most days we would stop by four or five other marinas. We had to refuel our boats with gas and ourselves with beer. We would also eat something real good, like oysters on the half shell or a fried-oyster sandwich, feed the jukebox, and shoot some pool. The eight ball games were played for beers, and I usually won more than I lost. I wasn't the best shooter, but I loved to compete. All competition was serious fun to me.

Sometimes it got too serious. All the marinas, like the honky-tonks, were beer-and-a-black-eye places. You could get a drink and a fight in any of them at any time. I always went out of my way to be friendly because I enjoyed talking to people, so I didn't have much trouble. But on occasion I'd run into a guy who wanted to brag that he had popped a professional football player. Usually I could talk off the gladiators. Or the people I was with would read the play and just ease the asshole out of the joint. But not always.

One afternoon I was shooting pool down at the Bear Point Marina with Billy Walker. We were drinking beer and laughing about some of our adventures over the years. Shooting pool with Billy was an adventure in itself because he had balls flying all over the table on every shot, hoping they would find pockets to fall into. "If you can't shoot good," he said, "shoot hard."

Billy Walker stands six-two and he weighed about 250 pounds at the time. He'd gotten a scholarship to Alabama seven years before I did, but as he says, "I just couldn't conform my freshman year, drank that whiskey too much. I had a runnin' feud with a student coach and finally had to knock him down. They redshirted me the next year, which pissed me off. So I went over to Jackson State and played some football."

He was sometimes a commercial fisherman, captain of his own boat, and for a few years he managed the Sportsman Marina. Billy was a good guy to have fun with. But you could tell at a glance that he was also a guy who didn't take any shit. With his coal-dark eyes, his deep-brown tan, and his black Viva Zapata moustache that turned straight down the sides of his mouth to his chin, Billy looked like one mean Mexican. We called him "Frito Bandito."

Still, while we were playing pool this day at the Bear Point Marina, two guys walked over and the biggest one said, "How 'bout we shoot a game with y'all for $5?"

"Thank you, no," I said, chalking my cue. "Shoot you for a beer, but I don't bet money on pool games."

I kept on shooting and the guys moved off. After pocketing two balls, I was bending over lining up another shot when the big guy was back by Billy.

"Y'all too chickenshit to play for $5?" the guy said.

"No, we ain't chickenshit," Billy said with a sneer. "Kenny just don't gamble for money. Now, why don't you just leave him alone? You don't know him. He'll get pissed off and knock you on your ass. And Kenny don't wanna do that."

I missed my shot and stood upright. I didn't even notice the guy was holding a cue stick. I did take notice when he hit me in the head with it. I guess all the shots I'd taken in football had callused up my skull. I just stepped in with a left and dropped the guy on his back. I jumped on his chest, but could see the guy was finished. I let him up.

Billy was furious. "You sorry sonuvabitch!" he said, reaching for the guy. He turned and ran.

"Let him go, Billy," I said. "Looked to me like you talked him into rapping me in the first place."

He laughed and ordered another round of beer.

You didn't have to be in a tough place to run into a tough guy. One night I had dinner with two buddies in The Jolly Ox, a nice steak-and-ale house on the beach. We talked about the new boats we'd ordered from the factory, and after eating moved into the lounge. We were standing by the dance floor, chatting and looking over the talent. Suddenly a guy walked right between the three of us, intentionally bumping shoulders.

"Excuse me, buddy!" I said, annoyed.

He swung around and punched me right between the eyes, knocking me backward. He wasn't that big—about six feet tall with a stocky build—but he sure hit hard. We started fighting, rolling around under tables, tipping over chairs. A bouncer broke it up.

My eyelid was bleeding, so I went into the men's room and washed up. As I was drying my face, I saw the sneak-puncher bent over the sink at the end of the row. I moved behind him, grabbed the hair on the back of his head, and smashed his face into the sink. He was yelling when the bouncer came running in and saved that guy from some real hurt.

I was told that his name was Joey Grow and that he had a reputation as a bar fighter around Mobile. My lawyer advised me to avoid such battles, and whenever possible I surely did. I took enough beatings during the football season. But when I got hit, I tended to hit back.

Potential violence just seemed to hover around Gulf Shores, like the salty air that blew in steadily off the Gulf. Particularly if Butch Firth was in a vicinity where vodka could be consumed. Butch was large, six-four and 240 pounds, and he was a mean drunk. Nobody wanted to be around him. But I got along good with Butch. I'd talk to him, while others would just walk away.

Butch owned a tackle-and-bait shop on Highway 182 across from the beach near town. I rented a beach house in that area in one of my first years with the Raiders and I lifted weights for six months to strengthen my body for football. I'd get up and pump iron for about three hours, eat lunch and lie on the beach for a while, then lift again in the afternoon. I got my bench-pressing up to 320 pounds and my weight up to 225.

So one day I asked Butch Firth if he wanted to lift with me. I guess that was why he liked me because nobody ever invited Butch to do anything except maybe leave a place when he was into the vodka.

Butch said he wouldn't mind joining me. "I got a set of 110 pounds over to the house."

"You work out pretty regular?" I said.

"Yeah, but that's not enough weight," he said. "I made a bench and I get under the weights and I get my wife to sit up on the bar. Then I bench-press until I get tired. Maybe thirty, forty times."

So we'd lift and drink beer, lift and drink beer. Butch was no problem on beer. But one night I had a big party at the house, about twenty-five people, and Butch was nursing his favorite drink, sitting out on the front porch by the weights.

A car full of young guys came skidding up into the yard and the driver asked if a Jack-something was in the house.

"No Jacks here," Butch said, walking to the car.

"Jack said he'd be here," the driver said.

"Did you hear me?" Butch said. "NO JACKS HERE!" he shouted.

"Well, all I know—" the driver began.

"All you know is you're getting wet," said Butch, who started peeing through the open window onto the driver. "Now get outta here!"

The car took off, and I thought that would be the end of it. But a little while later that car was back, along with three other cars full of guys. They all got out. We had about fifteen big guys and it looked like there was going to be a hell of a fight.

But Butch grabbed a solid steel weight bar and walked out toward the crowd. He swung that thirty-pound bar around the way you'd swing a thirty-one-ounce baseball bat. The crowd and the cars dispersed.

One weekend Randall Watson came down from his cabin in the woods for a visit. Butch got drunk and surly and I was sure he and Randall were going to go at it. Not a word passed between them, but the mutual animosity buzzed around them like a mosquito.

I took Randall inside off the porch with me, knowing he would not back down from anyone, and asked him to be cool. He was a very strong 185-pounder, but no match for Butch. "He's too big for me to fight, so I'm gonna have to cut off one of his arms," Randall said, pulling a six-inch penknife out of his back pocket. "Even up the odds."

I went out and convinced Butch it was time for him to go home. He was not pleased. But there was no way he could take on both of us —if it came to that. Not with one arm.

Butch Firth was shingling the roof of his shop some years later, and that night he went drinking in The Pinnacle. He got into an argument with Jerry Lowe, who, like Randall, did not believe in hand-to-hand combat with oversized folks. Jerry carried a gun. Butch was so big he didn't carry anything but a look that could shiver you. He shivered Jerry, who promptly brought out his .32 and shot Butch in the leg.

Butch was driven to the hospital for repairs. But the next morning he was back climbing a ladder to his roof with a rack of shingles on his shoulders. That .32 wound didn't slow him at all.

In another beer-and-a-bruise bar one night a full-scale war broke out across the room from where I was drinking. I was six-three and I was the smallest man in the place. Those big dudes were going at it like they were playing a scene in a John Ford film. Fists and bottles and bodies were flying. As the battle moved toward me and a beer bottle sailed past my head, I started to leave.

Then a short, skinny policeman burst in on the scene and shouted, "Break it up!" But the fighters must've noticed his size and the fact that he was from Silver Hill, a nearby town that's so small both of its CITY LIMITS signs are on the same post. They ignored the cop. He pulled out a canister of Mace and sprayed them down, and they hollered, rubbed their eyes, and dove for cover. In thirty seconds that little cop had restored peace.

Billy Walker, The Frito Bandito Kid, had a number of opportunities to do battle in honky-tonks. He and his wife Lois Gayle attended most of my games at Alabama, including the one against Auburn my senior year. It was played in a heavy rain and nobody could move the ball much. We were down 3–0 in the second half when I ran a play off-tackle, veered to the outside, and went forty-seven yards for the winning touchdown. There was a big controversy over the play. Auburn claimed the linebacker I'd run past was being held. The officials, bless their hearts, disagreed.

That night, back in Gulf Shores, Billy and his wife Lois Gayle were having drinks in The Flora-Bama, toasting our victory. Now everybody in the state follows college football, and half of them root for Alabama and the rest root for Auburn. Billy got into a heated argument about the big play with five Auburn fans seated at the next table.

"You know there was holdin' on that play!" said one Auburn fan. "Everyone could see it 'cept the damn ref."

"You're a goddamn liar!" Billy said.

The Auburn fans all jumped on Billy, who went crashing to the floor. One of the men clipped Lois Gayle as he lurched for her husband. She grabbed the stainless-steel napkin holder off her table and cracked the guy in the back of the head. He went down hard.

Meanwhile the other four were struggling with Billy, who wasn't faring too well on the floor. What the Auburn fans didn't know, though, was that The Frito Bandito Kid had a secret weapon. He wore a bridge in his mouth, the result of earlier skirmishes, and the plate was minus one tooth, leaving only the metal frame posted on his gum. One of his attackers flailed away and somehow stuck his thumb into that empty space in the bridge. Billy just clamped down hard on that thumb and bit it off.

The man screamed, yanked out his stump, and blood flew everywhere. None of the Auburn fans wanted to fight any more.

When the nine-fingered man was released from the hospital, he and his friends, along with Billy and Lois Gayle, were summoned before a judge. The judge, nodding at the bandaged man, asked Lois Gayle, "Did you see your husband bite this man's thumb off?"

"No, sir," she said. "All I saw was him spit it out."

I was spending so much time in bars that I decided to buy one in the late seventies. In fact, I went partners with a couple of other guys and bought two bars that we ran for three years. The first was Lefty's, which was a pretty classy little family place that served good quick-order food. There was a deck hanging over a lagoon in back where you could eat, drink, and watch the turtles cavort. We featured soft music days for the older crowd, but the high-dollar sound system jumped at night. We actually made a little money on Lefty's.

The other place was called The End Zone. It was bigger and featured a four-tiered bleacher against the wall opposite the bar, had a hold-onto-your-ears sound system, and was another roaring roadhouse. Just what Gulf Shores needed. The End Zone was a lot more fun than profitable.

We had a different band every week or so, some rock and roll but mostly country-and-western. A big crowd favorite was J. W. Slyde and the Closet Cowboys. We'd just pack them in that place from 6 P.M. to 2 A.M.

It was good having two partners because we'd split up time in the bars. I would open The End Zone, stock the bar, do all the glasses, and help bartend most nights. After closing the place, I'd hit some all-night restaurant like a Waffle Hut and have breakfast, get to bed by 4 or 5 A.M., and be up and out by 9. I had so much nervous energy that I seldom needed over four hours' sleep.

I spent money the same way I did most things: with tremendous enthusiasm. I was an impulse buyer of trucks, cars, motorcycles, and, of course, boats. Buying a new toy gave me a sense of achievement, a feeling of success, maybe because I hadn't been able to do that as a kid. Looking back now, at the age of forty, I often think: "I was eighteen years old for over twenty years!"

The boats kept getting faster. I moved from Checkmate speedboats to Hydrostream craft when that company took over the real fast outboard field. Randall and the others kept buying more speed, more speed. But I gave up those little speedboats when we started hitting 85 m.p.h. It got too scary. I had a career to think about and I couldn't keep courting disaster.

I was out to have fun, and that's what drew the girls to Gulf Shores by the carload. They came to play and I was there to play, so it all worked out fine for most of us.

My second wife, Debbie, was from the area but didn't like Gulf Shores. She preferred to stay year-round at our home near Oakland, a decision I couldn't understand. But I never pressed her to do anything she didn't want to. I didn't take the marriage as seriously as Debbie did, and it finally dissolved.

At about the time the divorce was finalized, I met a beautiful blonde in the lounge of the State Convention Center and Hotel overlooking the Gulf. She was twenty-three, barely five feet tall, with big eyes and a sleek, tanned figure. But I guess what got me most was her real bubbly personality.

"My name's Wanda," she said. "You can call me 'Wickedly Wonderful Wanda.' "

"What a pretty name," I said, laughing. "How did you come by it?"

"I earned it," she said through a dazzling smile.

Then she stuck her tongue out at me. That, I would discover, was something Wanda liked to do to people at any time and for no discernible reason. She was funny.

We started running around together and within a week Wanda moved into the house I had bought in Grand Lagoon on the Intracoastal Canal. She said she could cook, but that proved to be a slight exaggeration. She tried to heat up two TV dinners in the microwave without removing them from the boxes.

"Wanda," I said, "you may be the only woman I know who would scorch Jell-O."

She stuck out her tongue. About all we kept in the fridge were bottles of white wine for Wanda and bottles of beer for me and my cronies. As far as cooking went, the only time I expected a girl to fix a seven-course dinner was when I handed her seven beer bottles and an opener.

Wanda would sit on the top row of the bleachers the nights I worked at The End Zone, and attract a crowd. Everyone enjoyed her because she laughed and kidded and danced with our friends, drinking her white wine or a gin and tonic. A couple of nights after we closed, I brought J. W. Slyde and the Closet Cowboys back to the house with a bunch of friends and we had a private party.

During one of those gatherings, Wanda got me to demonstrate my skills as a juggler. I often practiced juggling around the house and could keep three tennis balls in the air for five minutes on a good day. The problem was that every time Wanda saw me practicing I'd miss.

"You could be a comedy juggler," Wanda said. " 'Kenny the Bumbling Juggler.' "

Well, after eight hours of bartending that night, I couldn't juggle my bank account. That was still on my mind the next night when we closed The End Zone and went for breakfast. I asked the waitress to bring me three raw eggs, then said to Wanda, "I'll show you some juggling."

I stood up and put those eggs in the air. *Splat!* One egg hit the floor, followed by a second. I caught the third, looking sheepish. Wanda laughed and said, "Kenny, if you had to juggle for a living, you'd starve."

Wanda was fun and we had a lot of good times, particularly after I bought a forty-two-foot Bertram Sportfisherman that I named *Honky Tonk.* Then we partied on land and sea. Wanda wanted to know, "When does your airplane get here?"

"The sky's my limit," I said.

The Bertram was like a seagoing luxury apartment. Up top was a large salon with a suede couch, chairs, a color television set, VCR, and a stereo system with tape deck. There was a V-berth stateroom in the bow. Down below was the owner's stateroom with a double bed, and a galley that included a microwave oven and a full-sized refrigerator, plus a table and seats for six. The cabins were air-conditioned. The boat's engines and generator were diesel-fueled, and with a 450-gallon tank we could stay out four days without refueling. It was a completely self-contained existence.

We did a little fishing in the Gulf, but mostly we just cruised around and partied, stopping at marinas and restaurants on the water all the way to Panama City, about 100 miles away. All the while the music would be cranking and the laughter would be loud. Randall Watson would join us and anyone else who wanted to go.

I docked the Bertram at the Sportsman Marina on Orange Beach. It wasn't far from the Bear Point Marina where we'd hung out with our speedboats, but I chose the Sportsman for *Honky Tonk* because it was managed by Billy Walker and his wife. I knew my $250,000 toy would be well cared for. I didn't want the curious climbing all over the boat, and I figured it would draw a crowd. It did.

"Everyone knows the *Honky Tonk*'s yours," Billy told me. "They want to get on it just so they can say, 'I been on Kenny Stabler's boat.' I think I better string a rope across the gangplank with a KEEP OFF sign on it."

He did, and the next day Lois Gayle accused Billy of roping off the boat so he could charge people for allowing them to climb the plank for a peek at the inside.

"Wish I'd thought of that," he said, laughing.

I spent a few hours signing autographs and talking football with the crowd that gathered—which I always enjoyed anyway—and then they dispersed. Some of them were awfully good-looking women, as Gulf Shores was full of such creatures, and I couldn't resist inviting them out for a cruise when Wanda was occupied elsewhere. One day Randall Watson and I had four young women on the *Honky Tonk* and that developed into a very wild party, naked bodies cavorting on the Gulf. We didn't tie up at the dock until midnight.

Luckily one of the girls could shift a four-wheel-drive truck and take us to my house. Otherwise Randall and I would have had to sleep on the boat.

I pretty much always had a problem with my wandering eye. Rather, my wives and girlfriends over the years had a problem with it. Looking back, I can't say now that I'm proud of everything I did. But it sure seemed necessary then.

Wanda was coming out of a marriage just as I was when we met, and I thought she was looking for some unrestricted fun like I was. Now, I liked Wanda, I really did, and we lived together almost two years, as she went back to Oakland with me. But soon after she moved into the Grand Lagoon house she seemed to think she had full dibs on my person. "Hell, my wives never achieved that kind of arrangement," I explained. Wanda was not interested in the past.

As it turned out, "Wickedly Wonderful Wanda" could also be "Terrible Tempered Wanda." The situation was that while she always slept at my house, I did not. Sometimes I wouldn't come home for two or three nights. When I did mosey in, Wanda would start throwing things at me. Bottles, ashtrays, whatever was at hand. As a quarterback, I had learned to duck pretty good. But Wanda's missiles were not limited to small items and once I had to play receiver. Wanda heaved a large expensive glass table lamp and, rather than see it get smashed, I had to stand fast and catch it.

I had a buddy with a house several miles away, closer to the beach than mine. If I was out jacking around and picked up a girl, I'd sometimes take her to my friend's digs. Unfortunately, Wanda had been at the house a time or two with me.

One night I was in bed with a girl there. The stereo was on and I didn't hear anyone enter the house. Wanda had not only slipped in, she had come into the bedroom behind me. She didn't say a word. She just picked up a metal trash can and cracked me in the back of the head. *Quarterbackus interruptous!* For a full minute my head was filled with those black stars you see when a flashbulb goes off in your eyes.

I jumped up naked, grabbed my clothes, and locked myself in the bathroom while I got dressed. It was 4 A.M. and Wanda was beating on the door and screaming as loud as she could. I came out of the bathroom and tried to get her to quiet down.

"The neighbors'll have the police on us!" I said.

She screamed louder and started throwing things at me, chasing me around the house. I saw lights come on in the house next door and decided to break and run. The other girl had already left in her car. I went out the front door and down the long, steep staircase toward my truck. Right behind me, still screaming, came Wanda, and she tried to push me down the steps.

"This woman may not be a real good live-in," I thought as I drove home. I wondered if she had really divorced her husband or if he had died. By her delicate hand.

My second season in Gulf Shores with Wanda, I tried to be more

I was always pleased when fullback Marv Hubbard was happy in a game because it meant that during that night's celebrations Marv would not break anything. (Photo: Russ Reed)

Jack Tatum was, pound for pound, the toughest player I ever knew. He hit so hard he loosened the fillings in your teeth. (Photo: Los Angeles Raiders)

Ted Hendricks, the dominant force as outside linebacker in my Raider years, was also fun off the field. (Photo: Los Angeles Raiders)

Otis Sistrunk did not attend college or barber school, but he was one hard-edged defensive lineman. (Photo: Los Angeles Raiders)

My last year with the Raiders I roomed with John "The Tooz" Matuszak and kept him out of jail. (Photo: Los Angeles Raiders)

"Man, that looks easy!" (Photo: Los Angeles Raiders)

Chatting it up with O. J. Simpson before a Pro Bowl game. (Photo: Los Angeles Raiders)

John Madden, a coach for all seasons. (Photo: Los Angeles Raiders)

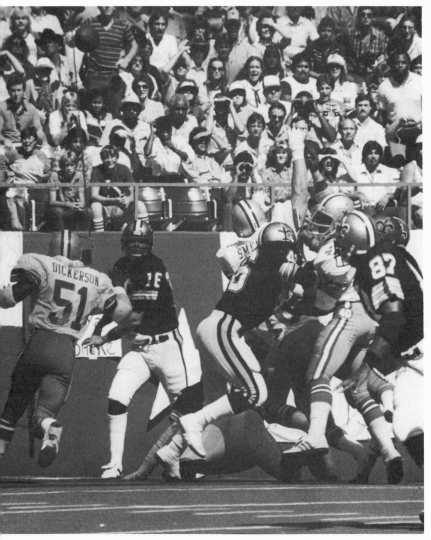

My last game with the Saints, when the Dallas Cowboys showed no respect whatsoever for an aging quarterback—me, number 16. (Photo: New Orleans Saints)

With Rose Molly, the love of my life. (Photo: Four Seasons Photography/
Rick Williams)

careful about where I took my other dates. They all loved the Bertram, and that became a second home at all hours. I often partied while the boat was right at the dock. But when I'd be missing for long, I'd get reports from friends that Wanda had been scouring the bars looking for me.

Then one day I had a close call at the marina. I hadn't been on the *Honky Tonk* more than thirty minutes when Wanda pulled in, Billy Walker told me later.

"Billy, you seen Ken?" she asked him.

"Not today," he lied, and she left.

When I finally came off the boat, Billy said, "You know, when I was telling Wanda you hadn't been around, I noticed that every other boat was riding steady in its slip. But the *Honky Tonk* was just rockin' away." He laughed.

"Good thing Wanda didn't see that," I said. "I can't take too many more shots to the back of the head or I'll have to start wearing a helmet to bed."

Then I saw that my new Diamond Jubilee Lincoln was gone. Most people would be upset if their car disappeared, but I realized how lucky I was. Had it been there when Wanda arrived, she would have surely boarded the boat and busted me again.

Billy explained that a mutual friend had borrowed the car for an hour. Someone at the marina was always borrowing that car. And one time I just misplaced it.

Billy Walker and I were out drinking and lost the Lincoln for two days. We went from roadhouse to roadhouse looking for it, stopping in each for a few beers, until one day folded into another. We finally decided that the police should be notified that the car had been stolen. As we were in no condition to do that, Billy phoned Lois Gayle and asked her to make the call.

"Is there a reward if the car's found?" Lois Gayle asked.

"Why?" Billy said.

"Because if the price is right, I might just turn up that car."

"How're you gonna do that, girl?"

Lois Gayle laughed so hard that Billy almost dropped the phone. "Well, it's parked right in front of the house," she said.

After that near-disaster at the marina with Wanda, I changed my style. Whenever I had a date on the *Honky Tonk,* I took her out aways and dropped anchor. Wanda was not a distance swimmer.

I had a new house built on Ono Island in 1978 and settled down for a couple of months while I checked on the construction. I became so engrossed in the project that I lost interest in running around. But, of course, that couldn't last indefinitely, and when I fell off that wagon I was gone for three days. I guess once I saw the house was coming along in good shape, I just had to celebrate.

When I did go home to Wanda at the Grand Lagoon house, I found she had closed the deadbolts inside the doors. I was locked out of my own goddamn house!

"Wanda, what's wonderful about that?" I yelled through the window. "I own the place!"

"Yeah, but right now you own the outside of it," she said. "You like being out so much, stay out!"

I knew what I had to do. I had to bribe my way back into my own house by coming up with a gift that was irresistible. I knew the perfect gift, a Yorkshire terrier puppy—the cutest little dog in the world. At this point, I had already bought five of them for various women, including my mom.

Wanda had been hinting that she wanted a puppy, and now I told her I would get her one if she would open the door.

"Go get me the dog first," she said.

I went to see Billy Walker, told him I needed a dog and why. He thought it was funny, but said he'd borrow his bosses' van to go get the dog. "Billy, I'm not going after a Great Dane. I'm looking for a Yorkshire terrier pup, a runt dog. All I need is a lunch pail to carry one of them."

I had seen a notice posted in a store up around Wolf Bay that offered Yorkshire terrier pups for sale. We had a few beers while making our plans, then set out in the Lincoln for the thirty-five-mile drive. It was beginning to get dark by the time we reached the store. The notice was gone.

"We'll have to go door-to-door," I told Billy. "Somebody around here's selling Yorkshire terriers."

We took turns going up to the houses in the area. Half of them had a three-color dog with a mean streak that was just waiting to chew on your shinbone. In the fading light, Billy went up to one house and he didn't see the dog under the porch. It was about the size of a Volkswagen Bug. Barking like mad, it charged out and all but tore that porch away. Billy just got the car door closed before the dog crashed into it.

We finally found the right house and bought the terrier, and by then we were in deep need of a beer. We stopped at a roadhouse, put the bluish-gray pup up on the bar between us in a shoebox, and started drinking.

"Oh, isn't he the *cutest* little thing!" a pretty lady said, leaning over me to pet the pup. "Look at that sweet little tan spot on his head!"

On the way home we stopped at four other bars, and in each of them the female customers fell all over us to get at the pup. "Kenny, I believe we've discovered something," Billy said, smiling.

"Yeah, we should take this dog home and go buy us another one to carry around. Girls sure do go for a guy with a runty pup."

The dog got me back in the house with Wanda. For about a week.

About this time I was offered $20,000 to go up to Nashville for three days to do a TV commercial. I invited Billy to go along. He'd never been to Nashville and he was all excited. We both loved a bunch of the music that came out of there. Randall Watson was also going with us, so I knew we'd have a blast.

But then Billy found out that an old friend of ours had been stricken with cancer. Henry Mattingly was his name, a good guy who ran the Bear Point Marina where we had hung out for years.

"You know, Kenny," Billy said, "we ought to take Henry out fishing on your boat. He loves to fish, but he's never found time to do much fishing. And I don't think he's got much time left."

"You want to go to Nashville or take Henry out on the boat?"

"It's up to you," Billy said. "You got the commercial deal."

"To hell with it. Let's go fishing."

Henry caught a four-pound redfish, and he was so pleased you'd have thought he hauled in a blue marlin. He was too weak to keep fishing after that, but he enjoyed the cold beer and just being out on the water all day. Henry's health failed so rapidly that we couldn't take him out again. He died three weeks later.

They say your happiest days with a big boat are the day you buy it and the day you sell it. The Bertram became a little too costly to maintain, and after two years I sold it to a commercial fisherman. My only regret was that I didn't get to do more fishing with her. With all the partying going on, I just never seemed to get around to much fishing.

If my teammate Dave Casper had owned the boat, he would have had lines in the Gulf every day. Big Dave was a nut on fishing. He bought a house in Oakland right on the water so he could fish off his back porch every chance he had.

During one off-season he even tried to produce a series of fishing shows for television syndication. He bought videotape equipment, hired a cameraman, and taped a show with Willie Nelson fishing in Texas. We'd both gotten to know Willie and loved him and his music. Dave even spent a month or two on the road with him, riding on his band bus.

Dave called to tell me about the fishing shows he was producing and asked if he could do one with me. "I know you do some fishing," he said.

"Recently I've been engaging in other activities on the water," I said.

"Well, you can bring along a friend who's a fisherman," he said.

I thought immediately of Billy Walker, who could catch anything. But as I've said, Dave could be a little strange and I didn't know if I wanted to put up with his shit in the off-season. I could just see Dave holding conversations on different subjects with me, Billy, and his cameraman all at once, while he tied lures and hummed "On the Road Again." But he said he wouldn't need more than two days to shoot the show, so I told him to come on.

He trailed in a beautiful bass boat and had all his videotaping and fishing gear in the back of his Blazer. Billy Walker joined us and we went right out on the Intracoastal Waterway. For some reason, the cameraman was left behind at my house. Either Casper saw this as a practice session or he was just so anxious to fish himself that he forgot about taping it. He was after speckled trout, which are fished on the bottom, using live shrimp as bait. The trout has a soft mouth and must be brought in gently or the hook will tear loose.

Casper was good, and in ninety minutes we reeled in so many speckled trout that we ran out of live bait. "We've got to go get more bait," I said.

"I don't want to go," Dave said. "I can fish with lures."

"How are we supposed to get in for bait?" I said. "Swim?"

Dave looked around and saw a four-by-four platform on top of a piling close to a nearby bridge. "Put me up there," he said.

Billy and I left him on the wooden platform and motored on in for bait. But it was hotter than hell, the temperature and humidity both up around ninety, and we were thirsty. We stopped at the nearest bar and started firing down beers. In a couple of hours, we began to feel better.

But we ran out of money. We hopped in my truck and drove to Lefty's. I grabbed a handful of cash out of the register drawer, feeling we really ought to get back to Dave. It had been over two hours since we left him, and he was probably getting right crisp out in that sun by now.

"Let's have a quick beer," Billy said.

What the hell? We had two.

The Outrigger Bait Shop was about five miles away, and as we drew abreast of it our thirst was up again. We pulled into the roadhouse across Highway 182 from the Outrigger, which looked out on the Gulf.

By the time we got the bait, we were buzzing right along. We put the pound of live shrimp in a Styrofoam cooler. As I swung the cooler up toward the bed of my truck, the cooler handles broke. All the live shrimp fell onto the sizzling concrete driveway. They were flipping and flopping every which way, trying to keep from frying.

Seeing those shrimp, the seagulls and blackbirds circling over the water dove at them—and at us. It was like a scene from Alfred Hitchcock's *The Birds*. I snatched the baseball cap off my head and swung at the incoming birds with one hand, while with the other I frantically tried to toss shrimp back into the cooler. Billy grabbed a paddle and took a beery swing at the birds, almost taking my head off.

When we finally got back to Casper with about three quarters of a pound of semi-live shrimp, four hours had passed. We thought he'd be angry. He hadn't had anything to eat or drink in all that time, he couldn't even pee, and he looked like a boiled lobster, sitting out in that intense sun. His skin was bright red.

"Look at this!" he said excitedly, holding up a very large trout. "Must be a five-pounder! Speckled trout don't come any bigger!"

He wasn't even interested in the two bottles of beer we brought him, so Billy and I emptied them.

Casper had a bucket of good-sized trout. The only thing that annoyed him was that the cameraman hadn't shot his catches. I didn't ask why he hadn't brought the man because Dave always had his own unique plans.

He decided to take the boat into the waters off the beach at my house and have the cameraman shoot him catching the big trout there. Pulling it out a second time and pretending it was a catch.

"Dave," I said, "you're always thinking."

"Don't seem right," Billy said, burping.

So Dave sat out in the boat with his line in the water, the big trout on the end of it. The cameraman stepped into the shallow water and walked toward Dave, taping away. The cameraman did fine for the first five yards offshore. Then, as Dave pulled the trout out of the water, the cameraman suddenly disappeared. He had stepped in a deep hole and the weight of the camera drove him straight down. There was nothing on the surface of the water but some air bubbles.

We had to run into the drink and drag the cameraman to the beach. The videocamera and tape were ruined. All Dave Casper got out of his trip to Gulf Shores were a bunch of speckled trout and a second-degree sunburn.

But as he packed up to leave, Dave just laughed. "At least the fishing was good," he said.

"Dave," I said, "everything's good on the Redneck Riviera."

9

"You've Got to Point to Someone, So Blame Stabler."

In January I was named winner of the twenty-seventh annual S. Rae Hickok Award as the professional athlete of the year. During the presentation of the bejeweled belt at the Washington Touchdown Club, I said I didn't know if I really deserved the award. It's hard supporting the notion that the best individual athlete in the country should come from a team sport like football where you get so much help from others. I liked to think I was the leader of the Raider team that had dominated football in 1976. But Chris Evert, who finished third in the Hickok voting, had dominated women's tennis all by herself. Of course, I didn't let this keep me from accepting the belt. It was valued at $20,000, $5,000 more than the winner's share of the Super Bowl.

In 1985 I had the gold and jewelry in the belt reappraised for insurance purposes. I took it to former Patriots' offensive tackle Tommy Neville, who has an appraisal business called The Source. As Tommy reminded me, I had taken money out of his pocket in that playoff game we won over New England in the last ten seconds. Now

I was asking him to tell me I was even richer. Neville said the glitter was worth $95,000. Not a bad increase.

Before the 1977 season, I presented my offensive linemen with custom-made cowboy boots, their numbers hand-tooled on the side, and thanked them for saving my ass so many times. We all felt we were going to win our second straight Super Bowl come January because we believed we would have the best Raider team ever.

Having done a lot of off-season weight work to strengthen the muscles supporting my knees, I personally felt better than I had in two years. I reported to camp at 210 pounds, figuring less weight would be easier on my knees. I would wrap them before every game and have them aspirated afterward by the team doctor. The doc would stick a six-inch needle in them and draw off the fluid that caused the swelling. It was no fun, always worrying about my knees. I had to be careful where I walked, watch each step. Even a slight stumble could cause pain. And seating myself to eat, I had to be careful not to bang a knee on a table leg. I had been walking around on egg shells too long.

This year I planned to leave off the knee wraps and to try to be more mobile in the pocket, better able to evade the rush. I felt I should have avoided a number of the twenty-eight sacks I took in 1976. I'd feel the pressure and just go down, protecting the ball and my knees. Another step or two in quickness might buy a bit more time.

But overall I really felt good. As I told one writer: "I think I'm one of the luckiest guys in the world. I'm doing what I love and getting paid for it. How many guys go to work every morning and feel like they are bleeding inside? Playing football is more than being a celebrity. It's creating something. You blend people of different size, shape, talent, and personality. You all work together for a common goal. And when you achieve it, that's it! Perfection. You feel like you own the world."

We got off to a good start in 1977, winning our first four games and extending our streak to seventeen in a row. The biggest victory came in Pittsburgh, 16–7, a game we controlled throughout. But it was another slugfest and we took a physical beating on the rock-hard artificial turf at Three Rivers Stadium. John Vella and Phil Villapiano were lost for the year. Jack Tatum, Carl Garrett, and Cliff Branch were all sidelined for several weeks.

We missed them in the next game, particularly Vella's blocking at tackle. Young Henry Lawrence replaced him and, along with the line in general, did not have a real good day. The Broncos were just sacking me around like a rag doll the whole game. I threw seven interceptions, as we got behind early and I just kept throwing, trying to come back in a game we eventually lost, 30–7.

After my fifth interception, I picked my ass up off the ground and referee Jim Tunney just shook his head. The referee is the guy who stands behind the backfield and keeps his eye on the quarterback, the official who's supposed to look out for you.

"I know you're having a hard time looking after me today, Jim," I said. "But if you'll count that team over there in the orange jerseys, I think you'll find there's thirteen or fourteen of them coming at me."

Tunney laughed with me. On days like that, you've got to laugh to keep from crying.

But we bounced back and won four more in a row, running our record to 8–1. Then I got knocked out early in our next game, as the Chargers won, 12–7. The left knee again. It was so sore I couldn't even practice all week. We hosted the Bills the following Monday, and just a few hours before game time I decided to try the knee.

When I limped onto the field, the crowd gave me a tremendous greeting. I thanked them by throwing three touchdown passes and left after three quarters of the 34–13 victory.

"When the crowd yelled as Ken came on the field," Art Shell told the press afterward, "a strange feeling went through me. He just exudes leadership. He's like a computer out there. He calls such a great game he makes it look easy to the people in the stands, and it is easy for us."

We finished the season with an 11–3 record, second in our division to 12–2 Denver. The Raiders led the NFL in scoring (351 points), total first downs (305), and total offensive plays (1,030). The defense led the AFC in allowing the fewest first downs (204). I had twenty touchdown passes, seven less than in 1976, as our running game was stronger. Mark van Eeghen rushed for over 1,200 yards and we gained 2,627 as a team on the ground.

We flew to Baltimore for the opening playoff game. Colts' quarter-

back Bert Jones and I had a shoot-out. Both teams moved up and
down the field as if we were in a track meet. The Colts led 31–28 with
a minute to play, but we got rolling and Dave Casper made a great
catch at the end. The guys called Dave "Ghost" after Casper the
Friendly, and I hit him with a forty-two-yard "Ghost to the Post"
pass that he reached up for, his back to me, and caught over his head.
With twenty-six seconds left, Errol Mann kicked a twenty-two-yard
field goal and we went into sudden death.

It wasn't real sudden, though. Neither team could score in the fifth
quarter. Just before it ended, John Madden made a smart move,
calling a time-out that forced the Colts to punt into a hellacious wind
that was whipping in from the open end of Memorial Stadium. We
got great field position and drove to the twelve-yard line. There was
an automatic time-out before the start of the sixth quarter and I
walked over to Madden.

John was his usual frenetic self in this kind of situation, bouncing
around, talking to assistant coaches, trying to come up with a play.
Meanwhile the 60,000 Colt fans were screaming and going nuts in the
stands. I looked up at them and said, "You know, John, these sonsa-
bitches are getting their money's worth today."

"Where in the hell are you?" John roared. "We've got a game out
there!"

"We've got that under control," I said. "No problem."

Calling plays is probably the most fun a quarterback has. It was a
chess game between me and the middle linebacker, who usually
called the defensive alignments. I called the plays by feel. Remembering what had worked and what hadn't, I'd put myself in the linebac-
er's spot and try to guess what he might be expecting in the situation
we were in.

I figured now the Colts had to play us for the run because all we
had to do was run three plays and kick a field goal. We used a three-
tight-end formation on first down and picked up two yards on the
ground. The Colts had everyone bunched in the middle. A lot of
things can go wrong on a field goal when the wind is swirling. So on
second down we play-faked, Casper drove inside, then went outside,
and I flipped the ball to him in the corner. We won, 37–31. You don't
kick extra points in sudden death.

The game only took one hour, fifteen minutes, and forty-three seconds of playing time, the third-longest in NFL history.

John Madden looked about as calm and relaxed as a man who had been out in a hurricane all day. His face was flushed, his shirttail was hanging out, and he appeared in need of oxygen. Last-second wins do that to coaches like Madden.

Trotting off the field beside John, I said, "That was kinda fun, wasn't it?"

"You know something, Ken," he said, "I'd like to take your pulse right now. I'll bet it's not up one tick. You don't get excited about *anything*."

"Well, John, I don't know about that. I think there are a few ladies who might testify different."

The following week we went to Denver for the AFC Championship Game, and I thought sure we'd win. The Bronco defense, known as "The Orange Crush," was tough. But I felt we had the weapons to control the ball and move on them.

We took the opening kickoff right down the field and Mann kicked a field goal. All told, we ran forty-one plays in the first half to Denver's nineteen, yet we couldn't put the ball in the end zone. The Broncos led 7–3. We also lost Freddy with a dislocated shoulder.

Midway through the third quarter, as it turned out, we lost the game. And not because Clarence Davis fumbled at our seventeen. The Broncos recovered, moved to our two, then halfback Rob Lytle fumbled diving into the line. Mike McCoy, a backup defensive tackle who played on goal line stands, picked up the ball and was running for a touchdown when the play was blown dead. Officials ruled no fumble, though television replays clearly showed that Lytle never had possession of the ball before he dove. What we ended up with was a penalty for arguing the bad call, and Denver scored on the next play.

In the fourth quarter Casper caught a twelve-yard pass to make the score 14–10. When we got the ball back, I threw an interception that was returned to our fourteen, and Denver quickly scored. But I went to Casper again with a seventeen-yard touchdown pass and we were only down by three, 20–17, with three minutes left to play. The problem was, we never got the ball back. The Broncos ran out the clock over The Tooz at left tackle. I don't think that would have happened if Phil Villapiano had been at left linebacker. But that kind of speculation is about as helpful as that official's call on Lytle. The Broncos went to the Super Bowl and we went home.

Richard Todd, who had followed me a few years later at Alabama and who was the New York Jets' quarterback at the time, also had an off-season home in Gulf Shores. We were casual friends and one day in the spring of 1978 he came by The End Zone and asked if I'd like to go out and throw a football around.

"Richard," I said, "in the off-season I train on booze. There are no games to play. I don't throw again until training camp. It's a long season, sixteen games this year, plus four exhibitions and the playoffs. You only have so many throws in your arm. About the only thing I'm doing is a little work on my knees. I ordered a new set of them, but they haven't arrived."

In training camp my arm was always sore for the first few days, then it was fine. I still lifted weights there and worked on the iso-tonic-isometric ropes to aid flexibility. One of my first days back in camp I was working in the weight room with center Dave Dalby. I was curling dumbbells and "Double D" was pulling on an isotonic-isometric rope. Suddenly the rope broke away from the post it was pinned to.

Upshaw and Shell were standing by it, laughing. I wondered if maybe they'd given that post a push. I grabbed another rope and said, "If Double D can do that, so can I."

"Why not?" Upshaw said. "You both weigh the same."

I laughed. I always carried a paunch at my waist from the beer, but I only weighed 215. I would be 210 when the season opened.

My long hair and the beard I'd been wearing for several years were now much more gray than light brown. I was thirty-two and Freddy, thirty-five, said I looked like I could be his father. Pete, thirty-four, said, "You'd make George Blanda look young."

I felt good until our league-leading offense had trouble scoring points in the preseason and in the opener, which we lost to Denver, 14–6. Errol Mann, who had led the AFC in scoring the previous season, missed the extra point. It was an indication of things to come.

We literally stole the next game. With the clock running down, we had to move the ball eighty yards against San Diego, which led 20–14. We marched to the ten, missed a pass, and there were only ten seconds left to play when I dropped back to throw again. But linebacker Woody Lowe charged in and hit me. As I went down at the twenty-four, I purposely fumbled the ball forward toward Banaszak, who tried to scoop up the ball and kicked it toward the goal line. Then Casper swiped at the ball, knocked it into the end zone, and fell on it for a touchdown. Time had run out, and after Mann's PAT, we won, 21–20. Someone called this play "The Holy Roller."

The Chargers protested the call, citing the NFL rule that says: "It is considered intentional grounding of a forward pass when the ball strikes the ground after the passer throws, tosses, or lobs the ball to prevent a loss of yards by his team."

"The ball went into the end zone and was recovered for a touchdown, that's it," said referee Jerry Markbreit. It was one of those judgment calls that only the referee can make. The rule was changed the next year because I admitted I had fumbled on purpose and Casper admitted he'd helped the ball into the end zone. I just wished we had gotten a judgment call like that in one of our playoff games.

We beat Green Bay handily, running for a club record 348 yards, then blew a 14–0 lead against New England, losing 21–14. A writer asked me if we were a better team than our 2–2 record, and I said, "I really don't know. Maybe we're not *that* good. We'll just have to see."

At this point, some members of the press were writing: "What's wrong with Stabler?" I had completed only 46 percent of my passes and I had been intercepted twelve times. I had also been sacked for losses eight times. In thirteen games the previous season, I had been sacked sixteen times. I wasn't throwing the ball well consistently, but I had started slow before and felt I'd get it going. I didn't know if our other problems would work out, though.

After our next game, a 25–19 overtime victory over the Bears in Chicago, I stopped talking to the press. I had always been cooperative with the writers and they had always been good to me. I hoped they would understand my silence, that they would see from the press box that the 1978 Raiders were having more breakdowns on offense than ever before.

Guard George Buehler and tackle John Vella were sidelined with injuries, as was tailback Clarence Davis. You don't lose three excellent blockers like that trio and have the same protection you had with them. Tackle Henry Lawrence, replacing the injured Vella much of last year, had trouble blocking the top ends. We often had to put Casper or a back over there to help Lawrence.

Davis, our best blocking back, had undergone knee surgery. In his place was rookie Art Whittington, a 180-pound speedster. Upshaw said to me, "Whit doesn't want to have anything to do with blocking. He just falls down and hopes they trip over him. But he can run like crazy—he's fast." He ended up rushing for 661 yards, but we couldn't call on him to block. So defenses knew that every time Whittington came into the game he was going to carry the ball, usually on a sweep, or swing out for a pass.

We also lost Freddy Biletnikoff after the first game, not to injury but to Al Davis's decision to replace him in his fourteenth season with a younger receiver. Mike Siani, tired of his reserve role, had asked to be traded and was sent to the Colts for tight end Raymond Chester. Morris Bradshaw, in his fourth year, was given Freddy's job. But he just didn't show the consistency you need from a wide receiver. Bradshaw ended up with forty receptions, but if he had caught all the balls he should have he would've had sixty.

And Cliff Branch, after catching forty touchdown passes in the last four seasons, caught just one in 1978. Part of that was my fault for not getting the ball to him. On a number of occasions, blocking breakdowns didn't give me the time to hit him for scores, and there were times when Cliff didn't catch passes that he had gobbled up in other years.

Everyone occasionally breaks down, fouls up, and blows plays in a football game. When those things happened on the Raiders, we tried to pick up one another. I spent a lot of the 1978 season trying to boost up players who were having problems. I always saw it as the quarterback's job to motivate his teammates and not let them lose confidence in themselves because they'd dropped a pass or turned in the wrong direction on a pass route. "We'll get 'em next time," I'd say. And when I'd miss an open receiver, guys would tell me not to worry.

We won game number six on a last-ditch pass to Casper, beating Houston 21–17. Three of our four victories had come in the final minute.

Then we beat Kansas City and lost to Seattle, 27–7. By now Madden was starting to lose faith in our kicking game and in our next game against the Chargers he had holder David Humm rise up and throw out of field goal formation. Later, with a fourth-and-one from the Charger eight, we went for the first down rather than try a field goal. We needed points and we needed to control the ball and keep our defense off the field. The Chargers opened the third quarter of the game by controlling the ball for over eleven minutes and eventually won, 27–23.

We won three in a row to lift our record to 8–4, but we were not the Raiders of old. In fact, ten of the players who had started for us in the Super Bowl less than two years earlier were now on the bench or off the roster. The Raider offense had always been the strength of the team, and the defense had usually picked us up with a great effort when we slumped. But the offense just couldn't set the pace any more.

In the next game, against Seattle, we failed to convert an extra point for the fifth successive week, the result of three Mann misses, one blocked, one on a high snap. Madden had Mann try field goals only three times in the last eight games, all inside the twenty-six, and he made two, one in this game. But because we were ahead by only two points, 16–14, we went for a bomb on a third-and-one from the Seahawks' thirty-eight. It missed, then we missed making a yard on the fourth-down run.

"Going for the touchdown pass on third-and-one," Al Davis told a writer afterward, "was like going for a home run when you need a sacrifice fly. I've got nothing against running on fourth down, but I would never have thrown that pass on a third-and-one. And it wasn't Kenny's call."

"If Ken connects, the game's over," Madden said. "But he didn't, so now I'm the jackass."

Some members of the press were calling me the jackass. Suddenly I was too old, too fat, and a carouser who couldn't do it any more. When I was a carouser who was leading the Raiders into the playoffs every year, I was a folk hero.

One writer quoted a veteran Raider lineman as saying, "For a while I tried to keep up with Snake at camp, but I had to quit. I told him, 'That's okay for you, Snake, but I've got to go to work tomorrow.' I like Snake. Everybody likes him. He's a hell of a guy. But for his sake I hope he gets his act together."

I suspect the player was defensive end Pat Toomay, the designated pass rusher who'd done a good job in 1977 and was yet to be heard from on the field this season. But Toomay was right when he told that same columnist why I wasn't talking to writers.

"I think the reason for that is that if Snake started opening up he'd put the blame on other people," Pat said, "and he doesn't want to do that. Look, right now there are two guys holding the offense together, Snake and Dave Casper."

I had never knocked a teammate and I wasn't about to at that point. Some quarterbacks yelled at players. I've heard that Bobby Layne cussed and kicked his linemen in the shins when they got him knocked around. I'd never had much reason to be annoyed with an offensive lineman on the Raiders until the 1978 season. Guard Mickey Marvin, a second-year man, had his breakdowns, but he was all heart and guts and just needed experience.

On the other hand, tackle Henry Lawrence had played five years, and I thought he was going to get me decapitated at times. I also thought he was the laziest number one draft choice I'd ever seen, a guy who never seemed to work hard. Maybe that was just his style because Lawrence later went on to play a whole lot of good football for the Raiders.

But not in 1978, and I let him know I wasn't pleased with his performance. When an offensive lineman's man got loose and beat on me, the blocker usually came back and helped me up, as if to say, "I'm sorry." That's all part of the game. The bad part of the game was when, time after time, it was Lawrence's man who rang my bell. Henry would come back, stick out his hand to me, and I'd slap it away. I'd get up myself, not saying a word to him.

And when I'd pull up a stool among the offensive linemen before games, I'd position it so my back was to Lawrence. Then I'd go down the line and ask Shell, Upshaw, Dalby, and Mickey Marvin how they were feeling. As I had always done, I'd bring a sheet of plays and ask each of them which ones they liked. I knew that if I called plays the linemen liked best, they'd really put out for them. It was almost as if they got to call some plays, which everyone loves to do. But all the while I was going through this routine, I'd ignore Lawrence.

We lost two of our last three games—scoring exactly six points in each of the defeats—and in one of them Lawrence said something that really pissed me off. I was out there busting my ass and I didn't need him to tell me how to do my job because he was getting beat regularly and I was paying for it. I picked myself up off the ground after another hit from his man, and as we moved to the huddle Lawrence said, "Snake, you got to get rid of the ball quicker."

I didn't say anything, but I thought, "If you'd just make a little contact with that end, Henry, I wouldn't need to get rid of the fucking ball quicker."

Besides, I couldn't get rid of the ball until a receiver came open, which was another problem. The only guy who came open consistently was Dave Casper, who had nine touchdowns among his sixty-two receptions. At least a dozen of those catches were great ones.

Just about everyone on the offense knew that Freddy Biletnikoff should have been starting. The coaches seemed to think he'd lost a step, but that was impossible. Freddy didn't have a step to lose. He'd never had any speed. He got open on slick, not speed. He was a great mechanic who ran the best sideline and comeback routes on the team. In addition, Freddy and I read each other like the Corsican Brothers.

For example, if Freddy ran down fifteen yards and cut straight across the field at a 90-degree angle on an end route, he'd have to read my situation and the linebackers strung out there. He'd have to decide whether to pull up between the backers or take the route all the way across the field. Meanwhile Freddy would sense whether I had to hurry the throw or could hold the ball longer for the best opening. At that point, I would absolutely *know* which choice he would make.

It was like money in the bank to have mental telepathy with a clutch receiver like Biletnikoff. Freddy played in the season's last two games, and I couldn't have been happier when he caught a touchdown pass in each, the guy who had sat on the bench all season. I think now that had Freddy played every game we might have won two more in 1978 and finished 11–5 instead of with a 9–7 record. Denver, 10–6, won the Western Division.

Fred Biletnikoff was not invited back by the Raiders in 1979. He ended his career with 589 receptions, 8,974 yards, and 76 touchdowns. I don't know why he's not in the Pro Football Hall of Fame, but he's in mine.

Before our fifteenth game, Merlin Olsen, who would be broadcasting it for NBC-TV, asked me to do an interview with him. I admired Olsen, a Hall of Fame defensive tackle who had always gone out of his way not to hurt a quarterback. He had retired in 1977 after the Rams lost in the playoffs to Minnesota, 14–7, and after he'd played fifteen years and made fourteen trips to the Pro Bowl. I remembered seeing him on television when he walked off the field as a player for the last time. His helmet hung from his hand and his head was down. I thought, "All those years, all those great plays he made, yet Merlin never made it to the Super Bowl."

I think that's why I agreed to give him a brief interview. I tried to be tactful when he asked what was wrong with the Raiders: "What do I say? That I've got a couple of new linemen who haven't played much and aren't giving me the protection I'd like? I know they've got to get more experience before they can be expected to give me that kind of protection. Do I say that I've also got a new wide receiver and we're still learning how to work together? It takes time, all that adjusting."

Then I admitted I had to take some responsibility for the Raider offensive performance. "I have not played good football," I said. "But I'm willing to take the lumps with the good."

The next thing I did was go out and take a few lumps in a loss to the Dolphins. I completed twenty-four of thirty-six passes, and I felt only three of those throws were bad. But all three were intercepted, along with two other passes that caromed off receivers.

One went off Cliff Branch and I felt real bad for him. He finished the year with forty-nine receptions, but he didn't have a good season. Rumors had it he had been having personal problems. Once he had been a no-show for practice, and sometimes he seemed to be elsewhere mentally. Maybe that's where he was on the interception that went through his hands.

I threw the ball low and to the sideline so that the defensive back couldn't get near the ball, and Cliff made a nice move, sliding feetfirst toward it. But the ball bounced off his chest and into the hands of a Miami defender who ran it back forty-six yards for a touchdown. I made my way through the guys on the sideline to Cliff, who was standing alone with his head on his chest. I walked over to him, and tipped his chin up. "It's not your fault, Cliff," I said, and patted him.

I threw almost a hundred more passes in 1978 than in any other season, completing 58.4 percent of them. But only sixteen went for touchdowns and thirty went to the other teams. I was also sacked thirty-five times.

I had grown closer than ever to John Madden during this trying season, as he and I took all the heat from the media. We felt almost deserted by the front office. Al Davis said nothing in our defense. At one point, John said to me, "Basically, all we have is each other, Ken."

The press kept asking John about my interceptions, a number of the writers saying my arm appeared to be weak. I was having some troubles with my left elbow, but I refused to use that as an excuse. John acknowledged that my arm wasn't as strong as it was when I was younger. "But whose arm is as they get older?" he said. "Over half the interceptions were not Kenny's fault. They came off a receiver's hands or shoulder pads, or they came with time running out—in desperation situations."

Al Davis didn't see it that way, and he blamed the disappointing season entirely on me. "You've got to point to someone, so blame Stabler," Davis told the writers. "He makes the most money. He gets paid to take the pressure. I'm certainly not going to make excuses for him, but he doesn't do any work in the off-season. I'm dissatisfied with the condition of the team and with the coaching staff for allowing the players to get out of shape.

"It has been our offense that has controlled the game. The defense played the same this season as it always had. But this year Cliff Branch caught only one touchdown pass. If you can't get the long ball to your wide receivers, you can't win. It all starts with the lefthander."

I was furious and my teammates were shocked. Al Davis had never criticized one of his players before. Some of them suspected, as I did, that Davis was trying to cover for his mistakes in putting together the 1978 team. Al hadn't had a first-round draft pick in three years, having traded them for Hendricks and Mike McCoy. His last number one pick, Neal Colzie in 1975, hadn't developed into a starter. His top pick two years ago, Philyaw, was a joke, but Davis hated to admit he'd made a mistake and kept Large Charles. We still couldn't mount a pass rush unless the linebackers blitzed.

A few weeks after Al Davis blasted me and expressed dissatisfaction with the coaching staff for the team's alleged lack of condition, John Madden retired. I was happy for him. The pressure was just eating him alive. He was always swallowing Maalox and antacid pills. I had seen him throw up on the plane going to games, during half-time at games, and on the plane coming home from games. If he had stayed on as coach of the Raiders, he might have needed surgery for his ulcers.

John Madden was only the second NFL coach to win over 100 games in ten years. He had won the AFC championship, won the Super Bowl. Now it was time for him to relax with his wife and kids. He called me in January and said that's what he was doing and he never felt better. We talked for about forty-five minutes. His wife Virginia owned a bar and John would go down there and shoot pool and play pinball, laugh, talk, and just hang out.

The more I thought about Al Davis's blast at me, the angrier I got. When a writer from the Birmingham *News* called me, I said, "I have lost all respect for the organization. I don't want to stay where I'm not appreciated. I have contractual obligations to the Oakland Raiders and I will fulfill them. I'd be letting down my teammates if I took a powder. I will play as hard as I can because I have loyalties to my teammates and myself. I have two years left on my contract and an option year. I'll honor that and go from there."

A writer asked Pete Banaszak if he thought I had overreacted, and he said no. "Davis came out and lambasted Kenny. During the season Kenny swallowed it, and now that the season is over he is spitting it back—punch and counterpunch. He took too much heat from everybody this year and he's got a right to give some back."

Willie Brown said he hoped my statement did not mean I would not be back with the Raiders. "To me, Ken's the finest quarterback to ever play," Willie said. "It would be difficult to replace him, to say the least."

After my sound off on Al, I just tried to forget about last season. But it wouldn't go away. Bob Padecky, a writer who covered the Raiders for the Sacramento *Bee,* visited Foley and Gulf Shores, trying to dig up all kinds of garbage about my life-style. He asked a number of my old friends, including Mayor Arthur Holk, Police Chief James Maples, and Billy Walker about my drinking, my driving, my speed-boats, how many fights I'd been in, and so on.

Padecky wrote a three-part series and his theme was: "Stabler enjoys a good time. Some say too much of a good time."

He got very few people to say negative things about my life-style and virtually none about me as a person. But I didn't think my private life was any of Padecky's business.

I may have become a little paranoid, wondering if Al Davis had sent Padecky to dig up dirt on me. Al was suddenly all hot about my physical condition. Yet not one of my teammates had ever said I was out of condition. Gene Upshaw told a writer, "Hey, I'll tell you what. Snake's never out of condition. We all had an off-year this season because the Raiders are not used to losing and didn't know how to deal with it. But Snake's a winner and we'll be back. The winning condition's all that matters."

But Padecky was the first writer Al Davis spoke to when he decided to knock me. It was on the plane coming home from the Miami loss. Davis compared me to "a 24–8 pitcher who was having a 17–10 season" and Padecky wrote it. I couldn't blame him for that, but I was damn pissed off about the series he'd done.

I phoned Padecky and invited him to come back to Gulf Shores and talk to me. I wanted to find out what else Al Davis had said to him about me, and to find out why he had flown three thousand miles just to crucify me. But when I met with Padecky, I didn't find out anything. I was so angry that all I did was chew him out for writing such crap.

The next thing I knew, Padecky had been arrested on what turned out to be an obvious phony drug bust. Someone had planted a magnetic key case containing a bit of cocaine in Padecky's rented car. Padecky was quickly released, went home, and wrote a story that I felt implied that I had set him up for the drug arrest. The story went all over the country.

"I had absolutely nothing to do with it," I told a news conference called by Chief Maples, "and I'm a victim of something I had no control over. I'm embarrassed about the whole thing. Even to be associated with this is absurd.

"What they found in the car could have already been there. It was a rental car from Florida. You can speculate that I was being set up. What if I'd been in the car when he was arrested? Or maybe someone loyal to me thought they were doing me a favor. They weren't."

I'm pretty sure I know who planted the drugs in Padecky's car. The man never told me he did and he's dead now, so it couldn't be proven.

I thought for a time there that the Snake had been snakebit. First we had a totally horseshit season, then Davis rapped me for his failures, then a writer tried to con old friends into rapping me, then my name was linked with drugs.

Fortunately, people in Gulf Shores were empathetic, coming up to me every day and saying, "They just won't leave you alone, will they?"

Al Davis wouldn't, as far as I was concerned. He was asked to comment on Ken Stabler's situation after the phony drug bust, and Al refused, saying the draft was coming up and he had higher priorities to take care of. I didn't think there was a higher priority for the head of a football team than his quarterback.

But Davis liked to play mind games with players. He had the Raiders release statements about how well backup quarterback Jim Plunkett was throwing in the off-season, as well as another quarterback they'd signed, Randy Hedberg. The idea was to build a fire under me. I was supposed to think, "Hey, I'd better get my ass in gear and get to work." I said to myself, "That dog just won't hunt."

I realized football was a cold, ruthless business, but somewhere along the line I felt there should be some sort of gratitude shown for all the good years I'd given the Raiders. I thought about all those times I'd stayed after practice to throw to anybody who asked me to, even when my knees were hurting. For five years running, I'd led the team into the playoffs and given everything I had to try and win.

And I couldn't understand why Al Davis had suddenly started knocking me. As Al said, I did make the most money, $342,000 in 1978, I did get paid to take the pressure, and I thought I had handled it very well. But I didn't think he had to say those things and exert more pressure on me. It hurt. There was enough pressure applied during the game itself, and I applied pressure on myself to be better all the time, to be the best quarterback in the NFL. I didn't need any extra pressure from management.

I never heard the Steeler management knock Terry Bradshaw when he was having his problems and people were calling him a dummy—which he sure as hell wasn't. I never heard any other team owner go to the press and criticize his quarterback. It wasn't professional.

Al Davis's slogan for the Raiders was "Pride and Poise." I wondered if he was proud of himself for losing his poise and popping off to the press about me. It certainly told all of the Raiders how much regard he had for his players.

As much as I cared for my teammates, I finally decided that I just couldn't play for Al Davis any more. I announced to the press that I had no intention of reporting to the Raider training camp come July. I said I wanted to be traded, and had my lawyer phone Davis with that request.

Then writer Lawrence Linderman did a magazine interview with me and I got everything off my chest about Davis and what had gone wrong with the Raiders. Asked if I had talked to Davis, I said, "I wouldn't talk to him if he walked through the door right now. Davis wanted to talk to me when he came to the Blue-Gray Game in Montgomery, Alabama, and he called my lawyer, Henry Pitts, to set up a meeting. He wanted me to come up to Montgomery and meet with him to bury the hatchet. I'd like to bury the hatchet—right between Al Davis's shoulder blades."

I also talked about the problems with our offensive line, saying, "Henry Lawrence didn't play very well, and sometimes when I went back to pass, it felt like I was standing in the middle of a freeway. He got me banged around a little, which also resulted in my throwing the ball before I wanted to. And we had problems with our outside receivers because another one of Al Davis's brilliant moves was to bench Freddy Biletnikoff. 'The Genius' went to a youth movement and put Morris Bradshaw in there. Well, Morris doesn't play very well, and Cliff Branch didn't play very well either last year."

As soon as the interview was published, I was sorry I'd complained about my teammates. John Madden called me and said, "Kenny, you really shouldn't have done that. Even if guys ever have something bad to say about you, don't sound off because that would just lower you to their level."

I was hoping I'd be traded to Atlanta, a good team and one that would allow me to stay in the South. I heard Al Davis shopped me around to several teams, but not seriously. He demanded two number one draft choices and two "quality players" in exchange for me. No team was going to pay that price for a quarterback with gimpy knees who would be thirty-four at the end of the season.

Training camp opened in July 1979 and I didn't report. Tom Flores, a good guy and the former receivers' coach, was now the head coach. He phoned and asked if I was coming in. I said I didn't know. But every year at this time for the past twelve years I'd been going off to Santa Rosa to get ready for a football season. A few days after Flores called, I knew I couldn't stay out of camp. Jumping in my Porsche 911 SC, I got on Interstate 20 and headed west. I always liked the cross-country drive, usually stopping at friends along the way. But this year I aimed to drive straight through.

Everything was fine until I reached Midland, Texas. I had a flat that could not be repaired. The Porsche had a temporary spare that was not supposed to be driven more than fifty miles and not at speeds over forty. And no one in Midland had a tire for the 911, though one garage owner said he'd have one for me in the morning. I left the car and went to the nearest bar.

I had tired of scotch a year or so ago and discovered a fondness for Jack Daniel's, which had a nice tang. Jack over ice was awful nice. I got into a bunch of Jack while shooting pool and hooked up with this girl who was playing the same Willie Nelson and Waylon Jennings songs I was on the jukebox. About 2 A.M. she took me home with her, which was a trailer a few blocks away. She fed me eggs and we flopped together till morning.

At eight o'clock I gulped a can of Coke and walked to the garage. The tire, I was told, wouldn't arrive for two more days. "Fuck it," I decided. I set out on that temporary spare bearing the red sticker, CAUTION, DO NOT DRIVE OVER 50 MILES, and drove over 800 miles on it. Straight through. Close to twenty hours without sleep. On my last gas stop before Oakland, I phoned Dave Casper, who was home, holding out for a better contract, and told him where I was.

"Dave, I am dead tired and need to lay down," I said. "Can I crash with you?"

"Come ahead," he said, and when I got to his house Dave didn't say a word. He just led me to a bed. I felt like a horse that had been rode hard and put up wet. My cowboy boots felt like they weighed forty pounds apiece. I barely got them off before I collapsed and slept for eighteen hours.

The next day I sat around with Dave, recovering. We played guitars, fished off his back porch, and talked. In desperation last season, we had used Casper on an end-around play and had even let him try a pass off a tight end reverse. He had a strong arm, but his pass was about five yards off-target. Of course, he wanted to try the pass again this season. "If I ever report," he said.

"David, I think you'll stick to catching the ball and leave the throwing to me."

"Flores may put in the play," Dave said.

"Yeah, but he won't be out there to call it," I said, laughing.

Late that day I went out to my car, which was filthy, covered with squashed bugs, road tar, and mud. It was also listing to the temporary spare side. I said good-bye to Dave, drove to the Porsche-Audi dealer, and I traded in the 911 for a $33,000 928. It felt good driving into camp a week late in that nice new silver-and-black machine. They were the Raider colors.

I arrived about 11 P.M., and the first guy I ran into was Gene Upshaw, who grabbed me in a bear hug. "Snake! Damn, it's good you're here!" he said. "And I don't want to hear any more of that shit about you wanting to be traded. We all like you, you like us, and we're all in this together. You're the leader of this team and you said what you honestly felt. You wouldn't be the competitor you are if you didn't react to criticism."

The players I had criticized also welcomed me back and told the press they just wanted to forget last season. Henry Lawrence said, "Kenny gave his own honest opinion of what was right and what was wrong here last season. Although his opinion of me was negative, I'm a team man. There were a lot of things I could have done better, the same as some other players, but I'm too mature to dwell on what happened."

Then he decided getting his name in print so much wasn't half bad. "It really puts me in a pretty good spot," Henry said, smiling. "Now people know who's playing right tackle for Oakland. Maybe now I'll get some of those votes for the All-Pro team."

In the morning I met with Coach Tom Flores, who asked me to please shitcan the trade talk, which made sense to me.

Then I met with the press and answered everyone's questions, indicating I planned to be cooperative again. Except with one writer. When Bob Padecky asked a question, I said, "Fuck you."

Most of the questions concerned my relationship with Al Davis, and I said I didn't have one, that I hadn't spoken to Al and didn't plan to. "If Al had something to say, he should have called me into the office, looked me in the eye, and said it. I don't think you should criticize someone to the media. Management asks loyalty from the players. Why can't a player ask some loyalty from management? When you win, you hear how it always starts at the top—good team, good management. It's possible that losing starts there, too, but you never hear about that.

"I just think the situation could have been handled a little better by Al. But that won't affect the way I play the game. I have a great relationship with the players, and that's the only thing that's important."

I also told the writers who had questioned my life-style that I wasn't about to change it. "Some of you wrote that I party too much and said, 'You can't do that as you get older.' Well, if I can't and it hurts my game, I'll get out. But I'm not going to let football control my whole life. I'm going to live the way I want to live because I don't know any other way. Last season some idiot in Oakland wrote that maybe I should stop going around with all the 'Wonderfully Wicked Wandas' of the South. What the hell does that have to do with football?"

One of the writers said he hardly recognized me without a pot belly. I told him I'd done a little running in the off-season. I just didn't tell him how little, but I said, "That ought to throw a monkey wrench into some people. They think all I do is drink, raise hell, and stay out all night, and they're pretty close to the truth."

Then we went out to the field for the morning workout. On one of my first passes, I threw a fifty-yarder to Morris Bradshaw behind the coverage, and everyone on the offense turned and started cheering me. Goddamn, it was good to be back!

10

<hr>

"Keeper
of The Tooz"

On a team of Hall of Fame carousers, John Matuszak was a man who almost always needed to go a little farther than the pack—if not a whole lot farther.

The Tooz, as he liked to be called, was a six-eight, 280-pounder who could run like an antelope and play defensive end like a raging bull when he was in shape. It often took two people to block him. The problem was that John didn't always take care of himself.

When we broke training camp in 1979, Coach Tom Flores sent for me. I went over to his office, wondering what was up. I found Tom pacing around with his head down, looking concerned. "Must be serious," I thought.

Tom looked up at me and asked, "Who're you rooming with in Oakland, Snake?"

"Just like last year, Tom," I said. "Nobody."

"Well, would you mind rooming with Matuszak?" Flores said. "We'd like him to move out of the trunk of his car."

I laughed.

"It's no joke. Last season, when he wasn't living with some woman, I hear he actually spent some nights in his goddamn car. Now we need performance out of John this year and it'll help if he's settled in one place. Will you take him in?"

"Will I qualify for hazardous-duty pay, Tom?"

Flores smiled. "You're about the only guy on this team who can handle The Tooz."

"I don't know if anyone can *handle* The Tooz," I said, remembering our loss to Denver in the 1977 playoffs. John had partied the pregame night away. When he got back to the hotel in the morning, he decided he didn't like the window draperies, so he tore them down —rod and all. A hotel employee tipped the Broncos that Matuszak was in bad shape, and the Broncos ran out the clock over him. They had The Tooz gasping for oxygen in that high altitude the whole final quarter. That wasn't the reason we lost, but John was real depressed on the flight home.

"I like John. He's basically a good guy," I said. "And I know he felt bad about that 1977 playoff game. I don't think that'll happen again."

"We can't afford to have it happen again," Tom said.

"I'll see what I can do." I thought it might be kind of fun, being "Keeper of The Tooz." I'd never had a 280-pound pet before.

I had leased a condominium in Alameda, California, near the Oakland Coliseum and the Raider practice facilities. The condo was on a little island just off the coast in San Francisco Bay. It was a real nice duplex that you entered on the ground floor and there was a large hot tub out on the patio. The first floor consisted of a spacious living room, a dining room, a kitchen, and a bathroom. Upstairs there was an oversized bedroom, a bath, and a smaller bedroom for John. It was commodious compared to the trunk of his car.

I went out to the parking lot looking for John and saw his big curly-haired "natural" rising above the vehicles. He was packing his car. The biggest player on the team also had the biggest car. It was a 1978 Lincoln Mark V, about twenty-five or thirty feet long. It looked like it had to have somebody to turn the front and somebody to turn the back.

As I walked over, The Tooz was shoving suitcases into the backseat. The open trunk was already filled and it resembled a Goodwill Industries collection container. Thrown into it were several pairs of jeans, a few pairs of double-knit pants, a bunch of T-shirts and wash-and-wear button-downs, a vast assortment of brightly colored suspenders, and several go-to-hell hats—cowboy, Teddy Roosevelt, cab driver. The Tooz also had strewn much of his paperwork in there: playbooks, receipts, bills, traffic tickets.

Although I'm obsessive about keeping my cars, duds, and living quarters organized, everything neat and polished, I told John he was welcome to join me in the condo.

"Hey, Snake, that's damn nice of you," he said. "But I'll have to see the place before I decide."

"You have other offers?"

"The Tooz always has offers for his person," he said, pushing out his chest.

The moment John looked through the sliding doors and spied the hot tub, he cried, "Goddamn, Snake, this is *me!*" He got right on the telephone. And before we had even unpacked, The Tooz, myself, and three airline stewardesses were all cavorting naked in the hot tub.

John began tossing a girl into the air and catching her in the water. He grabbed a second girl, who couldn't have weighed over 100 pounds soaking wet, which she was. When he threw her skyward, the girl must have sailed up about eight feet. The Tooz gave an appreciative roar, and the girl let out a piercing scream. An upper-floor window came open and a woman yelled, "A little quiet, please!"

John hollered, "Quiet *this,* you—" and I reached out and clamped a hand over his mouth. "Tooz, we don't want to get thrown out of here the first day," I said. "We can have fun without riling the neighbors."

He floated on his back and waved his dick at the upper window, whispering, "Quiet this, neighbor."

The first thing you note about John's personality in his overwhelming need to be noticed. "Hey, look at me" was written all over his behavior and getups. Typically, he would go out wearing a flashy, multihued shirt, red-white-and-blue suspenders, tight jeans, flip-flops or cowboy boots, and a pair of New Wave wraparound sunglasses, usually chartreuse.

God knows what people thought he looked like, but it was massive and it was very, very different. And no one ever made a comment on John's attire that he could hear. No one dared.

I don't know how many times I've seen The Tooz walk into a bar, grab his shirt at the chest with both hands, rip it open to the waist, and growl like a lion at the top of his lungs. That tended to get everyone's attention.

A young woman, on first meeting The Tooz, asked me if he ever tried to intimidate anyone. "Everybody that he ever came in contact with his entire life," I said.

He particularly enjoyed stomping into the gay bars in San Francisco and scaring the shit out of everyone in them. Eyes glaring and muscles bulging, he would let out that roar and it would rattle glasses on the bar and just freeze everyone solid. The Tooz did instant statues. He loved to see fear on people's faces.

His favorite cry when he entered a bar with me was: "Stabler will arm-wrestle anybody in here for $5!"

"You crazy bastard," I'd say. "*You* arm-wrestle." He never did because nobody would challenge him. But despite the fact that John had great big arms and was very powerful, he might well have lost an arm-wrestling contest to someone who had practiced the techniques of the sport.

The Tooz never practiced anything hard. Given his size, speed, and competitiveness, he was a natural football player. But there's no telling how great Matuszak might have been if he had pumped iron to increase his strength and worked diligently on techniques to perfect his skills the way other players did. John never picked up a weight. He never expended much energy in practice. What he brought to ball games were his natural gifts—period.

John was a natural as an actor, too, as he had demonstrated in his first film, *North Dallas Forty,* and in many parts that followed. But, hell, that figured. The Tooz was always acting. He was an intimidating-looking sonuvabitch and he played the part to the hilt.

Never with women, though. John's taste in females ran to little old ladies that he enjoyed sitting around talking to, and little young women that he could lift with one hand up onto his shoulders and parade about.

We went into a sedate San Francisco restaurant one night. An attractive and petite young woman wearing a tailored suit was seated at the bar near the entrance. As John walked by, he scooped her up onto his shoulder, saying, "Get on up there, little lady." He kept walking until he reached another pretty and diminutive woman at the bar. "You too," he said and hoisted her onto his other shoulder. He carried them to a table in back and gently sat them down.

"Now, what would you gorgeous girls like to drink with The Tooz and his partner here, The Snake?" asked The Tooz, charming the women, who ended up at the condo with us.

At a disco one night, we met two young women and decided to take them to a quiet bar across Jack London Square. John picked both of them up on his shoulders as we walked. Approaching the open door to the bar, John bent down and the girls ducked too. But they couldn't get low enough. One girl screamed as John crossed the threshold, bumping the girls' heads on the doorframe.

"You big dumbo, couldn't you see we wouldn't fit?" one girl said.

"And didn't you hear me yell?" said the other girl, holding her head.

"I'm used to women yelling around me," John said, rubbing her head. "I'm sorry. But, hey, you got to play with the small hurts, as Vince Lombardi used to say."

Women loved John. When he wasn't drinking hard, he was just a double-wired big old kid. He was fun and he was funny.

John and I each had three semiregular girls that we invited to the condo, and we mixed in others in between to keep things lively. There always seemed to be volunteers around to do the laundry and dishes. And someone had to pick up John's clothes that often seemed to be scattered all over the place. I still can't imagine how they got there, but I once found a pair of his shorts in the freezer.

A major goal of ours was to see how many women we could get in the hot tub with us at the same time. We advanced from three to six, stuck there for a while, then topped out at seven.

"If I put two more on my shoulders with their feet in the water," The Tooz asked, "will that count as nine, Snake?"

"Why?"

"I'm thinking about sending it in to the *Guinness Book of World Records.*"

"Why don't you go for twelve girls? In addition to the two on your shoulders, get a long-legged one to sit on your head and two itty-bitty gals to sit on your thumbs."

The Tooz liked that idea, but thumb-sitters were hard to come by.

Being so close to the Raiders' practice field, the condo became kind of a halfway house for teammates on their way home. Anybody who wanted to stop in for a drink, some food, and festivities was welcome. We soon needed a register and turnstile to keep track of all the people who wandered in. If we had hung out a neon sign, we could've opened a club.

It was a good thing for all of us that we had practices interrupt the partying.

We had to keep the condo liquor cabinet and larder pretty well stocked, but luckily I didn't have to keep a wide variety of food in for The Tooz. His meals basically consisted of Cheese Whiz smeared all over bagels. That's about what he lived on—Cheese Whiz, bagels, and Crown Royal.

John became friendly with the little old lady who lived next door to us. She invited him in for coffee and bagels the week we moved in, and every morning thereafter she would come by with a bag of bagels for him.

"I know Johnny loves these," she'd say when I answered her ring at the door. "Got to keep his strength up."

If The Tooz was awake when she came, he'd sit and talk to the bagel lady for an hour or more. If not, once he did rise and shake the debris out of his head, he would go next door and chat with her until it was time to leave for practice.

As you might imagine, the sounds from our duplex tended to grow a bit loud during some parties. Police were called about every third week and we'd have to tone down. But the party decibels never matched the frightening sounds that erupted from the place when John engaged a girl in his bedroom.

The Tooz had installed a custom-built bed up there, and naturally it was double-sized; hell, his billfold was double-sized. And when he had a girl in that bed it would just dance, bucking and bouncing around the room like two mating frogs. The whole place shook.

In addition, John's girls tended to be downright expressive in their love sounds. The cries and screams, shouts and hollers, high-decibel moans and groans combined with the lindy-hopping bed to make the activities sound like an ongoing mugging.

One evening I was downstairs awaiting a date's call to tell me where to meet her. The Tooz had gone upstairs with a young lady who appeared to be about a size two. He was soon into his apemanin-heat act, and I wondered if the tiny girl would get through it without subsequent need of medical assistance. The bed banged, the ceiling over my head trembled, and the screams about raised goose pimples on me.

Then the doorbell rang. "What can I tell the police?" I thought. "My roommate's making love, not war?"

I opened the door and the bagel lady said, "Oh, you're here, Kenny! I started to call the police. I was worried about Johnny if you had burglars. You know, Johnny's a big boy and some nasty people like to pick on big boys. Just because they're big."

"She's worried about the monster, but not about the aging quarterback," I thought as the final sounds of John's skirmish faded with an *"OOOOooooooooh. . . ."*

"Is Johnny all right?" the little old lady asked.

"Yes, ma'am," I said, thinking quickly. "John's been rehearsing for a part in a new movie he'll be in. He'll be working on that for a while, so if you hear that sound again, don't worry."

"Oh, isn't that nice. Johnny's in another movie."

About that time The Tooz came bopping down the stairs, trailed by his drained-looking friend.

"Hi, Johnny," the bagel lady said. "How did it go up there?"

John stopped still on the stairs, his smile dying. He looked quizzical, then embarrassed. The bagel lady may be the first person before whom The Tooz was ever embarrassed.

"I was talking about you rehearsing for a new movie, John," I explained, and he was relieved.

John insisted on walking the little old lady twenty steps down the hall to her door.

"Glad to see you're still breathing," I said to the girl, smiling. "Did the bed survive?"

The Tooz was a confirmed bachelor after his one bout with marriage, and he loved to tell stories about how his former wife Yvette was always warring with him. One year he snuck her into the training camp dorm when he was with Kansas City. As he was walking back from a meeting one evening, Yvette, angry about something, tried to run him down in their car.

"I don't remember what she was pissed about, but I saw her coming right at me," he said. "I ran off the road across a field, and that crazy bitch turned and came bouncing along right behind me. She had no damn respect for my new car. But I cut into this cemetery by the field and Yvette finally had to stop. She couldn't run over all those graves to get me in one. Yvette sat in the car calling me names, and I just stood behind a tombstone laughing my head off."

During the season, the Matuszaks moved into an apartment complex in Kansas City. Yvette bought herself two immaculately groomed, pedigreed white poodles and took them with her everywhere she went. The problem was, when the dogs were in the apartment they barked all the time and other tenants complained. Again and again. The building management sent the Matuszaks a warning and finally threatened them with eviction if the dogs were not kept quiet.

One night Yvette made a quick trip to the store without the dogs. They barked and barked. "Quiet, you artificial dogs!" The Tooz yelled, not knowing how to make them stop barking. "Why don't they lie down and go to sleep like normal dogs?" he wondered, taking another hit on his Crown Royal. Then he thought of it. He'd give the dogs what he gave himself when he couldn't doze off. Sleeping pills.

"In two minutes flat, those dogs stopped barking," John said. "Permanently."

He had OD'd the animals. When Yvette came home and found them, she tried to brain John with a skillet. "Again, quick feet saved The Tooz," he said, laughing.

John was so big and had such a capacity that he could drink Crown Royal all night, often washing down a couple of Quaaludes along the way. But when The Tooz did drink real hard, he'd get ornery, often downright mean. People would see him come roaring into a bar and disperse. He cleared out a lot of saloons.

Most people were afraid of him, including teammates who just didn't want to be around John when he was deep into the Crown. But I could handle The Tooz by talking him down, making him feel guilty when he acted up and caused a disturbance in public. We'd be in a bar or restaurant and he would yell at someone, say, for supposedly staring at him. He particularly liked to yell at groups of three or four guys.

"John," I'd say, "you're fucking up a good time. You keep being loud and making a scene, they're gonna ask us to leave. Now, I'm enjoying myself. You know this is my time out you're screwing up, too, so just behave."

John would look down, contrite, and be quiet for about thirty minutes. Then he'd start in again, suddenly yelling something like "What's the matter with you, goat face!"

"Damn it, you know you're getting a reputation," I'd tell him. "You don't need that shit, people not wanting to see you in their clubs. And look, Tooz, we've got too much going for us as a team now. We don't need anything that can hurt the ball club, anything that could disrupt the concentration it takes to go for a championship. Like getting in a fight and getting put in jail."

Again, that kind of talk would quiet The Tooz for a while. Until he was seized by that recurring need to let people know he was present. Then I'd have to get him out of the place and drive him on home.

I do believe that throughout my one season as "Keeper of The Tooz" he showed up at all our home games in good shape. How he fared when we traveled that year I can't say. I did not room with The Tooz on the road. Thank you, Lord.

No matter what plans you made with The Tooz, and he would fully agree with them, they never seemed to come to pass. Any number of times we would decide to low-key an evening: get all dressed up and just go out for a nice dinner at a top restaurant, like Ernie's in San Francisco. It was a real classy place, with good food, and a sophisticated clientele.

"We'll have a few drinks, eat, and call it a night, Tooz," I'd say.

"Right, Snake, get back early."

Wrong, Tooz. We'd get back late, both of us all fucked up.

Even on those rare evenings when we didn't get ripped, I never knew what The Tooz might do. Count on it to be a new treat.

One night in a favorite restaurant in Jack London Square, we had a fine meal, quiet conversation about our upcoming opponent, and John was on his best behavior. I got the check and we stood up to leave. John looked around to see if anyone was watching him, then he grabbed the big wooden peppermill off the table, shoved it inside his waistband, and buttoned his sport coat.

"Oh, shit," I thought, and hurried out the door. I kept walking fast until I was a block away from the restaurant. John caught up with me and pulled out the peppermill, smiling proudly.

"For chrissakes, Tooz, we love that restaurant," I said. "They always treat us like kings there. Now what the hell do you want that peppermill for?"

"We can use it at the house when I cook," he said.

"When *you* cook?" I said. "Oh, yeah, it'll come in handy with your Cheese Whiz specials."

Among the Raiders, Tuesday was known as "Tooz Day." That's because everyone else partied after Sunday's game and came back to earth on Monday. Everyone except The Tooz. His postgame celebrations stretched well into Tuesday. The Tooz would go right through the training room treatment on Monday, the early morning meeting on Tuesday, and the light workout that afternoon—and he would still be *roaring*.

Any time I got a call on Tooz Day, I knew John was up to something that required my immediate attention. One Tuesday I was about to head home for lunch after the meeting and John said he was going for a haircut.

"I'm gonna get it *all* cut off," he yelled with that wild look in his eyes that always accompanied his mornings-after when the Crown coals still glowed.

"Are you crazy, Tooz?" I said, eyeing his huge natural, a head of hair that would just about fill a bushel basket.

"Gettin' down to the skin!" he said, sliding into his car.

"Tooz," I said, imagining him shaved bald, "wait till tomorrow to get it cut. You may—"

He took off, tires squealing out of the parking lot. "You'll be sorry, Toozer," I thought, knowing how proud he was of his natural. I started to follow him to the Razor's Edge, the shop where most of us had our hair cut in Alameda. But I figured Dick Kellogg, the owner, would talk John out of the Otis Sistrunk look. Sistrunk, another of our defensive linemen, had shaved his head, and that led Alex Karras to say during a Monday night game telecast, "Otis is from the University of Mars." I guessed John had heard about that and wanted the notoriety that balding his head would bring him.

The telephone was ringing when I walked into the condo. "Come on down here and get John," Dick Kellogg said. "And, Snake, please hurry."

I pulled up to the Razor's Edge and Kellogg's other barbers and four customers were standing outside the shop, peeking in, one of the customers with shaving cream on his face. Kellogg was standing by the chair with The Tooz in it. "Cut it, goddamn it!" John was hollering.

Kellogg was afraid that if he didn't cut John's hair the big madman would wreck the barber shop. But he feared that if he did cut the hair John would look in the mirror afterward and not only wreck the place but maybe pinch Dick's head off.

I did some fast talking and told John he was making another bad scene for no reason. I convinced him that if he agreed to wait until the next day and still wanted his head shaved, that I would come with him and personally see that Dick razored him clean and shiny.

"Tooz, I'm just not sure that you want to look like you're from the University of Mars," I said. But I knew it was far more likely that Tooz was from outer space than Sistrunk.

As The Tooz rose from the chair, he spotted on a shelf the big bowl of hard candy that Kellogg gave to kids after they had haircuts. Tooz reached one huge hand into the bowl and then the other, scooping out candy and stuffing it into his pockets. Four lonesome pieces were left in the bowl.

"Now, what're you gonna do with all that candy?" I asked him on the way out of the shop.

"Feed it to the sourpuss," he said.

"Who?"

"Al Davis. The man's always scowling these days. Gonna sweeten him up."

Al Davis often used the weight room, and I could just see The Tooz hanging him up on one of the coat hooks there and force-feeding him hard candy. Thankfully, Al was not at the afternoon workout.

One day John said to me, "Snake, I need to get myself a gun."

I looked at him in disbelief. "You don't need a gun, Tooz," I said. "All you need to carry is a comb."

He laughed. "Hey, I just want a gun for a little target shooting."

"Yeah, I guess you don't have to worry about being attacked. Anyone who tried to mug you would have to be carrying a ladder."

I wasn't real thrilled about The Tooz having a handgun, but could

I tell him he shouldn't buy one? I figured he'd pick up a little .22 for plinking.

He came back in an hour later, all excited. "Look at this baby," he said. He showed me a .357 Magnum pistol, the gun that helped make Dirty Harry's day. I wondered what it might do to my nights.

A few days later I got a call at halftime of the Monday night football game. It figured, Monday being Tooz Day Eve. The caller was Matuszak's lawyer. "Kenny, you've got to come help me with John," he said urgently.

I wasn't sure I wanted to hear the rest of this, but I had no choice. "What's the matter?" I asked.

"The police arrested him out on the freeway for shooting at road signs. Actually, he was zigzagging from the freeway onto the service road and back."

"And firing that Magnum," I thought. Still, a few road signs, that wasn't so bad—considering the countless other possibilities. I climbed into my Porsche and drove to the small town just outside Oakland where John was being held.

The first person I met at the station house was the arresting officer, who shook hands and said he was glad to meet me. He also said he had been scared to death when he saw Matuszak emerge from his Lincoln in the dark.

"That's understandable, officer," I said. "You're a normal-sized person, and in the dark John looks kinda like a Coke machine with a head on top."

"Well, your friend really cursed me and my partner when we booked him," the officer said, smiling faintly. "And when we told him to strip, there were a few items that he flat-out refused to take off. Knowing he's with the Raiders, we decided not to argue with him. I think he's finally calmed down."

He showed me into a rear room. John was standing outside a cell, wearing only handcuffs, his Super Bowl ring, and a pair of powder blue elephant-skin cowboy boots. I couldn't help laughing. "That's my roommate," I said, "I'd recognize him anywhere!"

The sergeant laughed and said, "Good to see you, Ken. I'm told you're the man who can control him."

"He's a mighty big responsibility, but I try," I said. "Now, can we discuss getting John clothed and out of here?"

One thing about playing for the Raiders, the police around Oakland, all of them fans, tended to be understanding about player indiscretions. The Tooz was released in the care of The Snake. It was no big deal having a few holey road signs along the freeway.

Of course, The Tooz wasn't entirely happy. The police wouldn't let him drive his car home until he had sobered up, and his gun was history. "I don't know why they won't give me back my Mag," he said, pouting on the ride home, his shoulders pressing me against the door of the little Porsche.

"They'll probably let you have a bow and arrow, Tooz," I said. "You can't shoot one of those while driving a car. Come to think of it, though, the cops might insist that you get rubber-tipped arrows."

I missed The Tooz a lot when I went to Houston in 1980. He was a nice guy, a fun guy to run with when he wasn't laced. John did give me the hardest hit my former teammates put on me in the playoff game against Oakland, but it was an accident. He jumped offside, charging hard, and bumped me over.

"I believe you're offside, Tooz," I told him.

"I believe you're right, pardner," he said.

John had a major role in the movie *Caveman* that was released that off-season. He phoned me to say he'd be in Houston to promote the opening and that he'd visit me. He said he'd given up ludes and cut way down on the booze. "I'm a changed man, Snake. You might not recognize me."

"You mean you don't walk in bars, growl, and rip open your shirt any more?" I said.

"That's the old Tooz."

I told him where he could find me when he got in. "Look forward to seeing you on Wednesday," I said.

I was sitting with several people at a table in a bar on Wednesday when someone said, "Kenny, here comes John Matuszak through the door."

"My God," I said, "get your girlfriends off the street and your wives behind locked doors!"

The Tooz saw me and waved. But as he walked past the bar, he halted by a man who was smoking a cigarette with his beer. John reached into the man's shirt pocket and pulled out a pack of cigarettes as if he were going to bum one, except John never smoked. He crumpled up the cigarette pack and threw it down, then took the cigarette out of the man's fingers and stomped on it.

"You shouldn't smoke," The Tooz said. "A terrible habit. Take up pocket pool."

He strode over to me, and I said, "Good to see you've changed so much, Toozer."

"Wait'll you see me in *Caveman*," he said, smiling. "I had to run around the whole picture wearing a fur jock. I'm still itching." He reached down and scratched his nuts.

John Matuszak's retired now, living with a girl in Los Angeles. We keep in touch and he's always living with some girl, usually in her place. Which is better than living in his car.

The natural showman is now a full-time, very successful actor. In the fall of 1985 he was playing a continuing role in a television series, portraying a gay ex-football player. A strange role for John Matuszak? Not at all. John's been playing a strange role all his life. He's been playing The Tooz.

11

~~~~~~~~~~~~~~~~~~~~~~

Bummed Out in Houston

In 1979 The Santa Rosa Five was down to one—me. With Freddy and Pete gone, camp wasn't the same. Even The Circuit of bars every night wasn't as much fun. Most of the older renegade Raiders were now history, including Clarence Davis, Warren Bankston, Willie Brown, Skip Thomas, and George Buehler.

Ten rookies made the team, with not a so-called blue-chipper among them. When we split our four preseason games and Dave Casper still hadn't reported, I phoned him and said, "Dave, get your ass in here. We're not gonna do shit without you this season."

"Al won't give me what I'm worth," he said, "and I'm not coming in until he does."

A few days later, just before the season opener with the Rams, Casper reported. He was in shape and in several extra-long workouts, Dave and I got our timing down. He was an amazing athlete. But I don't know if he was satisfied with his contract. We had barely lost to the Rams in overtime during the preseason and everyone except Dave felt we would beat them.

Just before we took the field in L.A., Dave stood in the dressing room and shouted, "How does it feel, you guys, to know you're gonna get the shit beat out of you today?"

The rookies gave him strange looks. I figured, "That's just Dave.

He'll probably play a great game." He did, catching a couple of touchdown passes in the 24–17 win.

But we took a beating in the offensive line that day, and proceeded to lose our next three games. By then we had thirteen players on the injured-reserve list.

Just before the NFL trading deadline on October 9, Al Davis called the Bears' general manager, Jim Finks, and asked if he would be interested in acquiring me. Finks later told a writer, "We were never close to making a deal. We think Vince Evans, Mike Phipps, and Bob Avellini all have the ability to be a winning quarterback in the NFL." Finks was wrong about that, which may be one reason why he is no longer the Bears' GM.

With so many new players in and out of the lineup, we had to do a lot of adjusting. After losing three out of four, we went to a two-tight-end offense full-time, with Casper and Ray Chester. We won three straight, then lost to the Jets, 28–19, when I passed for a career-high twenty-nine completions and 360 yards. I also had five interceptions, three of which were turned into Jet touchdowns. Any time you have to throw the ball forty-seven times, as I did in this game, you're almost sure to lose.

Then we won two and I got some raves in the press. Casper said, "We're not the team we were three years ago, but Kenny is probably just as good. Sometimes he's better."

"He is better and it's because he's in shape," Pat Toomay said. "They put us all on a weight-lifting and running program after the season ended last year."

I had to laugh when I told the press, "I didn't do anything this off-season that I haven't done for eleven other off-seasons."

My body did have a little more tone than in recent years because Al Davis had hired a strength coach and bought a batch of Universal workout machines that I had used regularly all through training camp.

I guess I looked better with my shirt off because *Partner* magazine asked me to pose topless with stripper Carol Doda. Oiler quarterback Dan Pastorini had posed in the first issue, so I said sure. It wasn't real painful to lay my head on Carol Doda's blimp-sized breasts. I understand that issue of *Partner* sold out in Oakland and San Francisco.

"When are you going into porn flicks, Snake?" The Tooz wanted to know.

He had missed the first five games with a torn bicep and we hadn't had any pass rush without him. Since I joined the Raiders, we rarely put much pressure on a quarterback unless we blitzed the linebackers or a safetyman. That hadn't changed.

On the offensive line, only Gene Upshaw and Henry Lawrence stayed healthy all year, as Art Shell, Dave Dalby, and Mickey Marvin missed games due to injuries. We were an up-and-down team throughout the season. When we were playing well, we could handle the top teams in our division, like Denver and San Diego. When we weren't playing well, we couldn't beat the Little Sisters of the Poor.

After the 1–3 start, we won eight of eleven and had an outside shot at the playoffs if we defeated Seattle in the season finale. We lost, 29–24.

Still, it had been fun playing in a situation that wasn't ideal, going to a whole new offense and making it work. It would have been a hell of a lot better if we had been in the middle of the race all year. It would have been great if we'd won the last game.

But what I realized was that I loved the game more than ever because I was now totally confident of my skills. I was still aiming to win the big one again, but every game was a big one now. Every time I stepped out on the field, I felt like a kid. My beard was gray and my knees were fifty years old. But I knew that as long as I could get out there and compete, I would always be young.

Our most exciting game in 1979 had occurred on Monday, December 3, in New Orleans. In all my years with the Raiders, we only lost one Monday night game, that by one point, but it sure looked like we were going to lose this one. The Saints led 28–14 at the half, and I had fumbled and thrown an interception to set up two of those scores. Then, midway through the third quarter, I threw another interception that linebacker Ken Bordelon returned for a touchdown. I went after him and defensive tackle Barry Bennett hit me with a hell of a block. My head banged off the artificial turf and I didn't know where I was for some time.

I made it off the field somehow. Tom Flores said later that he talked to me, but I didn't respond to anything he said. I was so woozy that I just sat silently on the bench with the offensive linemen. When they got up to go back on the field, I followed them. The only thing I said, Upshaw told me later, was: "Well, I dug this hole, now let's climb out of it."

As we moved into a huddle, I saw Jim Plunkett running toward us, and I waved him off. I was still a little fuzzy and didn't know that Flores had sent him in, but I wanted to win this game. Although the Saints were up 35–14, there were eighteen minutes left to play.

We went sixty-two yards for a touchdown, and I still was not playing with a full deck as I headed for the sideline. I shook my head a few times, trying to clear it.

Upshaw said, "What's up, Snake, the wooze not gone?"

"Gene, what it feels like is an awful bad hangover," I said. "Luckily, I've had some practice with those."

The defense, which had changed from a three-four to a four-three in the second half, got the ball right back, and kept doing so. On our next possession we marched seventy-two yards for another score. I passed for the final seventeen yards to reserve tight end Derrick Ramsey in the end zone.

On the following series, Cliff Branch made a great play to tie the game. Flores had not started Cliff because he'd missed his third practice of the season that week. But Cliff was in there now, and I threw to him on a little sideline pass. He grabbed the ball, cut by the charging cornerback, and raced sixty-six yards down the sideline for the touchdown with 3:19 showing on the clock.

Pat Toomay set up the winning score. He hit Saints' ballcarrier Chuck Muncie so hard that he broke his face mask and caused a fumble. Mike Davis ran the ball back nineteen yards to the Saints' twenty, then lateraled to Ted Hendricks, who carried it to the thirteen. A few plays later I hit Branch with an eight-yard touchdown pass, and we won, 42–35.

"My job was on the line," Cliff said as we ran off the field.

"I think you'll keep it," I said.

Gene Upshaw threw a big arm around my shoulders and said, "Snake, there have been a lotta games we pulled out in the last seconds. But that was the most amazing game I've ever seen you play. Just amazing. And you were knocked silly there, just like against the Bears that time."

"Maybe I should have someone ding me in the head before every game," I said, laughing. "But, you know, I never thought we were out of it."

"None of us did," Gene said. "We never think we're gonna do anything but win when we go out there with you."

Tom Flores thought I had my best season ever in 1979, better than the Super Bowl season. "Taking into consideration the fact that we aren't as strong a team and the fact that Ken had to make so many adjustments playing with different personnel constantly," Flores said, "I think he had a remarkable year."

I had to agree. In 1976 I completed 66.7 percent of 291 passes for 2,737 yards and twenty-seven touchdowns. I had seventeen interceptions that year. In 1979, playing a sixteen-game schedule instead of fourteen, I completed 61 percent of 498 passes for 3,615 yards and twenty-six touchdowns. I had twenty-two interceptions. With a few more wins, I'd take those numbers any time. Of course, the only numbers that really mattered were the team's record.

Al Davis phoned me in late February, the first time we had exchanged words in over a year. "Ken, do you still want to be traded?" he asked.

"Yeah, Al," I said. "I think that'll be best for everyone."

"You're sure that's really what you want?" he asked.

"That's it," I said stubbornly.

I had the feeling, though, that if I hadn't been so pigheaded Davis would not have traded me. I may be wrong about that because I've heard that Tom Flores was against my being traded, yet Al went ahead. And the deal he worked out was for Dan Pastorini, who was three and a half years younger than me and had a much stronger arm.

Al loved bombers, and I wasn't ever a picture passer. I sometimes threw sidearm, three quarters, overhand, across my body, off the wrong foot. I never cared about pretty pictures of me throwing the ball. All I was interested in was completions. And my career completion percentage at this point, 59.9, was the highest among quarterbacks who had thrown at least 1,500 passes.

John Madden said, "Al always believes in getting rid of a guy before he has pissed the very last drop. But Ken's like Bobby Layne and Billy Kilmer. Even if he has lost a little arm strength, he'll find other ways to piss on you."

John also wrote a column about me for the San Francisco *Examiner* that was headlined: NOBODY CAN REPLACE STABLER. He concluded it by writing: "Ken has many special qualities. He is tough enough to stand up under fire, he is a natural leader, he has a mind that absorbs knowledge easily, and he is one of the coolest people under pressure I have ever known. Oakland has been good to Ken Stabler, and Ken Stabler was good for Oakland."

That was a fair assessment.

I knew that I was going to Houston several days before the trade was announced. I was looking forward to taking over the Oilers, who had put together an 11–5 record in 1979, only to get beat by the Steelers in the AFC Championship Game for the second year in a row. With the Raiders, I'd had some success against Pittsburgh, which was probably why Oiler coach Bum Phillips wanted me. I thought I'd like to play for Bum. He had begun his college coaching career under Bear Bryant at Texas A&M in 1957.

I had stayed in touch with Coach Bryant over the years, helping him some with recruiting and attending various charity affairs with him. And I made a lot of the banquets that the university held for ex-players in their hometowns. I remember walking into one in the early seventies when I first grew my hair long. Coach Bryant was standing with some buddies outside the banquet hall entrance when he spotted me and said, "Well, goddamn. Here comes Davy Crockett!"

I got him back at a banquet for quarterback Terry Davis. This was the year that Auburn beat Alabama by blocking two punts and running the ball in each time for touchdowns. Coach Bryant had caught a lot of flack about that game, and he was deep in conversation when I walked up behind him. I tapped him on the shoulder and said, "Hello, Coach, how's your kicking game?"

He turned around with fire in his eyes, then laughed and said, "Stabler, you sonuvabitch!"

I was at a banquet in Mobile and Coach Bryant was at the dais making a speech when someone slipped him word of my trade. He broke off his speech and said, "Is Kenny Stabler still here?"

I stood up and said, "Yeah, Coach."

"Well, you have to be the luckiest man in the world," he said. "You're getting out of Oakland, you're going down to Houston with all those cowboys, and you'll be playing for Bum Phillips, who is one hell of a man."

I talked to Coach Bryant afterward, and he told me that Bum had called him to ask about me. "I told him," Coach Bryant said, " 'Bum, don't believe everything you've heard about Kenny. He's a great kid. He'll do whatever you ask of him. He's a winner.' "

The next day I flew to Houston for a press conference with Bum. Afterward I went to his office. He was leaning back in a chair with his ostrich cowboy boots propped up on his desk. He had on a pair of ragged old Levi's and a cowboy shirt and his hat was cocked back on his head. He was spitting tobacco juice into a Coca-Cola cup. I said to myself, "This is my kind of guy. He's just an unpretentious cowboy who happens to coach football."

I settled right into Houston that spring. I bought a condominium on Clear Lake in Pasadena. That's the real cowboy and pickup truck side of town, where I had to be. Then I bought me a bunch of new toys. I got a four-wheel-drive Ford Bronco, added a six-inch lift kit under it, and mounted thirty-six-inch wheels all around. I bought a 1,000 c.c. Harley-Davidson Sportster with a low-rider seat, and a Cadillac Coupe de Ville that was as long as a whore's dream, a big old pimp's ride.

All the vehicles were black and I had them striped in red by Ray Milburn of Stripes by Milburn in Pasadena. I asked Ray to paint THE SNAKE on the Bronco's doors, which he did. But he also painted a diamondback rattler, coiled and ready to strike, on each door. That wasn't my style and I had them painted over. I didn't want people to think I was a snake peddler.

I also bought a thirty-foot Scarab, a speedboat that weighed three tons and was powered by two 525 h.p. big-block Chevy engines. It would do 85 m.p.h. without being any threat to your life like the little speedboats I'd had in Gulf Shores. The Scarab was just a fun boat to run around in on Clear Lake.

I knew I was on the right side of town when I found I could pretty much throw a quarter in any direction and punch up some country music on a jukebox. I hung out mostly at Gilley's, the huge saloon where *Urban Cowboy* was filmed. It housed about fifty pool tables, a hundred and fifty pinball machines, and a couple of mechanical bulls for the shift workers from the oil and chemical plants to ride. The place could get rowdy.

One of the first guys I got to know at Gilley's was the chief bouncer, David Ogle, who was called "Killer." We rode our bikes together and became friends. So I always had a good seat at Gilley's and nobody messed with me because nobody wanted to test Killer.

Mickey Gilley and Johnny Lee provided the live music, and they were just great. I shot a lot of pool with Mickey and did a lot of bike riding with Johnny. One day Johnny and I went too far on the Harleys and hit too many honky-tonks. We had to race back for Johnny to make his first gig of the evening. Arriving five minutes late, we said, "Fuck it, let's go on in." And we rode the bikes right into the bar. Sherwood Cryer, the majority owner of Gilley's, told us to get the machines outside. I guess he thought those Harley fumes didn't go too good with that long-necked Texas beer.

Sherwood got worried when I told the writers where I hung out. He was afraid I'd get upset if people started besieging me for autographs. I told him it didn't bother me. I really got off on folks bringing me cocktail napkins and business cards and matchbooks to sign. I figured that folks did that only because I had done something they liked.

Some of the writers were shocked when I told them how much I enjoyed the nightlife in Houston. "There have always been some people who thought my life-style would ruin me," I said. "I like to get out and get after it, always have. So what if I go out and drink, shoot pool, chase women, stay out late, don't come home. Everybody's system is different. Some people need six to eight hours of sleep a night. I can often get by on two hours just fine. Yeah, I carouse. I'm honest about it. I don't try to hide anything."

Mickey Herskowitz of the Houston *Post* heard that admission and wrote: "Stabler is not afraid to reveal himself. There seems to be absolutely no tension in him and no evasiveness. He is a refreshing change from other athletes."

Before heading for training camp in July, I went through the Oiler media guide and last year's injury report so I'd get to know everybody. Players were surprised when I spoke to them by name and asked about their injuries. It was all part of my campaign to get them to like me and have confidence in me, which would in turn help me motivate them in games. My interest in the guys won them over quickly.

The camp was at San Angelo State University, in the heat of West Texas. I'd heard that on real hot days Bum would cut practices short, and he did that early on one blistering day. He took his hat off, wiped his forehead with a handkerchief, and said, "Come on, guys. Let's go drink some beer."

It was easy to see why the Oiler players busted their asses for Bum Phillips. They loved the old cowboy. He ran a loose camp with only occasional bed checks. And when there was no evening meeting, he would announce there would be no bed check at the eleven o'clock curfew. Yet few players seemed to take advantage of Bum.

I didn't have much opportunity to run around after curfew, even if I had wanted to. Bum roomed me with 280-pound center Carl Mauck and he let me know he expected me to be in bed by eleven. Carl had some experience in the job of corraling fun-loving quarterbacks. He had roomed with Dan Pastorini, who like myself had been known to party hard the night before ball games. Dan had lived on the edge. In his time, he had wrecked his speedboat, wrecked his car, and punched a writer. Carl said Dan had also skipped some meetings.

"That's just not using your head," I said. "Sounds like Dan was his own worst enemy."

"Well, from what I hear you and Dan are a lot alike," Carl said, "both self-destructive. I tried to save him. Now I'll try and save you."

I smiled. "I guess everybody has their own style."

Including Carl Mauck. He didn't drink much, but when he drank he was just like a Tasmanian devil. And the man Carl drank with was Mike Stensrud, a 295-pound defensive end. All you need to know about Mike is that he was called "Mongo" after the character Alex Karras played in *Blazing Saddles,* the guy who punched out a horse.

An Oiler fan in San Angelo had a real nice place out on the Concho River that he let a bunch of us use in the evenings. We'd drive out there after the meetings, just to relax and get away from the college and the dormitory where we stayed. We'd drink some beer, pitch horseshoes, and listen to music by the river. And we usually took some girls along with us and had a little party.

One night six of us went out there with six women, and we were all sitting around on the banks of the Concho. We heard a car pull up out front, and Mauck and Stensrud came walking toward us. They didn't say a word as they strode out on the dock, unzipped their flies, flopped out their dicks, and pissed in the river. Then they turned around and shook their dicks at everybody.

"Mauck," I said, "get the hell out of here."

He cussed me and everyone else on the way out. The next thing I heard was pounding sounds out where we had parked our vehicles. I got up and hustled on out front. By the time I got there, Mauck and Stensrud were driving off.

Those crazy bastards had just pummeled my Bronco. They had knocked in both doors and both quarter panels with their fists, good old Mongo and Mauck.

When I got back to the room, Carl was snoring. I shook him and said, "No more drinks for you until you get toilet-trained!"

He mumbled something and went right back to sleep. I could have sued him for truck molesting, but I never troubled my center. He meant too much to my health and well-being on the field.

After one preseason game, a writer asked Mauck how I had fit in with the Oilers. "Like family," Carl said. "I call him 'Easy Rider' 'cause he never loses his cool."

By the time the season opened, Ken Stabler had become a kind of cottage industry in Houston. I was going to make more money off the field in one year in Houston than I had in ten years in Oakland. I had signed an endorsement deal with a department store, there were Snake T-shirts, Snake rattles, Snake hats, and even a soft drink called Snake Venom. It tasted about like its name. But it seemed like everything with my name on it sold. A guy named John Norman, who worked at the Hughes Tool and Die plant, wrote and recorded a song called "Snake Bite" that became the hottest-selling single in Houston.

Robert Gilliam, who already owned about fifteen nightclubs, opened two more and called each of them Ken Stabler's Diamondback Saloon. He gave me a percentage of the profits and that worked out fine. Gilliam paid off the $250,000 note on the first Diamondback in four months. People just lined up to get in them to drink and buy Diamondback pins, T-shirts, suspenders, and caps.

I also hosted a weekly television program, a thirty-minute talk show that we taped on Tuesday and was broadcast on Saturday afternoons. We featured an Oiler "Player of the Week" and a high school "Player of the Week." The talk wasn't all football, as we brought on athletes from other sports, like pitcher Nolan Ryan, and film stars like Burt Reynolds. I enjoyed hosting the show, which reportedly got good ratings.

Houston looked like it was going to be the perfect place for a guy from the Redneck Riviera. But I was a little concerned about the Oiler offense. And not because of the players. My receivers were similar to those I had in Oakland. Ken Burrough was a burner like Cliff Branch, backed by Billy "White Shoes" Johnson. On the other side Mike Renfro was a possession-type receiver like Freddy B. At tight end Mike Barber resembled Dave Casper, and Mike was backed by another good one in Rich Caster.

Barber was the happiest over my arrival. He claimed Pastorini had suddenly stopped throwing the ball to him last season. Others said that was partially true, and it happened right after Mike stole Dan's girlfriend. The woman, I was told, was the former wife of Atlanta Falcons' quarterback Steve Bartkowski. The whole thing sounded to me like a plot for a soap opera.

But Mike Barber proved to be a real temperamental guy. When he wanted to play, he played hard and was a damn good receiver. When he got upset, you couldn't get much out of him. He just wouldn't go hard. And he got upset and popped off to the press when Houston traded for Dave Casper in late October. We'd been playing a two-tight-end offense by then and Casper became a big plus for us.

Our ongoing problem, though, was that we couldn't develop a big passing game out of the run-oriented I formation. About all I did was turn around and hand the ball to Earl. As Earl Campbell was the best runner in football—he would rush for almost 2,000 yards this season—I couldn't tell Bum Phillips to change his offense for me. He had used the I formation and a good defense to get into the last two championship games.

But in the season opener against Pittsburgh, when we fell behind early 17–0, it was apparent that the I formation was not a catch-up offense. Once you're behind, defenses ignore your play-action fakes and just blast in on you. With Campbell running and the score close, linebackers had to respect your faking a handoff to him because when it wasn't a fake Earl was running over people. And when the fake held the linebackers, we could throw the ball behind them.

Bum's philosophy was to establish the run, mix in short high-percentage passes, and control the ball. That's what we did in beating the Browns 16–7 on a Monday night in Cleveland. We controlled the ball so well that our defense was on the field less than four minutes in the second half. I felt like I was driving a tank up and down the field. Afterward Robert Brazile, our fine linebacker, said, "It took so long for the Browns to get back on the field, I'm surprised they could remember the plays."

Brazile missed two days of practice later in the season and everyone wondered what was wrong with him. We found out he had dyed his hair and the chemicals had caused his eyes to swell so that he couldn't see. When he came in, he was not pleased with his dye job. His hair was bright orange.

After a slow start, we began to gel and reached the halfway point of the season with a 5–3 record. In no game did we score over twenty-four points. The offense was just too conservative for my taste, coming out of the wide-open Oakland attack, but I learned to adjust and be patient. Just turn around and hand the ball to Earl Campbell thirty to thirty-five times a game.

I was genuinely concerned about that, worried that he was going to get killed. Every time you gave him the ball, you knew there was going to be a collision. Earl did not go out of his way to avoid tacklers. He had the legs of a guard. A big guard. His thighs were as big around as the waist of most defensive backs, and they moved like pistons. Late in games you'd see backs who had taken him on earlier now moving over and trying to hit him from the side, wanting no more of those pumping thighs, and that just wouldn't get it done.

But Earl wasn't only power. He'd break a run down the sideline and outrun a little halfback seventy-five yards to the end zone. And if one happened to catch him from behind, Earl would just shrug him off or carry the guy in for a score.

Of all the guys I played with and against, I've never met one I respected more than Earl Campbell because of what he is on and off the field. He's just a solid, all-effort person. I remembered what he had done to us in Oakland in 1979. Leading by three points, the Oilers had to kill the final six minutes on the clock. Eating up two minutes at the end of a game is tough enough, but the Oilers had no problem chewing up six with Earl. They just kept giving him the ball and moving the chains.

Another guy I have nothing but respect for, Jack Tatum, also expressed concern about the pounding Earl's legs were taking. Jack had been traded to the Oilers in 1980, too, and he knew about battered legs now. His knees were worn out and he couldn't move much any more. In Houston he played mostly as the fifth back in the nickel defense. He was, pound for pound, the toughest sonuvabitch I ever saw, but he could no longer hit guys and knock the taste out of their mouths. Unable to fire off his weakened wheels, he couldn't play his game of separating receivers from the football. But he played with his head so well that he ended up leading the team in interceptions with seven. He did it on two wasted knees that forced him to retire at season's end.

I became better friends with Jack in Houston. We had that bond from Oakland and I liked him a lot. We'd go out for drinks together and I showed him Gilley's and the Diamondback Saloon. Jack had a pinkie on one hand that made a right angle at the first joint and stuck out weirdly every time he raised his glass to drink.

"I guess I should've had it repaired," he said, "but it's too late now."

I guess that pinkie sticking out might have looked funny if Jack was a tea drinker. He wasn't.

Jack and I both enjoyed traveling with the Oilers. With the Raiders, no drinks were served on the plane—not even beer. That forced a lot of us to smuggle booze on the plane for the flight home. In the last years in Oakland, Dave Dalby and I took turns smuggling a bottle of Jack Daniel's aboard. But with the Oilers, you could have all the beer you could drink on the return trip, probably because Bum Phillips loved beer.

When Bum wasn't coaching, you could always find him in the coaches' meeting room, drinking Budweiser and playing dominoes. He drank so much Budweiser we called it "Bumweiser."

With Oakland the scene on the airplanes was mostly card games and secret sipping, everything relatively quiet. With the Oilers, about every other player carried a big ghetto-blaster, most of them playing great black sounds at full volume, from jazz to the Commodores to

R&B to Stevie Wonder and Ray Charles. Then you had a bunch of guys, including Earl Campbell, carrying boxes that knocked out Willie Nelson and Waylon Jennings. The Oiler planes just rocked. Forget about sleeping. There wasn't enough beer, codeine, and sleeping pills to bring sleep in the midst of all those high-decibel sounds.

When we won, we just took over the airplanes. But when we lost a big game, it was so quiet on the flight home you could hear a rat peeing on cotton.

The Oiler players were all good guys, and one of the nicest was backup quarterback Gifford Nielsen. I enjoyed working with him and discussing strategy. The only thing was, I never got to sit down and have a drink with Gifford. A Brigham Young graduate, Gifford was a devout Mormon and just as straight as a string. He didn't smoke and he didn't drink. I don't think I ever got used to the smell of milkshakes on his breath.

One morning, after a night of revelry with a dark-eyed beauty, I was late for practice. I barreled down the highway and skidded into the parking lot at the practice field. I went running toward the fieldhouse. I saw Bum and Gifford standing together outside the door. "What the hell am I gonna do?" I thought as I ran, sweat pouring off me, hung over, my mind just racing.

Now, Bum never really jumped on anybody. What he would do when he was going to scold you was tip his cowboy hat back on his head, push his glasses down on his nose, look over them at you, and calmly lay out your sins.

As I stopped in front of Bum, he pushed back his hat, pushed down his glasses, and said, "Kenny, you know what time practice—"

"Wait up!" I said. *"Pheew!* I am just glad to see Gifford's here and all right. I have been looking for him *all* night. I mean, I stopped in every single bar on the South Side looking for him." I flicked sweat off my brow. "I am relieved!"

Bum couldn't help smiling, and I stepped past him and went in to get dressed. Bum never fined anyone anyway.

In Houston I partied regularly, but on the road Carl Mauck often made my night life pure hell. We always had a mandatory buffet dinner for the team at the hotel where we stayed, and after it Mauck would escort me back up to our room. But he went above and beyond the call of duty in trying to make sure I was ready for the game.

I usually watched TV or talked on the phone until one or two in the morning, or I'd sit around and chat with friends who dropped by. But Mauck would not allow visitors. One night around eight-thirty, Jackie Sherrill, the coach at the University of Pittsburgh, came by with his wife. "Is Kenny here?" he asked when Mauck opened the door.

"He's not seeing anyone," Mauck said. "We're trying to rest for the game." And he slammed the door.

People would call me, and Mauck would leap for the phone. "No, he can't talk. We got a *game* tomorrow." He'd slam down the receiver.

Promptly at 10 P.M., Mauck would turn off the TV and unplug the phone. Then he'd take off all his clothes, get into bed, and start scratching his ass. He'd sleep with one eye open, and if I tried to sneak over to the door, he'd say, "Sit down, Easy Rider. Get some sleep."

"Shit, Carl, it's goddamn ten o'clock!" I'd say. "You know I never get to sleep before one. I just want to go down for a cup of coffee."

"Coffee'll keep you up."

"What the hell am I supposed to do until one? I can't watch TV. Can't talk on the phone. I can't do anything but lay around here and watch you scratch your big ass."

"Try counting touchdown passes."

Carl Mauck drove me crazy, but we're still friends. He had the team's best interest in mind, which were also my best interests. It just didn't always seem that way to me.

When we went into New York to play the Jets in 1980, we stayed at a hotel just across the Hudson River in New Jersey. I liked to bop around New York and was determined to get over there. All through the buffet I kept looking for a chance to slip out. "This is some shit," I thought. "I not only have to escape from the coaches but from my own roommate!"

As the buffet wound down and guys began peeling off, I just walked out with middle linebacker Gregg Bingham and Mauck didn't notice. We were joined by a guy named Bobby Fingers, whose daddy was a wealthy furniture dealer in Houston and a friend of Bum Phillips. Bobby always traveled with the team and liked to pass himself off as a player when he went out.

The three of us grabbed a cab and drove to an East Side club called The Tittle-Tattle, which was owned by a guy I knew. About ten-thirty Bingham said he was going back to the hotel and asked if I wanted to join him. I said I was going to stay out a while. That turned out to be one of the stupidest things I ever did.

Bobby and I picked up a couple of girls and took them to the Playboy Club, then we went to a bar called Cody's to listen to some country-and-western music. We were having a good time. We got in a conversation with some guys about football, which I usually enjoyed. But one of these guys was a gambler with a bad mouth. He asked if I thought we were going to win tomorrow—which was now today, about 3 A.M.—and I said, "We're gonna try."

"Well, you ain't got a chance," the guy said.

"That's your opinion," I said. "Call your bookie."

"The reason you don't have a chance," he said, "is because you can't throw the ball over thirty yards any more."

I shouldn't have done it, but I'd had just enough Jack to say to myself, "Fuck it."

I popped the guy on the chin and knocked him down. The bouncers came right over and we cleared out of Cody's. Bobby and I went for breakfast at the Brasserie. From there I phoned Richard Todd and woke him up. "Richard, come on out!" I said.

"Hey, it's four o'clock, Ken. We got a game to play," he said.

"That don't matter. Come on out!"

Todd, of course, wouldn't budge. By the time Bobby and I got a cab to take us to New Jersey for $100, it was after six. I was still roaring pretty good when we reached the hotel. Some of my teammates had been going at it a bit too, as I could hear a lot of shit going on down the corridor beyond my room.

I walked in my room and Mauck wasn't in sight, but one of our backs was in there wrestling around with a woman who always showed up when the Raiders came to town. She was a big blonde who was really stuck together. She'd won some nickel-and-dime body beautiful contest, and the guy was trying to talk her out of some pussy. She wouldn't even take off her fur coat. The player got pissed, snatched off her coat, threw it in the shower, and turned on the water. "Miss Body Beautiful" raised hell, hollering and cussing him.

"Jesus Christ," I yelled, "it's rougher in here than it is in a game!"

I don't think I got over two hours' sleep, and I'm not sure that was enough before the Jet game. In the first half I threw four interceptions, and the Jets led 21–0. Then I told Bum, "I'm gonna throw the ball on just about every play. We're coming back."

All told, I threw fifty-one passes in this game, completing thirty-three, four for touchdowns. The last one, a long pass to Rich Caster, tied the game 28–28, and sent it into overtime. We lost the coin toss. The Jets took the ball right down the field and kicked a field goal for the win.

Afterward Richard Todd came into our locker room to see me. "How in hell could you see out there through those bloodshot eyes?" he asked, smiling.

"I could see well enough to have won that game if we'd gotten the ball in overtime," I said. "You didn't give me a chance, Richard."

A writer asked me how I felt about throwing four interceptions in the first half. "Well, I didn't throw any in the second half," I said. "But if we had played one more half I might have thrown four more. You put the ball in the air enough, you're gonna have some picked off. But you're also gonna get some touchdowns."

Still, I knew I'd done a dumb thing, getting into the booze so deep I lost sight of time, of my responsibility, and ended up punching some pencilneck and staying out all night. Having often partied before games for years and been successful, it was almost as if I was afraid to change my routine. But this was one time I should have quit earlier because we should have beaten the hell out of that Jet team. One of my interceptions was returned for a touchdown and another gave the Jets a touchdown from the four.

I thought about this on the bus ride to the airport, about the boozing, the scene in Cody's. "All of that shit is part of me; it all goes into making me whatever the fuck I am," I thought. "The trouble is, I don't know what the fuck I am."

We played better in the second half of the season, winning six of eight to finish with an 11–5 record and make the playoffs. But if we had beaten the Jets we would have won the AFC Central Division title and had the home field advantage in the playoffs. Instead we would play in Oakland.

I told the writers, "It's just another game to me." In truth, I wanted to win that game more than any I had played in since the Super Bowl.

On the films I saw that the Raider defense was much better than it had been in recent years. They were getting a pass rush out of an end named Willie Jones. Also, The Tooz was playing tough and tying up two men a lot, which allowed Hendricks to blitz from the outside.

We opened the scoring with a touchdown, and that was all the offense got all day. The Raiders put in a new blitzing scheme for this game. It had cornerback Lester Hayes and strong safety Mike Davis coming from the left side and they each got me twice. Hendricks and each of the ends got me once apiece. One problem was that our right tackle got hurt and the backup, who because of injuries himself hadn't practiced much, could not make the blocking calls that would have allowed us to pick up the blitzes. The other problem was there just weren't a lot of adjustments that could be made in the Oilers' conservative, old-fashioned offense. The machine just didn't have many adjustables on it.

I felt like a guy who had wandered into Oakland wearing a flattop haircut, wing-tip shoes, and carrying a slingshot, only to be set upon by a band of cutthroats bearing cutlasses. Fortunately, my former teammates took mercy on me. Six of the seven blitzes that got me came from the blind side and could have been hospitalization hits, but the guys just jumped on my back and rode me down. I appreciated that.

I guess overall I fared better than Dan Pastorini. He broke his leg in the fifth game of the season and never came back. Jim Plunkett took over and led the Raiders to victory in the Super Bowl, which is what I feel I would have done if I'd stayed in Oakland. Instead I'd gone to Houston with great expectations and got knocked out of the playoffs by Oakland in a 27–7 laugher.

Poor Bum. It was even worse for him. "They did things and we didn't have the adjustments," Bum said after the game. "We were outcoached."

As much as I loved him, I had to say he was right.

Still, I was shocked a few days later when Bum got fired and defensive coach Eddie Biles was named to replace him. But Bum was only out of work about twenty minutes before John Mecom hired him to coach the Saints.

Biles hired a new offensive coordinator, Jim Shofner, who said he would install a wide-open offensive system that would be more to my liking. That sounded good. Then Biles, who was a disciplinarian, started announcing that he would run a tougher training camp and said he expected Gifford Nielsen to make a serious bid for my job. That sounded like he was taking the fun out of football and that he didn't think much of my quarterbacking. Biles knew I was a Bum Phillips man.

Just before camp opened, I decided I'd had enough and announced my retirement. "We haven't closed the door on Kenny," Biles said, "but we are not going to actively pursue getting him to change his mind." Thank you very much, Ed.

But as July rolled into August, I was getting itchy to play football again. Late that month, Nielsen tore up his shoulder and I decided to come back. The Oilers were in a bind and my lawyer negotiated a two-year contract worth $800,000, but it wasn't the money that got my signature. This team had some excellent talent and with a new offense I felt we could win. My teammates welcomed me back. Two of the most outspoken supporters were, not surprisingly, receivers.

Ken Burrough, who had been sidelined most of last season with injuries, said, "All these years I watched Snake and I used to think, 'Oh my God, what would it be like to work with a quarterback like that?' So he becomes my teammate and I get hurt. Then I get well and he retires. When I look back on my career someday, that would be my biggest regret—not getting to play a full season with Snake."

"Snake can help us," Mike Renfro said. "He's a masterful quarterback. And he's fun to go out with because there's always a lot of women around him, and I need all the help I can get."

Biles, I learned immediately, was serious about curfews. At 11 P.M. he had the dorm doors locked so no one could get in or out. He had also made a rule that players had to be present at all meals. On that rule, one player lodged a small protest, and not surprisingly it was an ex-Raider. Dave Casper had arrived at breakfast one morning carrying his pillow and a blanket. He put the pillow on his plate, his head on the pillow, pulled the blanket around his shoulders, and went back to sleep.

Biles—who had fined a rookie $2,000 for bringing a girl into his room—did nothing to Dave. He had made All-Pro in 1980 for the fourth successive year (Mike Barber was second-team), and coaches make all kinds of allowances for real good football players. Besides, Dave was probably tired.

During the following day's practice, I wasn't sorry I had missed all those two-a-day workouts in the San Angelo sun. But I needed a good week of running and throwing to get my wind and my arm back. I told the writers it would all come relatively easy, that I enjoyed being back.

"This is much better than drinking beer and lying on the beach," I said. "Running plays and dying, that's much more fun."

Two days later the New York *Times* ran a story headlined: FOOT-BALL'S KEN STABLER IS LINKED TO A GAMBLER. It was then reported by every other newspaper and newscaster in the country. The story said that for the last few years I had associated with a gambler named Nick Dudich and was blown up all out of proportion. Because it also said that "according to a variety of law enforcement sources" I had been "subjected to physical surveillance and other investigations" in Oakland and in Houston, which had been dropped because I had done nothing wrong.

What I had done was have a few drinks over the years with a nice old guy named Nick Dudich, who said he had a string of beauty parlors in New Jersey. If I was guilty of anything, so was everybody else on the Raiders. As Phil Villapiano, who was now with the Bills, said, "Nick was one of our best fans, one of the boys, and we enjoyed having him around. But never at any time did Nick pump us for any football information. Never."

At one point in 1978, John Madden had told the whole team that Nick Dudich was a gambler and that we shouldn't have him in our rooms at camp or on the road. But Nick still showed up from time to time at airport or hotel bars, and a lot of us continued to have a beer or two with him. I didn't gamble on anything, but I never cared what other people did.

What was most upsetting about the *Times* story was that it reported that Dudich had been seen in our hotel before the Jet game, then said, "The Oilers, who were favored, lost, 31–28, in overtime. Four Stabler passes were intercepted."

I felt some people might imply from that that I'd thrown the game, which made me sick. It didn't make sense that anyone would throw four interceptions on purpose, then throw four touchdown passes. But you never knew what people might think. "Some shit," I decided, "you just have to live with."

Ladd Herzeg, the Oiler general manager, pointed out to me that in the *Times* story Al Davis said the Raiders had reported my so-called association with Dudich to the NFL office "at least fifteen times." Yet the league had not contacted me. It was as if Davis was trying to embarrass Pete Rozelle and the league office. Al had been fighting the NFL in court for the right to move the Raiders to Los Angeles, a trial that had recently ended with a hung jury.

Al was slick. You never knew what he might do, but if he smeared my name just to get at Rozelle, that was dirty pool. It was also absurd for Al to claim in the *Times* that for three years he had tried to get the league to have me stop seeing Dudich. If Al Davis really wanted me to stop my occasional beers with Dudich, he certainly could have forced me to. I worked for Al. And when Al Davis said jump, you jumped.

Sometimes now, though, I wished I hadn't jumped out of Oakland. The difference between playing with the Raiders and playing with the Oilers was not so much in personnel. The main difference was that the Raider players began every season with the belief that they were going to win, and that come playoff time they would be there. The Raiders played to win. The Oilers played not to lose. And that, subconsciously, was the attitude I felt among my teammates. They just hadn't been winning long enough to have that ingrained confidence that permeated the Raiders. Winning was expected, and that attitude all started at the top with Al Davis.

Ed Biles and Jim Shofner dropped the I formation, as they had planned. We ran a two-back offense and we won our first two games. When we lost the next two, we returned to the I—just turn and hand the ball to Earl. We hadn't given our line and backs time to adjust to the new blocking combinations. But in the I, defenses were stacking their fronts against Earl, and in that formation you can't get your backs out to catch the ball. It was frustrating.

The whole season was frustrating. While other teams were using modern, multiformation offenses that spread defenses and gave them room to run or pass, we were stuck in an antique system that had defenses standing on our toes before every snap of the ball. It had been bad enough the year before, when I had completed 64.1 percent of my passes for 3,202 yards. In 1981, I completed 57.9 percent for only 1,988 yards. When you run the I, you scrap the pass.

For the first time in my life, I missed two games in a season. I sprained my left wrist—of all things to sideline a gimpy-legged quarterback—when it struck a helmet as I followed through on a pass. But I can't say I missed much. The Oilers after Bum left didn't have much going for them. Ed Biles didn't have Bum's charisma, and I don't think guys put out for Biles like they had for Bum.

Biles ran the team like a Marine sergeant, and very few players applauded that. When we were in a hotel on the road, Biles actually posted someone by the elevators to see that no players slipped out.

Another thing that hurt Biles with the players was the fact that he talked out of both sides of his mouth. He'd come over to me and say, "Boy, our defense is struggling. I don't know what's wrong with Robert Brazile," and he'd tick off a couple of other names.

Then a defensive player would say to me, "Do you know what Biles said about you and the offense?"

"Well," I'd say, "I know what he said about the defense, so I can guess what he said about the offense. Of course, whatever he said about us is probably true because we're playing like shit."

For the first time in my football life—high school, college and pro—I played for a losing team. The Oilers finished with a 7–9 record.

I was a good soldier all season, too, never missing or even being late for a meeting or a practice. Except on November 11. I happened to get double lucky the night before, connecting with two women who stayed over at my place. In the morning we were still having so much fun that I couldn't get my ass moving to practice. Besides, there wasn't much I could do with a bum wrist. Later that Wednesday, I heard on the radio that it was a holiday. Great.

The next morning I read in the Houston *Post:* "I'm sure Kenny had a good reason for not being here today," Biles said. "I just wish he'd called."

I went right in to see Biles. "I'm sure you've got an explanation, Kenny," he said.

"Didn't you know what day yesterday was, Ed?" I asked.

"What do you mean?" he said.

"It was Veterans Day," I said. "I had to take off, Ed. I'm a twelve-year veteran."

Biles smiled. "It'll cost you $500."

The Veterans Day excuse became the joke of the week among the players. "What's your next holiday, Snake?" someone said. "Are you gonna take off Thanksgiving because you're an old turkey?"

It was nice to have a little levity. There wasn't a whole lot of it that year with the Oilers.

12

~~~~~~~~~~~~~~~~~~~~~~

Records, Like Rules, Were Made to Be Broken

I guess everyone needs a friend he can share his innermost feelings with, particularly when the shit flies the way it had been flying around me in recent years. I had a lot of good friends in and out of football, guys I liked a lot and enjoyed being with, but the only person I could ever really spill my guts to was Randall Watson. He was the brother I never had by birth.

I was always a private person in a public profession. Many people may have thought otherwise because I spent so much time out mingling with the public, sipping a drink, talking football, having a good time in full view of the folks who watched me play, and occasionally had considerable advice as to how I might do better on the field. I generally took the comments—good and bad—in stride.

I always tried to be calm, cool, in complete control no matter what the situation, in ball games or in bar games, and there were only a few slipups. I didn't show emotion on the field because I felt the quarterback should lead by example. I guess I adopted that unemotional style from the two major role models in my life: my father and Coach

Bryant. Both of them were strong, poised individuals who enjoyed being out and doing things among folks who tended to admire and respect them. They got a lot of love out of their socializing, as did I, and I loved them both.

I loved Randall Watson for a different reason. He was a total rebel who had no respect whatsoever for authority. I was a semirebel, a man pledged to live my life in my own way, but generally within the rules. I bent the rules, stretched them to their limits, but only occasionally overstepped them. To Randall, rules were meant to be challenged, ignored, circumvented, or flat-out broken when that course seemed the only appropriate one to him. Randall was an outlaw in the romantic sense of the word if you were his friend, and most people liked him either because of or in spite of that. But he was an enemy you would not have sicced on your own worst enemy. He played *hard* hardball.

I met Randall way back in 1967 through a guy I knew in Mobile when I was hanging out there after being suspended by Coach Bryant. Hollis Davis was a serious weight lifter. He told me he was going to Monroeville to pick up some steel plates from Randall Watson and asked if I'd like to ride along. I had nothing better to do on a lazy spring afternoon than take a two-hour ride and drink beer.

We pulled into a little country town—three stoplights and two cautions—and stopped at Watson's Auto Parts. Randall, a stocky, broad-shouldered guy who had obviously done some weight lifting himself, was outside the place working on his dragster. He had long blond hair that he parted in the middle and combed back on the sides. Facially he resembled Mickey Dolenz, the lead singer of the Monkees singing group, and he gave us a big smile. I later learned that Randall never met any strangers, that he talked to everyone he met about anything they wanted to discuss.

He said the weights were at his cabin up on the Alabama River, and told us to follow him. The cabin was twenty-seven miles out of Monroeville. We covered the last seven miles on a dirt road through thick woods and stopped at a cabin overlooking the river.

We got out and Randall said, "This place's so far back in the woods, in the old days you had to ride a pregnant mule into town so you'd have transportation back."

I liked him right away. There was just a natural chemistry between

Randall and myself that I'd never had with anyone else and never would have with another man. We both liked to hunt and fish. We both liked fast cars and fast boats. Randall not only had a race car but a hopped-up pickup truck, a motorcycle, and a twenty-foot bass-fishing boat with a 50 h.p. Mercury hung on the back. That was about twice the motor that fishing boat needed to get around quick. Randall just liked to get around quicker.

We sat around talking and drinking beer for a few hours that first day, and there is no way I could calculate how many drinks we had together over the next fifteen years. The word "countless" might apply. Randall came to see me play my senior year at Alabama and he caught a few games almost every year thereafter until he was killed in 1982. He'd jump on a plane and fly to Oakland, New York, Chicago, Denver, wherever. He really couldn't afford to lay out that kind of money, but somehow he found a way. Randall usually seemed to find a way to get things done.

How he got the cabin and all the land around it was with the insurance money he received after another house he'd built happened to burn down during a lightning storm. Unable to sell the house for what it was worth and wanting to move into the woods, Randall took matters into his own hands. He tied a burning cigarette to a string and hung it over an open jar of gasoline. He was miles away by the time the cigarette burned through the string and the embers fell into the gas.

Every off-season I would spend a week or so up at the cabin with Randall, and he regularly visited me in Gulf Shores. But I always looked forward to that time in the woods. I'd leave the crowds, the noise, the pressures, and the game wherever it was at season's end and just relax with my friend in total isolation. His backyard offered some of the best fishing and his frontyard some of the best hunting in the entire state.

We would fish, hunt, cook the fresh meat on his wood stove, feast, tell tales, and sip whiskey. No need to shave. No need to change clothes if you didn't feel like it, until your jeans got so stiff you could hardly bend in them. It was all a great release for me.

Randall, who was three years older than me, was a big family man. Even after he and his first wife divorced, his two oldest kids, Randy and Melanie, stayed with him summers and most weekends. Another son, Scooter, came along when he remarried about ten years later. And Randall gave his kids everything he could as they grew up, including their own motorcycles and their own boat. He hadn't had much himself when he was growing up as the only boy among seven sisters. That's why his kids always came first with him.

Like Slim, Randall's father was a pretty tough, demanding man. I didn't get to know him real well, as he died not long after Slim did. But from what Randall and I shared about our fathers, we decided they were similar men, both big influences on their sons. We both tried to impress our fathers, but we didn't seem to make them all that happy.

Perhaps it was this similarity in our backgrounds that underpinned our friendship and trust. But if I had a problem that I couldn't bring myself to talk about with anyone else, I'd get on the phone to Randall or go see him. He was the same way. We could say anything to each other, spill our guts about marital problems, work problems, life problems. I'd hold it all in with others, but with Randall I just felt comfortable opening up. Not that he helped me solve anything that was bugging me. He was just there—a good listener, understanding.

I played the same role with him and with a number of teammates over the years. When players came to me with problems, I always tried to make myself available. "Let's get a beer and chew on it." I'd listen, but I never offered opinions unless I was asked to. When the problem concerned marital difficulties, I'd say, "After two divorces myself, I'm the wrong man to consult. You can be sure my next career won't be marriage counseling."

Sometimes I thought it might be nice to have a teammate I could share my feelings with the way I could with Randall because just getting things out was a relief. But it just seemed that as long as I had a close friend like Randall, I didn't need anyone else. I felt that a quarterback had to be close to his teammates, yet he also had to keep a certain distance from them.

As I said, though, Randall had no regard for authority. He hated being told what he could or could not do. That was one reason why he chose to live way back in the woods, figuring he wouldn't be hassled there. But trouble was never far from Randall Watson.

He decided that most laws did not apply to him, and certainly none that were attached to hunting and fishing. He never went deer hunting to bring back one kill; he always shot at least four. He'd put away enough meat for two months and pass along the rest to the relatives he had all over Monroe County. He made the best venison sausage, mixing it with 40 percent pork, that I ever tasted.

Of course, the way he hunted was illegal. I was with him several times when he shined deer. We'd get a half gallon of Jack Daniel's and drive his pickup truck into the woods. Then we'd pass the bottle until we heard a deer, Randall would turn on his headlights, the deer would momentarily freeze, and we'd shoot it. As Alabama has the second-largest deer population of any state in the country next to Texas, shining deer did not seem illegal, particularly when none of the meat was wasted. We wouldn't pick up the deer until morning, after the rifles were left in the cabin. If you had a rifle and a dead deer in your truck at night, the law could nab you. But Randall had a dog that had pissed on every tree in his woods and he had no trouble finding the deer carcasses in daylight.

Randall also brought in all the fish he ate year-round. Some days he'd have smoked fish for breakfast, fried fish for lunch, and grilled fish for dinner. A typical serious freshwater fisherman will buy a tackle box and fill it with twenty different lures, two or three rods, and four or five reels with various test lines on them. Then he'll go fishing for eight hours and come home with twenty pounds of fish on a good day.

Not Randall. His tackle box wasn't heavy at all because he didn't have one. His rod consisted of two sticks of dynamite stuck in his belt and his tackle box was his jeans pocket containing dynamite caps and matches. He'd take that gear out in his boat for thirty minutes and come back with 100 pounds of fish. He'd have so many fish in his boat it would about sink.

But he wouldn't bring all the fish home. There were a lot of poor black families living along the Alabama River. Randall would spot an old man fishing off his broken-down dock with a cane pole and he'd turn the boat and head over there.

"Here comes Blondy!" the old man would holler.

Randall would pull up and throw the man a couple of catfish—some weighed up to twenty pounds—and maybe a brim and a largemouth bass. At every black home on the river, if someone was outside, Randall would toss them some fish.

Everybody in Monroeville knew Randall and most people called him "Blondy." All the hip young blacks who had cars, the shiny riders, would get their parts from Blondy and ask his advice about how to make their vehicles go faster.

After cleaning a mess of fish for himself, saving four or five days' of fresh meat, freezing some and smoking some, Randall gave away the rest to friends and relatives. A lot of poor folks appreciated his gifts.

But one day a new game warden showed up and said to Randall, "You know it's illegal to fish with dynamite."

"You mean people actually hang a line off a stick of dynamite and fish?" Randall said.

"I better not catch you," the game warden said. "Or I'll have to be confiscating your boat."

So Randall came up with another way to bring in a whole mess of fish quickly. This time silently. He just didn't have time to fish for hours, run his auto parts business, and work on his race car. Yet a lot of people counted on him to supply them with fish. So Randall bought a Hercules fence charger, which is normally used to keep cattle away from fences inside a pasture. He put the charger and a big car battery into his boat. He ran a wire from the charger to the battery, and attached another wire to a long chain that would drag the river bottom. And fish that swam within three feet of the charger would be stunned and float to the surface. Randall would just scoop them up in his net.

Watching him, it was almost magical, a guy putting along in a boat, net in hand, and fish floating up to him, as if Randall had cast a spell and the fish were just volunteering for the frying pan. It was certainly a more humane way to fish than any other method I'd seen.

Of course, Randall improved on his method. He reduced by half the amount of time he needed to catch 100 pounds of fish. All he did was hop up his Hercules fence charger. It worked off a set of points like those in the condenser of a distributor, the charge going out each time the points closed. By wrapping a rubber band around the points, Randall made them snap closed faster and thus throw more current faster.

But using the charger to fish was no more legal than using dynamite. And one day when Randall was unloading his catch on the dock near his cabin, the game warden stepped out of the bushes. The boat, motor, battery, and charger were all seized and held for ninety days.

Randall was not pleased. Not at all. He decided to send that game warden a message. Knowing the day the warden patroled that section of the river, Randall waited for him atop a 100-foot bluff some four miles from the cabin. He heard the whine of the outboard, peered through the scope on his .30-caliber rifle, and waited for the warden to come into view. When he did, his hand twisting the throttle arm on the outboard motor, Randall fired and blew the cowling off the top of the motor. The message was: Do not fuck with Randall Watson in his own backyard.

The game warden must have thought he'd motored into *Deliverance* because Randall seldom saw the man after that shot.

Whenever he was offended, Randall always got mad and then he usually got even. One spring, during the Easter school vacation, he brought Randy and Melanie down to Gulf Shores. He booked rooms for the weekend at the hotel in the State Convention Center, a beautiful new building on the beach. He was going to spend the rest of the week with me at my place. He drove down in his Lincoln Mark V and turned off Highway 182 into the center's long driveway. It wasn't until he was within twenty feet of the parking lot that he realized he was in the exit driveway. A big blue Mercury was coming at him.

They both stopped. Randall looked over his shoulder and saw he would have to back up some two hundred feet onto the highway. So he got out and walked to the other driver. "I'd appreciate it if you'd back up about twenty feet and let me get by," Randall said. "I know I screwed up, but I don't want to go backing out on that highway."

The other driver rolled up his window and sat there. Randall got back in his car and refused to move. Finally the guy got out and went to the convention center on foot, returning with two security officers. They put their heads together and decided, rather than have the other driver move his car the equivalent of seven paces, that Randall should back up two hundred feet.

Randall backed up and waited on the highway shoulder until the Mercury pulled out. It turned into a nightclub just down the road called Jerry and Wayne's. Randall kept going to the Holiday Inn a quarter of a mile beyond. He checked in there, got his kids settled, then walked to the nightclub. Opening the entrance door to the place, he heard deafeningly loud music. "Just what I figured," he said to himself.

Then he walked around the parking lot until he spotted the Mercury in back. He pulled a .357 Magnum from his jacket, shot through the engine block four times, and shot out the two near-side tires.

The first thing he said to me when he got to my place on Monday was the first thing he said every time I talked to Randall: "Snake, you'll never guess what happened to me the other night!"

There was no way I could ever guess, so I said, "I give up."

"I killed a cougar," he said. "A Mercury Cougar."

Randall had some real fast race cars over the years and he was a hellacious driver, absolutely fearless. He won a lot of drag races and loved the sport. Not for the money, as the prizes were only $200 or so, and keeping up the car was expensive. Randall just loved to compete. The only thing he loved more than competing was winning.

One of his top cars was a black '49 Chevy that he called "Big Iron." Painted on its doors were pictures of pistols with smoke floating out of the barrels. A crack mechanic in Pensacola named Jack Arnold put together the racing engine in that car and it could fly. But after a successful season with Big Iron, Randall started losing because other racers had more money to put into their machines.

That wasn't going to stop Randall from winning again. In drag racing, cars had to compete against others in the same class. The cars were classed by how much they weighed and how many cubic inches their engines displaced.

Randall welded a wide-pipe bumper on the back of his car and threaded a cap on each end of the pipe. He would open the caps and shove into the bumper about twenty cans that he'd filled with lead. That would add about three hundred pounds to Big Iron for the weigh-in. Afterward he would remove the cans and race against cars that were three hundred pounds heavier than his. Advantage: Randall. For a few months he just blew away the competition.

Then someone got wise and protested one of Randall's victories. When Big Iron was weighed after the race, officials took away Randall's prize money and his tin trophy. That was a mistake.

Randall put his race car in its trailer and drove home. But that night he went back to the track with some dynamite. He set the charge beneath the timing tower and attached a very slow fuse. About forty minutes later the tower blew over and fell across the race track.

"Snake," he said when he called me the next day, "you'll never guess what happened at Pensacola. They weighed Big Iron *after* I'd won the goddamn race! Ain't that a bitch!"

"Yeah. Well, I guess they won't be racing there for a while," I said. "I heard someone blew up the timing tower last night."

"Now ain't that a shame," he said.

Randall Watson didn't do many things in even a halfway legal manner. When he got caught, he usually came back at the catchers in a way where he couldn't be caught again. He believed in standing up for his outlaw rights.

But Randall would also stand up for other people he felt were deserving of help.

We both owned motorcycles we liked to cruise around on and boats we raced around the Intracoastal Waterway. But we never raced the motorcycles because I had a career to think of and they were just too dangerous. But it was fun sitting back on a bike with the wind whipping over you, not unlike the refreshing feeling you got in a boat with the salty air in your face.

One day Randall and I made a nice motorcycle trip to Sarasota, where I ordered a new speedboat. Back in Gulf Shores, we stopped at The Flora-Bama Lounge to have a beer and listen to some music. We had enjoyed the new singer we'd heard there the night before. He was on the little bandstand jutting out among the tables in the narrow room, just finishing a song as we took stools at the bar.

"I would really appreciate it if you all would listen to this next song," the singer said. "I just wrote the song, it means a lot to me, and I'd like to know how you folks like it. I'm kinda proud of it."

He was a nice-looking young man, lean, round-shouldered, with sad liquid eyes and a touching sincerity. Randall nudged me with an elbow and said, "This is gonna be good."

The place quieted down and the musician began playing his guitar and singing a song that was funny and sad and moving all at once. About midway through the song, three guys at a table in front of us started talking. One guy was real loud, laughing obnoxiously.

The singer stopped and said, "Hey, fellas, I'd really like you to listen to this. It's only about three minutes long, so if you please, just listen to it once." He smiled a small smile. "If you don't like it at the end, you can let me know then. Okay?"

He began again, and within thirty seconds the guy with the obnoxious laugh was heard from. Randall slid right off the stool and grabbed the guy from behind by both ears. He shook his head up and down real hard four or five times and the guy squealed. Then Randall glared down at the three guys and said, "The singer asked us to be quiet for three minutes. Now all of you shut the fuck up!"

It immediately got so quiet at that table you could've heard a mouse fart. Then the singer resumed, and finished his song without interruption. Those three guys clapped politely, paid their bill, and left.

But that was Randall, as soon as he was moved to do something, he did it. Screw the consequences. Essentially, he lived by his wits after he sold the auto parts business and gave up the American gas station he ran for some years. Then he took to buying, rebuilding, and selling cars and trucks. He also wheeled and dealed boats and lived simply in the woods. But once he outwitted himself when he tied in with a group of guys who tried to rob a bank in Mississippi. He had to serve eighteen months in prison, and my lawyer helped him get an early release.

Later, authorities put him away for another six months on a shitty charge. Randall had a fifteen-year-old nephew named Ashley who was a deaf mute. He bought the boy a .22-caliber rifle and taught him how to shoot it. But convicted felons are not allowed to buy firearms.

By the time Randall was released, I had been talking to a banker friend of mine about putting together a program to go for the outboard motorboat speed record. Outboard racing is superdangerous because the driver has little protection around him; the boat and motor together weigh only 800 pounds. We put $20,000 into a Hydrostream boat with a V-6 Mercury outboard built by Bill Sebold. It was designed to surpass the world record of 112 m.p.h. held by Wilbur Weeks of Jay, Florida. When I asked Randall if he wanted to go for the record, he didn't hesitate.

"Let's do it," he said. "I'd love to hold a world record." For Randall, records, like rules, were made to be broken.

Randall knew Wilbur Weeks and his son Wayne, and got them to help him set up our boat. But Randall was in charge, and he did everything his way. That was the only way with him, and there wasn't a lot of precision about the man. For example, every time a bug squashed on one of my vehicles I washed it. The only time Randall washed one of his vehicles was when he was ready to sell it.

I was playing in New Orleans in 1982 and Randall was working out the boat there. He entered a preliminary race in Shreveport, Louisiana, before going for the record. I was in Chicago that day to play the Bears. Later, I found out that Randall had started off fine. He was ahead of his opponent when suddenly the boat got loose on him, flipped up into the air, and as Randall came out of it the motor hit him in the head. His neck was broken.

Saints owner John Mecom called just before game time and told me about the accident, offering to send his private jet to fly me back to Louisiana. "Thanks, John," I said, "but I'm gonna play. There's nothing I can do except go help Randall's family when his body's shipped home."

After we beat the Bears, I flew to Alabama and took care of the funeral expenses, making sure that Randall's life insurance and homeowner's policy would cover the children's future.

It's funny, but throughout the day I spent in Monroeville I kept thinking that every time I pulled into Randall's gas station, I'd shake his hand and then get me a Coke from his machine and a bag of Tom's peanuts from the counter. Randall would do the same, and we'd pour nuts into the Coke, shake it up real fizzy, then drink and eat at the same time. I still had that taste in my mouth.

It was almost two years later before I found another person I could share my soul with as I could with Randall, my wife Rose Molly. Randall Watson was an original, a man who always went his own way, and I kind of liked the fact that nobody could ever change him. But I guess I always knew that he wasn't going to die in any old folks home.

I also know I'll always miss him.

13

"Save the Last Pass for Me."

I couldn't have been happier when Ed Biles put me on waivers in July 1982. I knew I couldn't play for the man some of the Oilers referred to as "The Shaky Corporal." I liked offensive coordinator Jim Shofner, who had tried to open up the offense, but Biles had been too scared to stick with it. He had kept the entire team in disarray all season, and I wanted no part of that again.

As a free agent, I could have signed with a number of teams. The only coach I would have played for no matter where he was, John Madden, was no longer coaching. But when Bum Phillips called, my decision was made for me. I respected Bum and he was coaching in New Orleans, a city I had loved all the way back to my college days. Also, the money offered by the Saints, $450,000, was top dollar. That was the figure on my last Oiler contract and my lawyer could not negotiate a higher figure because the Players Association and the league did not have a contract. But I was satisfied.

I reported to training camp on August 24. The Saints' starting quarterback, Archie Manning, was sidelined with a sore wrist and his backup, Dave Wilson, was on injured-reserve with a bad knee. On August 25 I passed a football for the first time in seven months. Three days later Bobby Scott started at quarterback in a preseason game against the Browns. We were down 17–3 when I relieved in the second half and took the team on two long touchdown marches to tie the score. Even though a field goal beat us at the end, I had completed eleven of seventeen passes for 149 yards and felt good.

"I think he got everybody's respect," end Jeff Groth said after that game, and that's what I was looking for. Once again I went through the media guide and educated myself on my new teammates' backgrounds so that I could get to know them quickly. I liked the looks of the team. Twenty-three of the players were only in their second year and there appeared to be good talent on the club. This was a franchise that had never had a winning season, and I liked the challenge of trying to turn things around.

"Kenny knew everybody's name as soon as he arrived in camp," center John Hill told the press. "He'll ask you things about your family or your hometown. And Kenny has a very relaxed nature which kind of exudes confidence."

"He makes everybody feel like an important part of the team and I mean *everybody,*" rookie wide receiver Lindsay Scott said. "Here's a guy I've watched on TV as a kid and I come in here and immediately I've got a good rapport with him. Everybody does."

The situation with Archie Manning was a little awkward. The Saints had been *his* team for a decade and I had tremendous respect for Archie, a good quarterback playing all those years with ball clubs that weren't up to his skills. All I could do was be complimentary about him as I fought to take his job. In the season opener against St. Louis, I generated only one touchdown drive before Manning replaced me in the third quarter. He didn't do any better and we lost 21–7. A few days later, Bum traded Archie to Houston for offensive tackle Leon Gray. That relieved any tension that might've been in the air.

Winning three out of our next four games helped build everybody's confidence and led Saints' owner John Mecom to say, "Bum kept telling this team they were capable of winning. They were beginning to believe. Then Kenny came along and showed them how."

Bum said, "I think Kenny Stabler is absolutely the best leader I've ever seen."

We couldn't sustain the winning record, though, and finished with a 4–5 record in this season that was shortened by a fifty-seven-day strike. Our major problem, in my view, was again Bum's conservative offensive philosophy. That kind of surprised me because Bum had told the press that he had been responsible for the Oiler offensive problems in the 1980 season in Houston. "My mistake," he said, "was not tailoring our offense to what Kenny could do best."

I was determined to push harder for a more wide-open attack in 1983 because I truly believed the Saints could be a winning football team. I knew I didn't have the physical skills that I'd had four or five years earlier, but I made the guys believe they had an opportunity to win and they broke their asses for me. I'd already been where they wanted to go and that carried a lot of weight with them.

So the aging process had taken some arm strength, but I'd never been a game breaker anyway. I was always a touch passer, which was why my completion percentage was so high. In 1982 I had completed 61.9 percent of my throws. The idea was to control the ball and move it into the end zone. Winning, that's all that mattered, and I was always sure I could find a way if I wasn't handcuffed.

At season's end I had a complete physical examination. I had two physicals every year because I had been concerned about my blood pressure, heart rate, and cholesterol level ever since my father had died suddenly so young. His brother Harold had also died young, as had my mother's brother. The doctor now told me my cholesterol count was high and advised me to change my diet. That touched my mortality.

I stopped eating meat, eggs, salt, and sugar, and I virtually quit smoking. Within the year I quit smoking entirely. I also cut out hard liquor, which I believed had combined with my father's smoking to kill him. I was amazed at how much better I felt almost immediately following the diet change. After going real hard for over fifteen years, I finally decided it was time to begin taking care of myself.

In the late spring I drove to New Orleans to sign for the 1983 season and I met with Bum Phillips for about forty-five minutes. I told him I knew that he and King Hill, his offensive coordinator, believed in the I formation, but I said it was almost impossible to build a big lead with that attack and it was totally impossible to come from behind using it. "We need to open up our offense and spread out the defense the way Oakland does. We have the personnel here to do that. We've got a big strong running back in George Rogers, and we've got backs like Wayne Wilson and Hokie Gajan who can run and also catch the ball out of the backfield. Now if we spread things out and throw the ball in short-yardage situations, we'll open up the medium passes and the opportunity for an occasional long one."

As I was talking, I put some stuff up on the blackboard and Bum kept nodding. When I finished, Bum said, "Go see King."

I went to see King Hill and repeated myself, including chalking up his blackboard and running down plays and personnel. King gave me the impression that he agreed with me.

But when we got to training camp, I still found myself in the I formation, taking the ball from the center, turning and handing off to George Rogers. Instead of playing to win, Bum and King still insisted on playing not to lose. That's what we did. We didn't lose and we didn't win. We played .500 football in 1983.

Our 8–8 record would have been 9–7 if we had won the season's final game, which also would have put us into the playoffs. Had we done so, the city of New Orleans would have gone absolutely berserk. The fans there were great, people who had waited so long for the Saints to win. I loved those people and their spirit. They loved to party, to eat and drink and celebrate life. The Mardi Gras came annually, but the French Quarter rocked year-round. I would have given anything to win for those folks.

But I couldn't get it done in that final game. We were trailing the Rams 9–7 early in the third quarter and, trying to bring us back, I threw a pass that I shouldn't have released. As I did, Jack Youngblood hit me and the ball was intercepted and returned for a touchdown. I was helped off the field and Dave Wilson came in. He led the team to two touchdowns and a field goal. We were leading 24–23 with ten seconds on the clock when the Rams kicked a forty-two-yard field goal to win the game.

So my season ended the way it began—in pain. On my first pass of 1983 I was hit and tore cartilage in the right knee, and I should have had arthroscopic surgery right then. Instead I kept playing, icing down the knee daily and having it drained all season. All told, I was forced to leave four ball games and in two others I couldn't play a down. I seldom practiced more than one day before any game. Bum Phillips told the press, "Kenny just doesn't need the work necessary for most quarterbacks. He could play—and play well—without taking one practice snap."

In truth, my timing would have been better if I had been able to get in more work. But playing on the artificial turf of the Superdome caused my knee to take on fluid for a week. Just moving about on that surface for a few hours would cause my knee to be three times as sore as it was after a game on grass.

Artificial turf was probably the worst thing ever created for football players. Ironically, it was supposed to be a godsend. Turf manufacturers claimed it would reduce knee injuries, but it has actually increased them. Turf does not give at all, so that a planted foot will not slide when you're hit—and then something has to go. Usually a knee or an ankle. I have seen players tear up knees and ankles just running and cutting on synthetic surfaces without being hit. And a number of top players like Jack Lambert and Larry Csonka have had to retire early after suffering what is called "Turf Toe," where the foot glues to the surface, causing ligament and tissue damage.

The fact is, playing on an artificial surface is like playing on asphalt. That is what's under the green synthetic carpet, and as the rug wears it gets harder and harder. Then it becomes more like concrete. That's why you see so many players suffer broken bones from simple falls on it. That's why so many players are helped off the artificial fields with concussions. They wear the best helmets that technology can produce, but when your head inside that helmet bangs off the turf your brain gets scrambled. It happened to me while playing for the Raiders in Chicago and in New Orleans.

Artificial playing surfaces are so destructive to players that coaches who care—as most do—will not let their teams practice on them. Only when the weather was bad did Bum Phillips's teams work out on a carpeted field. Even when the Raiders were going to play a team that had turf, John Madden and Tom Flores had us do only a light workout on it, just enough to get used to the traction.

If the Raiders of my day had had an artificial surface at the Coliseum, I would never have lasted fifteen years in the NFL. No player with gimpy knees lasts long on asphalt. And I was somewhat fortunate that the turf in Houston and New Orleans was inside covered stadiums because the turf in open fields magnifies the weather conditions, holding the heat or the cold. In Kansas City, for example, on hot days the turf burns your feet and on cold days it freezes them.

The only players who like synthetic fields are the fast receivers who can cut quicker on them and placekickers who admire a true surface. Everyone else just hates that plastic shit. Football was meant to be played on natural grass, which doesn't punish you. It gives. It prolongs careers. But the carpeted fields are cheaper to maintain than grass, and most owners play bottom-line football. They go for the profit and say to hell with the players. The bodies can be replaced cheaper than the turf. Hundreds of fresh new players come out of colleges every year. More fodder for the asphalt maimings.

Throughout the 1983 season it was hard for me to walk around a pool table, much less play football, and it was reflected in my stats. While I completed 56.6 percent of my passes, they gained only 1,988 yards and accounted for just nine touchdowns. That didn't keep the Memphis Showboats of the United States Football League from offering me $1 million to play for them in February. My attorney, Henry Pitts, reached "an agreement in principle with the Showboats," the Memphis *Commercial Appeal* reported, and that much money for one more season would have been nice. But I needed arthroscopic surgery on both knees and several months afterward to get my legs in shape. The 'Boats would have to float without me.

Besides, Bum said he wanted me back with the Saints, as did a bunch of my teammates. "Maybe it's the fact that he's a legend or maybe the fact that he's just the kind of guy he is," halfback Hokie Gajan said. "I've never been around a guy like him before. Dave Wilson's a great young quarterback, no doubt about that. But one of the biggest things that's helped Dave these last two years is having Snake here. He's a winner."

"Snake's meant an awful lot to me," said center John Hill, who had played for twelve years. "He's been kind of a catalyst to get this team the confidence it needed to do the things that it did."

My only regret was that I couldn't have done more. A .500 season was better than a losing record, but just barely.

Still, there were a couple of bright moments during the season. One was the occasion of Bum's sixtieth birthday, when the players threw a little party for him, complete with a massive birthday cake and a whole lot of "Bumweiser." I presented him with a large photo a photographer had taken of us together. I was standing with my arm around Bum's shoulders, my hair and beard coming out even grayer in the sunlight. As usual, Bum was wearing sunglasses and one of his thirty-five cowboy hats.

"Thanks, Kenny," Bum said, accepting the photograph. Then he held it up for all the team to see and said, "I ask you, which one of these sumbitches looks older?"

"The Snake!" everyone yelled, and I broke up.

The other bright moment occurred before some 65,000 people in the Superdome. We moved to a 24–10 lead over the Bears in the third quarter. But George Rogers was injured and we couldn't get a running game going, so the Bears kept blitzing. They picked off three of my passes to send the game into overtime. We first touched the ball in OT on our two-yard line, and I told the guys, "Check with me at the line."

I called all the plays from there so that I could see exactly what the Bears were doing on defense. Mixing four passes that gained thirty-six yards with six runs that gained thirty-eight yards, we marched to the Bear twenty-four. Our fine field goal kicker, Morten Andersen, put one through the uprights from the forty-one.

The ironic thing in this game was that Walter Payton—the greatest all-around running back I ever played against—almost beat us by himself. Not just by rushing for 161 yards, including a 49-yard touchdown run, but by passing the ball twice and completing both for touchdowns. After the game, as I was dressing, Walter came into our locker room and shook my hand. I thought that was damn nice of him, and told him so.

"But don't go passing the ball," I said. "They'll be making a quarterback out of you."

"Not me," Walter said. "Quarterbacks don't make enough money."

I laughed. Walter Payton had signed a 1983 contract that paid him $700,000 a year, a record salary at the time. Of course, all he did was deserve every penny of it.

In early January I had both knees cleaned out and began a rehabilitation program, using a stationary bike and some weight-lifting machines. In six weeks my legs felt like new. I owned a big house on a golf course in New Orleans and another house on the beach in Gulf Shores, and I spent most of my time there in the off-season. I had invested in a number of other properties and was now negotiating to buy a marina.

Of course, I was also having a good time. And one of those relaxed occasions in February 1984 turned out to be the most important day of my life. I was having a drink one afternoon in The Passport Inn, which is on the second floor of the Top of the Port, a little hotel that looks out on the Gulf. I was sitting with some friends when a waiter said I had a phone call from the bar downstairs. I picked up and said, "Ken Stabler."

"My name's Rose Molly Burch," a girl's voice said. "My friends here told me who you were when I saw you walk in and go upstairs. And I'd just like to buy you a drink."

I decided, "Why not? If she doesn't appeal to me, it's one beer and I'm out of here."

My friends were leaving when Molly came up, and she was just a gorgeous little thing, about five-three and 105 pounds. She was twenty-six, Miss Alabama of 1979, and she was the sharpest girl I had ever met. Her mother was a Japanese war bride, her father a career sergeant, and Molly was a member of the first women's class at West Point. But Molly soon tired of carrying a rifle and enrolled at the University of South Alabama, where she earned an undergraduate degree and a master's in business administration. She didn't care about football.

"What made you interested in me?" I asked her.

"I like your size, your gray hair and beard," she said. "Just the way you look."

She had an apartment in Eastern Shore, down near Mobile, where she had been working for IBM until recently. I drove her home that night and began dating her every few days, then every two days, then every day. I was smitten, and she moved in with me. I sold the beach house and bought another on Ono Island, and we took turns partying there and in New Orleans. I felt like a kid again. Molly was *special* special, someone I decided I wanted to spend the rest of my life with. The 1984 season would be my last, then I'd retire and we'd start having kids. Molly agreed to marry me in June.

Meanwhile she introduced me to a guy who became a very close friend. Monroe Falterman, co-owner of The 544 Club on the corner of Bourbon St. and Toulouse, was always there when I needed him. I started going to The 544 Club my first season in New Orleans because Monroe had some of the best rhythm and blues sounds in town. His star is Gary Brown, who plays alto, tenor, and soprano sax. His group is called Gary Brown and Feelings, and he is so popular that Monroe has featured him at the club for over eight years. Another favorite of mine was singer Luther Kent, who I'd catch at Storyville.

Monroe Falterman knew everyone in the French Quarter and he showed me all around town. He had an apartment above The 544 Club with a balcony hanging out over Bourbon St. That's where we watched the Mardi Gras right after Molly and I got together, along with four other guys and their girls. As the costumed marchers came down the street below us, some of the guys started yelling at the women in the low-cut bodices: "Show us your tits! Show us your tits!"

The women looked up, laughing, and several of them spotted me and yelled, "Show us your knees! Show us your knees!"

I tugged the legs of my jeans up over my knees. The women cried, "All right, Snake!" and tugged down their bodices, then pranced on by.

"Kenny, enough of that!" Molly said, laughing.

About 4 A.M. Molly said she'd had it, and I drove her home. But I was still raring to go, having had nothing but light beer all night. I went back to Monroe's, we hit a couple of other joints, and ended up on his balcony again at eight-thirty in the morning, just the two of us.

"You know, Ken," he said, sipping a vodka on the rocks while I finished a final beer. "I'd like to make all the quarterbacks in the league equal right now, all of them in your state and having to play a game in a few hours. And you know who I'd bet on?"

"Yeah, the favorite," I said, laughing. "Me." And I believed that. No matter what the circumstances, I believed every time I went into a ball game that I was going to win.

In June, Molly and I were married at our house on Ono Island. One of the Alabama alumni who had helped recruit me, Judge Farrell McRae of Mobile, performed the ceremony. Three days later we threw the damnedest wedding party at the Riverview Hotel in Mobile. We rented the Alabama Room, of course, a big ballroom, and spent $15,000 on the reception. Luther Kent and his band supplied the music. Al Hirt played his horn as an extra added attraction. John

Mecom, Bum Phillips, and some four hundred other people had a good time with us. John Mecom owned an island off the coast of Mexico and he offered to fly us down to his villa for a honeymoon week. We thanked him kindly, but we had too much to do before camp opened in two weeks.

I had been working hard and wanted to keep at it. My legs felt better than they had in years and my weight was down to 195 pounds. I knew I would have to be at my best because Bum had traded for my Gulf Shores neighbor Richard Todd, a good young quarterback who figured to be the team's future. I felt I was its present, though, and I told Richard, "You've got to understand one thing—I'm still the man."

I got along well with Richard and we roomed together in training camp. The Saints trained at Dodgertown in Vero Beach, Florida, which had an eight-foot-high fence around it and a security guard at the main gate so players didn't sneak out after curfew. In 1983 I'd gone over the wall and crawled through the bushes once for a night out, but it was too much trouble. I had contented myself with having a few beers with the guys at the bar a short walk from the gate, then coming in for curfew and staying.

But in 1984 Richard and I would put a cooler of beer between our beds and stay in after the evening meeting, reading and watching ESPN. We went out to a movie or two, and finally one night we stopped at the bar. Carl Mauck, my old Oiler roommate who had been offensive line coach of the Saints ever since I joined them, said, "Easy Rider, I know you've been a model citizen here. But this year it looks like you've retired from partying entirely."

"Well, yeah," I said, "pretty much."

Since I'd married Molly, I had no interest in carousing, plus I had a job to win in the preseason. And I felt I outplayed Todd in the exhibition games. I started all of them except the last one, but I knew then that Richard was going to be the number one quarterback and I would be the backup. I didn't like it, but I didn't say anything.

I should have seen the handwriting on the wall back when Bum traded a number one draft choice for Richard Todd and signed him for a lot more money than the $550,000 I was getting in 1984. Aging quarterbacks can't always see the reality around them when the career clock's running out of time. Every old quarterback wants his last pass to be the last play that wins the Super Bowl, and then to walk off the field with the cheers raining down on his head. I thought about writing a song: "Save the Last Pass for Me."

My last hurrah came in the third game of the season. I relieved Richard with the 49ers leading 17–0, and I had about as good a twenty minutes as I've ever had on a football field. It didn't start well. My first pass traveled fifty-five yards in the air and came down in the hands of a young receiver who dropped it. But then I led the team on four straight scoring drives. One ended with an eight-yard TD pass to Eugene Goodlow, another with a twenty-six-yard pass in the end zone to Hoby Brenner, and the other two set up Morten Andersen field goals. We led 20–17.

The 49ers came back with ten points in the fourth quarter, three set up by an interception. Still, we had a chance. We moved from our seventeen to the San Francisco forty-four with 3:38 remaining. Bum boldly decided to go for a first down on fourth-and-six. I loved it, feeling sure I could hit Wayne Wilson coming out of the backfield and move the chains. I hit Wilson, but I threw the ball a little behind him and it arrived as a linebacker banged into him. The ball fell to the ground.

A friend in San Francisco, where the game was played, sent me a column from the *Chronicle* by Glenn Dickey, who wrote: "In today's NFL, teams . . . have to attack continually on offense. You have to figure on outscoring opponents, not sitting on a lead. Bum Phillips can't do that. He's still wedded to the run-oriented offense with which he had some success at Houston. Bum's lack of imagination shows in many ways. One is his habit of running on first down. Even more telling is the Saints' lack of diversity; their playbook must be the smallest in the NFL."

Dickey ended his column by saying the 49ers are a team of the eighties: "The Saints aren't."

I also saved a quote from 49ers' coach Bill Walsh on my performance against his team: "When Stabler came into the game, we just tried to contain him. He's great at looking off the ball and throwing it away from where he's looking. He's a Hall of Fame quarterback if there ever was one."

On that note I should have packed up the battered, raggedy pair of shoulder pads I'd been wearing since 1968 and said good-bye. Rodger

Bird, a Raider defensive back from Kentucky, had given me those little pads that were now held together by nothing more than tape and history—much like myself. But as the man once said, you buy your train ticket and aim to get off at your stop, unless you happen to drift off. Then you go to wherever you wake up, and maybe that was just the destination that was meant for you from the start. But if Bill Walsh is right, I'll mount those beat-up pads in Canton anyway someday, and how I got to the end of the line won't matter.

I'm such a competitor, though, I tried to hang in, tried to show that I could still do it. I made two more appearances, against the Rams and the Cowboys, and couldn't do diddily shit. The Cowboys picked off two of my passes, caused me to fumble near the end zone, and recovered the ball for the tying touchdown in a game we lost in overtime, 30–27. The following Wednesday, Dave Wilson moved ahead of me as the number two quarterback, as probably he should have. But I couldn't see it, just as I couldn't see being number three and having to throw the defensive skeleton drills that day in practice.

I did it, and it depressed the hell out of me. I drove home to Molly after practice thinking of something Pat Peppler had told me confidentially earlier. Pat had been the director of player personnel for Bum in both Houston and New Orleans and he'd always been real forthright with me. He told me that in meetings, King Hill had laid off a lot of the team's offensive failures on me. King Hill had insisted on using a tired offense from the seventies in the eighties and blamed me because it wouldn't work when I'd been telling him that very thing.

Pat Peppler shook his head and said, "Ken, they've coached you from being the most accurate passer in NFL history into being a sub-50 percent thrower."

"That's a helluva coaching job, isn't it," I said.

Monroe Falterman had recently given Molly and me two bottles of Dom Pérignon, telling us to save them for a special occasion. We drank them that night, as I tried to shake my depression. It didn't work. I skipped practice the next day.

Bum called and Molly said, "He's sick."

"Well, send him in and we'll get him to a doctor," Bum said.

"Are you gonna send him to a physical doctor or a mental doctor?" Molly asked. "Bum, Kenny's depressed."

"Well, send him in."

"What if he doesn't report?"

"Then tell him not to come back at all."

I went in the next day, and Bum told me he was going with Richard and Dave, which was apparent. He also said that in two weeks he was bringing two players off the injured-reserve list and that I would have to go on it. That was the final gun. The game was over.

In an hour I was back home hugging Molly and saying, "I'm through, finished with football," as the tears ran down my face. I felt hurt, abandoned, as if I had been betrayed and just cast aside like an old worn-out jockstrap.

I guess every athlete who plays too long, who just can't bring himself to say it's over, goes through similar emotions when the folks in charge finally tell him it's over. I had played too long, probably two years too long. My knees were aching, but I was used to that, and my arm was steadily weakening, but I had convinced myself that I was smart enough to compensate for my lack of physical ability. I realize now that the only way I would have had a chance of doing that successfully was in a different system with an excellent supporting cast.

I believe that if I'd stayed with the Raiders I would have continued to win, but that's pure speculation. Jim Plunkett did a great job and I admire the hell out of him. People say that the Raiders won because they got Marcus Allen and also built a tremendous pass rush. I know for sure that if the Raiders of the seventies had put that kind of pressure on offenses, we would have earned a lot more Super Bowl jewelry. The Steelers got most of it—four rings—because they were the best. Still, when people say the Raiders of the eighties won two Super Bowls without outstanding performance from their quarterback, that overlooks one important thing. Jim Plunkett proved he's a winner.

That night I phoned Bob Roesler, executive sports editor of the *Times-Picayune* and announced my retirement. "I was unhappy with the situation," I said, "unhappy with my contribution, and unhappy where the team was and the inevitability that I wasn't going to get the opportunity to do anything. Before today, I always felt that if you keep plugging, something would happen. . . . But they wrote me off, so I just want to leave with class."

I also told Roesler I had seen the hurt in Bum when he told me his plans, and that he'd seen the hurt in me. "If Bum could draw it up again, he would draw it up a lot different. So would I. But the cards just didn't come up that way."

Then I said I had never liked Bum's offensive system because I didn't think it would win. Of course, it didn't win, and Bum finally quit himself the next season, a nice old cowboy coach that the game had passed by.

A couple of weeks before I retired, Bum even traded for Earl Campbell, a fullback he had already helped wear out by running him thirty to thirty-five times a game. It was apparent to everyone but Bum that Earl was no longer the great runner he had been. And once Earl was brought in to alternate with George Rogers, George pouted all the time. So Bum ended up with a pair of one-dimensional full-backs who couldn't catch the ball or block. It didn't make sense to a lot of the players on the Saints, but then neither did the I formation offense.

It seemed apparent to me that if the I formation could be a championship offense, other successful teams would be using it. But you look at those teams—San Francisco, Dallas, Oakland, Washington, Pittsburgh, Miami—and you see they all won by spreading out the defense and throwing the ball.

But Bum kept following the offensive philosophy he believed in, and I can't really fault a man for sticking by his beliefs.

That's why I'd like to mend my fences with Al Davis, who always stuck by his beliefs, which were all aimed at one thing—winning. His goal was always to dominate the NFL, and you'd have to say the Raiders have done a pretty good job of that. They always will as long as Al Davis is at the top of the organization because he spends every minute of the day working to strengthen the Raiders. The other owners are afraid of him and hate to deal with him. He plays *hard* hard-ball, not unlike my late friend Randall did, except Al also plays smartball.

The Raiders have always been among the best-paid players in the game because Al Davis knows you have to spend to be the best, and that's the only thing he wants to be. In his lawsuit against the league, Al won $55 million in damages, and whatever portion of that money comes through after the appeals could make the Raiders unbeatable.

Top players will be lining up to wear the silver-and-black with the patch-eyed pirate on their hats.

Looking back now, from a little wiser perspective at age forty, I think I understand why I got so angry with Al Davis. I guess I always wanted more from Al, just as I wanted more from my father, than he could give or was interested in giving. It wasn't in either of them to give a lot of praise. I wanted my relationship with Al to be more like what I had with Coach Bryant and, even more so, with John Madden. I always did my best to try and make people like me, and I needed to know they did.

I knew Al Davis respected me and my football abilities, but I never knew if he liked me because he never said it. Of course, I see now that that just wasn't his style. Hell, anyone who didn't like John Madden had a bunch of pages missing from his playbook, and I know Al liked him. But I'd be surprised if he ever told John that. I kept wishing Al would open up a bit with me, and that was naïve on my part. He wasn't going to change his style any more than my father was going to change his, any more than I was going to change mine. So be it.

All of my good years in the National Football League came when I was playing for teams that Al Davis put together and John Madden molded, and I thank them for giving me the opportunity. There aren't too many teams that would have given a second chance to a young quarterback with a surgical knee and a weak arm who had run out of camp the year before. The Raiders were always willing to take chances on fuckups who could play a little. I just wish I'd played a little longer with them . . . like my entire career.

The day after I retired, Molly and I packed and drove to Gulf Shores. I needed to get away from the city where a major part of my life had ended abruptly. I got together with a friend named Bob Williams and told him I was going through a kind of painful withdrawal, but that it would pass. His company has a suite at the Superdome and he invited me to join him for the upcoming Monday night game in New Orleans. "I'm taking a bunch of customers and friends and it'll be great for you," he said. "We'll party, as usual."

I wasn't sure. But then Jim Lampley of ABC-TV called to say he wanted to interview me at halftime of the game, so I went with Bob. The ABC booth was halfway around the stadium from Bob's suite.

As I walked around to do the interview, Saints fans recognized their grizzled ex-quarterback and applauded me every step of the way, many of them standing. "Damn," I thought, "I may be gone, but I sure ain't forgotten!"

It wasn't an easy transition going from football player to civilian without any preparation, and I felt damn lucky that I had Molly. It seemed like I came to love her more and more each day. She was the only woman I didn't dominate in a relationship. I like that. Molly was the only woman I've dealt with on an equal basis and made an effort to make the relationship work.

Molly's a lot like me in that she likes a good time, she's got a lot of energy, she's stubborn, and she's smart. She's been good for me in every way, and she's really helped organize my finances. For several years I had been buying property and I suddenly realized that my monthly debt service was over $15,000.

I woke up one morning and said, "Molly, I've got shit scattered from asshole to appetite. We own this house, the one in New Orleans, and I still haven't sold the Houston condo. I also have a boat here, a boat in New Orleans, a marina in Pensacola, a $400,000 piece of commercial property on a lagoon here, and another undeveloped plot of land out on a point of Ono Island."

"Yeah, we're land-rich and liquid-capital-poor," she said, laughing.

But Molly quickly put her MBA training to good use. We sold off most of the real estate and put the money into an investment package that would allow us to live well on the interest for years. Molly also did some careful tax planning for us, pointing out, "If you'd done a bit of that years ago you wouldn't have had to buy Uncle Sam an airplane, or whatever he did with the taxes you paid."

I decided to take my time in pursuing a future career. But I hope I'll be able to do something that will satisfy my ego, my ambition, and my need for recognition the way football did. I know I'm ambitious and that I have so much nervous energy I seldom can relax. I've always felt that I had to keep striving to get all I could out of myself in whatever I did, that life is a never-ending struggle to keep pushing to do better, to achieve and keep achieving. I have never yet achieved total contentment because I've never fulfilled all my ambitions, and I never will. There will always be something else to go after. The only semblance of contentment for me has been in the striving.

Molly said, "People who keep pushing and pushing usually die earlier."

"Not if they take care of themselves," I said. "You have to keep going because if you accept the end, you lose. For a competitive sonuvabitch like me, there can't be any limit, any end in sight. When you've done something successfully for a long period of time, some people might not think they can do something else as well, but I want to see if I can. I think I can, and I have to find out one way or the other."

Molly and I began working on having children and planting roots in the area. We put the beach house up for sale because an island is no place to raise kids. But we've got our eye on some other property in the area and there's no rush. And Molly put me on a budget for the first time in my life. I've thought about all the money I've pissed away on cars, boats, trucks, motorcycles. I finally got rid of all those toys. I may be growing up after all.

It really feels good to finally pull over out of the fast lane and just cruise along with the woman I love.

One nice thing about retirement was that I got to see more of my family. My mom had finally remarried a few years earlier, and she'd gotten a fine man in J. C. Burnett, a merchant seaman who was as mild-mannered as Slim was unpredictable. J.C. buys her anything she wants and Sally, who turned sixty a few weeks before I reached age forty on Christmas Day 1985, just works part-time now for something to do.

My sister Carolyn's doing just great, too. Her husband is six-four, 325-pound Miles Bishop, a good old boy from Fairhope, Alabama. Carolyn's a big girl, so naturally their thirteen-year-old son Scott is a big 'un. He's also a good athlete and I enjoy throwing a ball around with him.

I spend the rest of my time, in between unloading real estate, making some recruiting calls for Coach Ray Perkins at Alabama, visiting with friends, and doing a lot of fun-type charity work. Molly and I attended a number of banquets like the March of Dimes Gala in Mobile, in which she was one of the celebrities who prepared food for some five hundred guests at $300 a plate.

What I enjoy most about my civilian life are the charity golf tournaments I now can play in every couple of months.

The best tournament I ever played in was the Sahara Amateur Classic in Lake Tahoe, California. Not only was it probably the best amateur tournament in the country, it was there that I finally got to meet Bobby Layne. And that was no small thrill.

Due to a delayed flight, I didn't arrive at the Sahara until about 4 A.M., but I was up and in the lobby at seven-thirty. I knew I was paired with Bobby and I couldn't wait to get together with him. Tee-off time wasn't until nine, so I was just walking around. Then I felt a hand come down on my shoulder from behind, and a voice said, "Hey, Lefty, let's go get us a drink."

I turned around and it was Bobby Layne. "All right!" I said.

We moved into the bar, and when Bobby was about ten feet from it he stopped and reached into his pocket. He pulled out a roll of money as thick as your fist, with a rubber band around it. He shook the wad of bills up by his ear and rolled it against the bar, crying, "Seven, dice!" Then he picked up his money and bought everyone in the bar a drink.

After having a few bloody marys, we went out and teed off. It was the perfect tournament for me and Bobby. At every hole there was a little bar set up with pretty girls to serve us. And at every hole Bobby would walk up to the bar, kiss the girl, and say, "Honey, fix me a real *tough* scotch and water."

Bobby would drink his scotch, hit the ball, and he did that all around the course, eighteen holes. It was one of the great days of my life.

I had another one in September 1984 at the Second Annual Ed Podolak–Jimmy Buffet High Country Shootout in Aspen, Colorado, a charity golf tournament in which people pay to play with celebrities. I knew it would be good because the invitation announced: TEE-OFF PROMPTLY AT THE CRACK OF NOON.

The first day I ran into John Mecom, who had sold the Saints for $70 million and he was so goddamn happy to be rid of that team. "John," I said, "it's kinda different for both of us. You don't have to wake up Monday mornings and read about another loss, and I don't wake up sore all over."

John laughed. The Saints had already lost their first game of the season.

But on Monday night I got together with Billy Kilmer, the man they called "Whiskey" and a quarterback who got as much out of his ability as any since Bobby Layne. Billy and I watched the Cowboys beat up the Redskins. Billy, no fan of Joe Theismann's, gave a raspy laugh every time the quarterback he left behind was intercepted—five times in that game.

"Jurgy was my man," rasped Billy, speaking of Sonny Jurgensen, who was quarterbacking the Redskins when Kilmer joined them in 1971 after four years with the 49ers, four years with the Saints, and one year trying to rehabilitate his body. That was in 1963, when he was so seriously injured in an auto accident that the doctors said he'd never play again.

"You know who called me when I was lying in the hospital," Billy said, "just to tell me to hang in there and keep fighting, that I'd make it? A guy from the other league, the AFL, a guy named Al Davis. I'll never forget it. I think everyone else wrote me off."

Billy and I sat up all night—him sipping his nickname, me sipping beer—and talked football. I loved it, two beat-up old quarterbacks exchanging lies, roaring about how much fun it had been. "Jurgy used to say, 'Between us we couldn't put together one good body,' " Billy said, laughing. He only played for sixteen years.

Molly wasn't too happy about me sitting around with Kilmer until the sun came up because she doesn't understand the camaraderie guys like us share. I just wish I could've sat there with old Whiskey for two days.

When we got back from Colorado, I had good news on four fronts. I had sued NBC-TV for defamation of character after several of its stations had reported my association with gambler Nick Dudich, showed his picture, said Dudich had been seen at the hotel where I stayed with the Oilers—then showed one of my passes being intercepted by the Jets in an overtime loss to them. Some viewers may well have been led to believe that I had thrown the game. NBC settled with us out of court. All I cared about was clearing my name completely.

I also got an invitation to play football again with a bunch of old worn-out guys like myself. Ray Malavesi, the former Rams' coach, was putting together two teams: one from the AFC, the other from the NFC. "The Legends of American Football," as he called it, would play a game in Tokyo within the next year, each player to receive $5,000 plus a share of the profits. It sounded to me like a blast. And we would get to play a second game a week later in Osaka —if any of us could still walk.

In February I went partners with Ron Blackburn in a company that will represent athletes called Stabler Sports Management. We are negotiating with Freddy Biletnikoff to run a California office of SSM and with Steve Mix, the former Philadelphia 76ers player, to head an SSM basketball office in Ohio.

I was also notified that at the end of February 1986 I would be inducted into the Alabama Sports Hall of Fame. That turned out to mean as much to me as any honor I've ever received.

But there is one honor that would mean more than all the rest, of course. I remember when Bobby Layne retired in 1962 after playing for fifteen years. Five years later, as soon as he became eligible, he was inducted into the Pro Football Hall of Fame. I become eligible in 1989.

I hope I'm invited to Canton, Ohio, that August, with Molly at my side and maybe two or three kids in tow. By then I might even be driving a station wagon. I wonder if anybody would recognize The Snake in one of those?

KEN MICHAEL STABLER
QUARTERBACK
Career Passing Stats

YEAR	CLUB	G	ATT.	CMP.	PCT.	GAIN.	TD P.	INT.	AVG. GAIN
1970	Oakland	3	7	2	28.6	52	0	1	7.43
1971	Oakland	14	48	24	50.0	268	1	4	5.58
1972	Oakland	14	74	44	59.5	524	4	3	7.08
1973	Oakland	14	260	163	62.7*	1,997	14	10	7.68
1974	Oakland	14	310	178	57.4	2,469	26*	12	7.96
1975	Oakland	14	293	171	58.4	2,296	16	24	7.84
1976	Oakland	12	291	194	66.7*	2,737	27	17	9.41*
1977	Oakland	13	294	169	57.5	2,176	20	20	7.40
1978	Oakland	16	406	237	58.4	2,944	16	30	7.25
1979	Oakland	16	498	304	61.0	3,615	26	22	7.26
1980	Houston	16	457	293	64.1	3,202	13	28	7.01
1981	Houston	13	285	165	57.9	1,988	14	18	6.98
1982	New Orleans	8†	189	117	61.9	1,343	6	10	7.11
1983	New Orleans	14	311	176	56.6	1,988	9	18	6.39
1984	New Orleans	3	70	33	47.1	339	2	5	4.84
NFL TOTALS: fifteen years		184	3,793	2,270	59.85	27,938	194	222	6.89

* led the league
† fifty-seven-day strike season

Played in AFC Championship Game following 1973 through 1977 seasons.
Played in Super Bowl XI, January 1977.
Played in AFC Wild Card Game following 1980 season.
Played in Pro Bowl (NFL All-Star Game) following 1973, 1974, and 1977 seasons.